THRESHOLD

Cambridge Pre-GED Program in Social Studies

Pamela Check

00-3196

 CAMBRIDGE Adult Education
Prentice Hall Regents
Englewood Cliffs, New Jersey 07632

Library of Congress Cataloging-in-Publication Data

Check, Pamela, 1953–
    Threshold: Cambridge pre-GED program in social studies/Pamela
Check.
      p.   cm.
    Includes bibliographical references.
    ISBN 0-13-111089-6 (p)
     1. Social studies—Problems, exercises, etc.   2. Social Studies—
Study and teaching (Secondary)   3. General educational development
tests—Study guides.   I. Title.   II. Title: Cambridge pre-GED
program in social studies.
H62.3.C48   1994
300'.71'273—dc20   93-49665
                                                              CIP

Executive Editor: JAMES W. BROWN
Editorial Supervisor: TIMOTHY A. FOOTE
Senior Editor: ROBERT MCILWAINE
Production Editor: JANET S. JOHNSTON
Desktop Production and Electronic Art: KEN LIAO
Managing Editor: SYLVIA MOORE
Buyer and Scheduler: ED O'DOUGHERTY
Interior designers: JANET SCHMID, JANET S. JOHNSTON
Cover coordinator: MARIANNE FRASCO
Cover designer: BRUCE KENSELAAR
Cover photo: BRYAN PETERSON/THE STOCK MARKET
Photo researchers: ELLEN GRATKOWSKI and KEN LIAO
Permissions: MARK COHEN

©1994 by PRENTICE HALL REGENTS
Prentice-Hall, Inc.
A Paramount Communications Company
Englewood Cliffs, New Jersey 07632

Printed in the United Sates of America

10 9 8 7 6 5 4 3

ISBN 0-13-111089-6

Prentice-Hall International (UK) Limited, *London*
Prentice-Hall of Australia Pty. Limited, *Sydney*
Prentice-Hall Canada Inc., *Toronto*
Prentice-Hall Hispanoamericana, S.A., *Mexico*
Prentice-Hall of India Private Limited, *New Delhi*
Prentice-Hall of Japan, Inc., *Tokyo*
Simon & Schuster Asia Pte. Ltd., *Singapore*
Editora Prentice-Hall do Brasil, Ltda., *Rio de Janeiro*

CONTENTS

ACKNOWLEDGMENTS

CAMBRIDGE Adult Education thanks the men and women enrolled in ABE and Pre-GED courses who read parts of the Threshold manuscripts and offered valuable advice to the programs' authors and editors.

We also thank the following consultants for their many contributions throughout the preparation of the Threshold Pre-GED programs.

Cecily Kramer Bodnar
Consultant, Adult Learning
Adult Literacy Services
Central School District
Greece, New York

Pamela S. Buchanan
Instructor
Blue Ridge Job Corps Center
Marion, Virginia

Maureen Considine, M.A., M.S.

Learning Laboratory Supervisor
Great Neck Adult Learning Center
Great Neck, New York

ABE/HSE Projects Coordinator
National Center for Disability Services
Albertson, New York

Carole Deletiner
Instructor
Hunter College
New York, New York

Patricia Giglio
Remedial Reading Teacher
Johnstown ASACTC
Johnstown, New York

Diane Marinelli Hardison, M.S. Ed.
Mathematics Educator
San Diego, California

Margaret Banker Tinzmann, Ph. D.
Program Associate
The North Central Regional Educational Laboratory
Oak Brook, Illinois

INTRODUCTION

The instruction in *Threshold: Cambridge Pre-GED Program in Social Studies* is organized by a hierarchy of critical-reading and -thinking skills. Unit 1 concentrates on basic comprehension skills: preparing to read, finding the main idea, and finding details, using both verbal and graphic materials. Unit 2 covers inference skills: figuring out the meanings of words from their contexts, making inferences, and inferring unstated main ideas. The final unit covers critical thinking skills: applying, analyzing, and evaluating information.

Except in the practice feature called Readings, the five social studies content areas are integrated throughout, so that students become familiar with a wide variety of topics that they are likely to encounter on the GED. All the reading passages in the book explore topics in history, geography, economics, political science, and behavioral science. Many of the passages present basic concepts or important themes. Others discuss a variety of contemporary issues related to social studies—including environmental issues and the state of the U.S. economy. In each unit, however, standard topics are treated. For example, the passages in Unit 1 cover American history, including the geography of the colonies, the early government of the colonies, the Revolutionary War, and the writing of the Constitution.

The social studies program's organization—a hierarchy of critical-reading and -thinking skills in an integrated social studies context—provides an excellent way for students to improve their reading skills while simultaneously becoming familiar with social studies topics.

You will profit in several important ways by using this book as you begin to prepare for the social studies test of the GED:

- You will improve your reading skills.

- You will expand your knowledge about the five main branches of social studies.

- You will gain experience answering questions like those on the GED.

- You will become more confident of your abilities.

To Find Out About Your Current Reading Skills and Social Studies Knowledge . . .

Take the **PRETEST**. When you have finished, refer to the **ANSWERS AND EXPLANATIONS** at the back of this book to check your answers. Then look at the **CHARTS** that follow the Pretest. They'll give you an idea about which parts of this book you need to concentrate on most.

To Improve Your Reading Skills and Expand Your Social Studies Knowledge . . .

Study the **LESSONS**. They present instruction about reading skills and give examples that show how the various skills can be applied to passages about social studies. Some of the examples—called **TRY THIS** and **NOW TRY THIS**—let you apply the reading skills to social studies passages. Each lesson has one or more **EXERCISES** for you to practice your reading skills. They have questions about social studies passages on various topics.

Study the readings in the **SOCIAL STUDIES READINGS** sections, too. They come right after the lessons in each unit. Each reading is about a different topic in social studies. The questions in each set of readings give you more practice with all the reading skills you will have studied up to that point in this book.

To Gain Experience in Answering Questions Like Those on the GED . . .

Take the **GED PRACTICE** at the end of each unit. The GED Practices are made up of passages and questions like the ones on the social studies test of the GED. They offer you test-taking experience that you will find useful when you take the GED.

Before you finish with this book, take the **POSTTEST**. Like the GED Practices, it is similar to the GED Social Studies Test. Look at the **CHARTS** that follow the Posttest. If you compare your Pretest and Posttest performance, you will probably find that your skills and knowledge improved as you worked through this book. The charts can give you an idea about which parts of this book you should review.

Pretest

The following Pretest is similar to the Social Studies Test of the GED. Taking it will help you find out what you need to study most in this book.

The Pretest has 32 multiple-choice items—half as many as there are on the GED. The items are based on readings in history, geography, economics, political science, and behavioral science. The questions test your understanding of the readings and your ability to apply information and to think critically.

To begin preparing for the Social Studies Test of the GED, take this Pretest. Work through it at a pace that is comfortable for you. You don't need to study anything before you take the Pretest. The information you need to answer the questions is given in the readings.

The Maine Coast

SOCIAL STUDIES PRETEST

Directions: Choose the one best answer to each item.

Items 1 and 2 are based on the following paragraph.

States raise money with taxes and charges for services. They also receive tax money from Washington. In the last twenty years, states have looked for ways to broaden their revenue bases. More than half now run lotteries. In one year alone state lotteries earned $4.5 billion. That sum was left after some lucky winners became millionaires. Most states spend their lottery money on programs like education.

1. States probably began using lotteries to raise money to
   (1) cause excitement in the state
   (2) give everyone the hope of becoming rich
   (3) share some of the extra money lotteries would make
   (4) get money without raising taxes
   (5) give people jobs

2. A state's revenue base is made up of
   (1) all its lottery tickets
   (2) the programs it gives money to
   (3) all its sources of income
   (4) the money people in the state earn
   (5) $4.5 billion

Item 3 is based on the following paragraph.

A news report stated this: Jobs in manufacturing will keep decreasing, especially in the steel, leather goods, and textile industries. Service jobs will keep increasing, especially in health care and computer technology.

3. Gloria is in her last year of high school. She likes to work with her hands. She also wants a good job. She could best use the information in the news report by
   (1) taking some computer technician courses
   (2) dropping out of school to find a job
   (3) going to work in a textile factory when she graduates
   (4) waiting until the job market gets better to look for work
   (5) finding a job in a leather goods workshop

Item 4 is based on the following paragraph.

In 1968 the United States was involved in the Vietnam War. Fifty-two percent of the people asked said the country's worst problem was the war. But times change, and so do people's ideas about the nation's problems. Ten years later, in 1978, the economy was going through hard times. That year 54 percent said the worst problem was the economy. In 1988 44 percent said the worst problem was drugs.

4. What is the main idea of the paragraph?
   (1) In 1968 the country was involved in Vietnam.
   (2) Fifty-two percent said the war was the country's worst problem.
   (3) Times change, and so do people's ideas about the country's problems.
   (4) In 1978 54 percent thought the economy was the worst problem in the country.
   (5) Many thought drugs were the worst problem in the country during the late 1980s.

Item 5 is based on the following map.

The Four Regions of China

5. The map suggests that most of China's one billion people live

   (1) in the northwest
   (2) in the east
   (3) in the west
   (4) in the southwest
   (5) along the northern border

Items 6 and 7 are based on the following paragraph.

We allow only certain people close to us. Spouses, lovers, children, close family members, and professionals such as doctors or haircutters are allowed within eighteen inches of us. That is intimate space. Friends are allowed within eighteen inches and four feet of us. That is personal space. We relate to other people from a distance of four to nine feet. That is social space. Any space beyond that is public space. If strangers are forced into our personal or intimate space, such as on a crowded bus, we avoid meeting their eyes or making other social contact with them.

6. What is the general topic of the paragraph?

   (1) The relationship between space and intimacy
   (2) Intimate space
   (3) Family members
   (4) Social contact
   (5) Touching

7. Which of the following people would you probably keep outside your social space?

   (1) a girlfriend
   (2) a doctor
   (3) your grandfather
   (4) your child
   (5) a store clerk

Item 8 is based on the following graph.

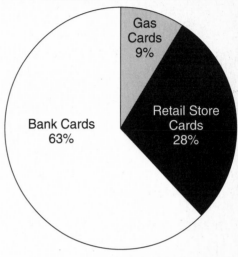

8. Which of the following conclusions is supported by the graph?

   (1) Few charge cards are bank cards.
   (2) People find bank cards the most convenient type of charge card to use.
   (3) Bank cards are used less than other cards.
   (4) Gas cards are not very useful to people.
   (5) People should charge more on store and gas cards.

Item 9 is based on the following information.

The Supreme Court has the power to make sure every law follows the Constitution.

9. Which of the following illustrates that power?

   (1) In 1981 President Reagan named the first woman to the Supreme Court.
   (2) The Supreme Court meets in Washington, D.C.
   (3) Congress approved Clarence Thomas as a Supreme Court judge.
   (4) Nine judges make up the Supreme Court.
   (5) In 1972 the Supreme Court said states could no longer put criminals to death.

Items 10 through 13 are based on the map below.

10. Which areas of the country had free states in 1854?

    (1) all of the South
    (2) all of the North
    (3) the Northeast, the Upper Midwest, and the Far West
    (4) the South and the West
    (5) the Northeast, the Southeast, and the West

11. If people in the undecided territories had voted for slavery,

    (1) more than half the country would have allowed slaves
    (2) the Civil War would have resulted
    (3) free states would have had to allow slaves too
    (4) the Northeast would have been the only free area
    (5) Native Americans would have become slaves

Free States and Slave States, 1854

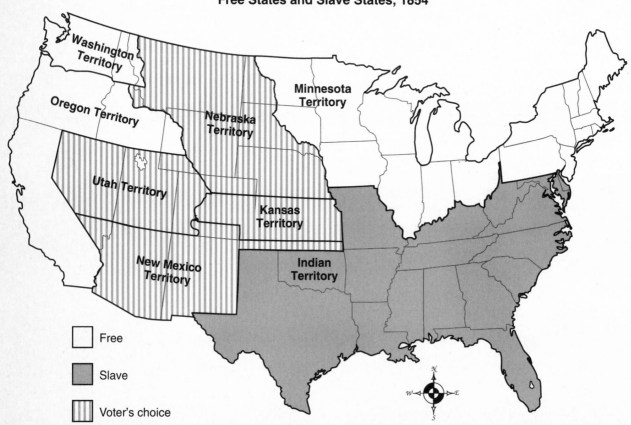

12. Which of these conclusions is supported by information in the map on page 4?

    (1) The South was alone in wanting slavery.
    (2) Slaves who moved to the Nebraska Territory were free.
    (3) The North could easily win a war against the South.
    (4) Slavery had split the country.
    (5) People in the West were not concerned about slavery.

13. Which of the following statements is NOT a fact that can be supported by the map on page 4?

    (1) Fifteen states allowed slaves.
    (2) Slavery should not have been allowed anywhere.
    (3) Some territories did not allow slavery.
    (4) The West Coast was a free area.
    (5) Washington was a territory in 1854.

Items 14 and 15 are based on the graph below.

14. In the 1980s farmers had economic difficulties. Which of the following pieces of information could be used to support that conclusion?

    (1) The value of farmland never fell below $500 billion in the 1980s.
    (2) From 1980 to 1981, farmland was valued just below $800 billion.
    (3) By 1986 the value of farmland had sunk to a low of $500 billion.
    (4) Farmland had about the same value in 1989 as in 1984.
    (5) By 1990 the value of farmland was up to about $700 billion.

15. Which of the following people would probably have most interest in the information in the graph?

    (1) a senator from a wheat-producing state
    (2) a salesman in a New York clothing store
    (3) a retired couple in Florida
    (4) a housewife in California
    (5) the mayor of Atlanta

Value of U.S. Farmland

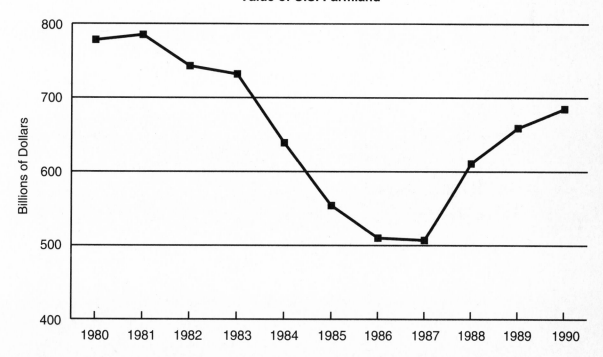

Items 16 through 19 are based on the following information.

Here are descriptions of five kinds of climates.

Tropical wet: Hot all year round. Heavy rainfall all year round. Rainforests.

Desert: Hot or cold. Very little rainfall. Scrub plants, cacti, and grasses if any plants at all.

Continental: Warm to hot summers, cold winters. Rain in summer, snow in winter. Trees and grasses.

Mediterranean: Warm to hot summers, mild winters. Dry summers, wet winters. Grasses, scrub plants, some trees.

Tundra: Cool summers, cold winters. Little rainfall or snowfall. Grasses, mosses, lichens.

16. Barrow, Alaska, has January temperatures below −10°F and July temperatures below 45°F. It gets less than 8 inches of rain a year. Caribou feed on short ground plants. What kind of climate does Barrow have?

   (1) tropical wet
   (2) desert
   (3) continental
   (4) Mediterranean
   (5) tundra

17. San Diego, California, has temperatures near 80°F in summer and 55°F in winter. Most of its 10 inches of rainfall comes from November to March. What kind of climate does San Diego have?

   (1) tropical wet
   (2) desert
   (3) continental
   (4) Mediterranean
   (5) tundra

18. New York City has summer temperatures around 82°F and winter temperatures around freezing. Rainfall or snowfall amounts are nearly even each month. What kind of climate does New York City have?

   (1) tropical wet
   (2) desert
   (3) continental
   (4) Mediterranean
   (5) tundra

19. To see if Timbuktu has a desert climate, you should check all of the following EXCEPT

   (1) the amount of rain it gets
   (2) the number of people who live there
   (3) the kind of plants that grow there
   (4) the summer temperatures
   (5) the winter temperatures

Items 20 and 21 are based on the following paragraph.

In the 1760s and early 1770s, the American colonists increasingly opposed Britain's attempt to exert control over the colonies. The colonists protested British policies by writing to the king and to Parliament. Leaders of the colonies got together to plan the opposition. The colonists refused to buy British goods or to pay certain taxes, and they threatened British officials. They believed that a break from Britain was necessary. Eventually, war broke out between the colonists and Britain at Lexington and Concord, Massachusetts, in 1775.

20. Which of the following sentences from the paragraph expresses its main idea?

   (1) In the 1760s and early 1770s, the American colonists increasingly opposed Britain's attempt to exert control over the colonies.
   (2) They protested British policies by writing to the king and to Parliament.
   (3) Leaders of the colonies got together to plan the opposition.
   (4) The colonists refused to buy British goods or to pay certain taxes, and they threatened British officials.
   (5) Eventually, war broke out between the colonists and Britain at Lexington and Concord, Massachusetts, in 1775.

21. From the information in the passage, you can infer that
    (1) many colonists wanted independence from Britain as early as the 1760s
    (2) the king and Parliament did not reply to the colonists' protests
    (3) threatened British officials attacked colonists at Lexington and Concord
    (4) the Battle of Lexington and Concord was a victory for the British
    (5) some colonists were for independence and others were for remaining British citizens

Items 22 through 25 are based on the following passage.

Divorce is much more common than it used to be. For every two marriages, one ends in divorce. That's 2½ times as many divorces as thirty years ago.

Our attitudes about marriage have changed. In the past, marriage was considered mainly a matter of supporting and caring for children. Today most couples still expect to raise children, but husbands and wives also expect love and friendship from each other.

Our attitudes about divorce have changed too. In the past divorce was considered wrong. Today most Americans accept it.

In the past most women did not earn money. They were less able to support themselves after a divorce, even with alimony payments from ex-husbands. Today most women work outside the home. One researcher has suggested that working women feel more free to end a bad marriage.

Laws also have changed. In the past, divorce was allowed only for extreme causes, like cruelty. Now "no-fault" divorces are allowed. A couple can get a divorce if they just can't get along.

22. Today there is one divorce for every
    (1) 30 marriages
    (2) 3 marriages
    (3) 2½ marriages
    (4) 2 marriages
    (5) 1 marriage

23. What probably caused divorce laws to change?
    (1) Lawyers wanted more money for divorces.
    (2) Too many people were getting divorces.
    (3) Children were not getting enough in support payments.
    (4) Couples were not having as many children.
    (5) Changes in people's attitudes led lawmakers to change laws.

24. What explains why women divorce more often than they used to?
    (1) The rate of divorce has gone up 2½ times in thirty years.
    (2) Women used to get alimony from their ex-husbands.
    (3) Women expect more from marriage these days.
    (4) Laws have changed to make it easier for women to divorce than for men to divorce.
    (5) More women earn money and feel freer to leave their husbands.

25. Which of the following would be a direct result of the present divorce rate?
    (1) more children being born
    (2) more children living with one parent
    (3) fewer children in school
    (4) children being born to older mothers
    (5) children getting more attention

Items 26 and 27 are based on the following graphs.

Top-Selling Cars, in Thousands

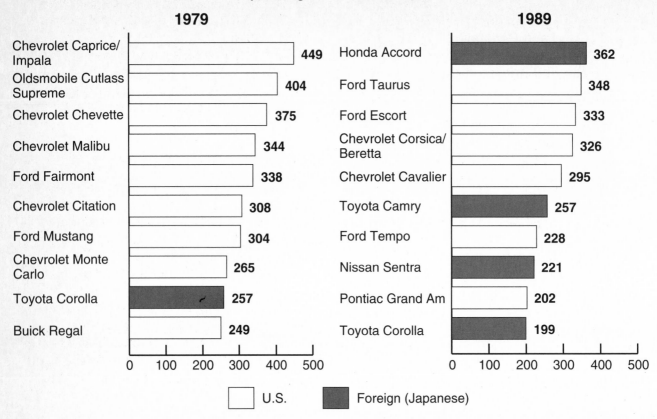

1979	
Chevrolet Caprice/Impala	449
Oldsmobile Cutlass Supreme	404
Chevrolet Chevette	375
Chevrolet Malibu	344
Ford Fairmont	338
Chevrolet Citation	308
Ford Mustang	304
Chevrolet Monte Carlo	265
Toyota Corolla	257
Buick Regal	249

1989	
Honda Accord	362
Ford Taurus	348
Ford Escort	333
Chevrolet Corsica/Beretta	326
Chevrolet Cavalier	295
Toyota Camry	257
Ford Tempo	228
Nissan Sentra	221
Pontiac Grand Am	202
Toyota Corolla	199

☐ U.S. ■ Foreign (Japanese)

26. Which of the following sentences states the main point of the graphs?
    (1) Toyota Corollas sold poorly in both 1979 and 1989.
    (2) Chevrolet sold fewer cars in 1989 than in 1979.
    (3) In 1989, Japanese cars took a greater share of the market than in 1979.
    (4) The Honda Accord was the least-sold car in 1989.
    (5) The Toyota Corolla is the only car to show up twice on the graph.

27. A man looked at the graphs and thought, "Americans bought more foreign than American cars in 1989." The man was
    (1) right because the top-selling car in 1989 was Japanese
    (2) right because four of the top ten cars were Japanese in 1989
    (3) wrong because foreign cars aren't better made than American cars
    (4) wrong because more American than foreign cars were bought in 1989
    (5) wrong because only 199,000 Toyota Corollas were bought

Item 28 is based on the following information.

President Franklin Roosevelt said: "The test of our progress is not whether we add more to . . . those who have much; it is whether we provide enough for those who have too little."

28. Based on that statement, which of the following would Roosevelt have supported?
    (1) low income taxes for high-income people
    (2) Social Security payments to the disabled
    (3) research for new defense systems
    (4) fewer controls on business
    (5) more elections

Item 29 is based on the following table and paragraph.

| | 100th Congress | | 101st Congress | |
	Dem.	Rep.	Dem.	Rep.
Senate	54	46	55	45
House	258	171	255	176

Dem. = Democrats
Rep. = Republicans

People who study politics have noted two facts: (1) The number of Democrats and Republicans elected to Congress tends to stay about the same. (2) Voters return the same people to office.

29. Which of the following is a conclusion that can be drawn from the information?

　(1) Congress truly represents all American people.
　(2) Voters are always interested in new faces.
　(3) There should be fewer Democrats in Congress than there are.
　(4) Republicans should run for office more.
　(5) Office holders have a decided advantage over new opponents.

Items 30 and 31 are based on the following passage.

The Internal Revenue Service (IRS) has the right to collect taxes. But over the years some people feel it has abused that right. In 1988 an act was signed into law. It included what some people call the Taxpayer Bill of Rights. Some suggest it will lower the amount of taxes the IRS ends up collecting.

The bill includes these rights: (1) the right to be told how the IRS audits, or checks, your tax return, (2) the right to have an accountant deal with the IRS for you, and (3) the right to tape your meeting with the IRS.

30. Which of the following is an hypothesis based on the passage?

　(1) The IRS has the right to collect taxes.
　(2) The Taxpayer Bill of Rights was passed in 1988.
　(3) The IRS will collect less money than it used to.
　(4) Accountants can attend audit meetings with the IRS for you.
　(5) The IRS must allow a taxpayer to tape audit meetings.

31. Which one of these statements is a fact about the IRS?

　(1) The IRS has the right to collect taxes.
　(2) The IRS has abused its right to collect taxes.
　(3) People should not complain about the IRS.
　(4) Taxes are almost always unfair.
　(5) The IRS could not be run any better than it is.

Items 32 is based on the following paragraph.

A clever study helped show that children's thinking develops in stages. A scientist took two glasses of the same size. He filled them with equal amounts of lemonade. Five-, six-, and seven-year-olds all agreed the glasses held the same amount. Then the scientist poured the lemonade from each child's glass into a taller, thinner glass. He left his lemonade in the original glass. Five-year-olds said they now had more lemonade than the scientist had. Six-year-olds weren't sure. Seven-year-olds knew the amounts hadn't changed.

32. Which of the following best describes one thing the scientist found about children?

　(1) Children usually want more than you give them.
　(2) Six-year-olds have trouble making up their minds.
　(3) Children realize when you don't share equally.
　(4) Children's thinking improves as they grow older.
　(5) Children prefer lemonade in tall, thin glasses.

Check your answers on page 209.

SOCIAL STUDIES PRETEST SKILLS CHART

To study the reading skills covered by the items in the Social Studies Pretest, study the following parts of this book.

		Item Number
Unit 1	**Comprehending What You Read**	
Chapter 1	Preparing to Read	6
Chapter 2	Recognizing Stated Main Ideas	4, 20
Chapter 3	Understanding the Details	10, 22
Unit 2	**Inferring as You Read**	
Chapter 1	Inferring Word Meanings	2
Chapter 2	Inferring Details	5, 21, 23
Chapter 3	Inferring Unstated Main Ideas	26
Unit 3	**Thinking Critically as You Read**	
Chapter 1	Applying What You Read	3, 7, 9, 16, 17, 18, 28
Chapter 2	Analyzing What You Read	1, 11, 13, 24, 25, 30, 31, 32
Chapter 3	Evaluating What You Read	8, 12, 14, 15, 19, 27, 29

SOCIAL STUDIES PRETEST CONTENT CHART

The following chart shows the type of content each item in the Social Studies Pretest is based on.

Content	Item Number
History	4, 10, 11, 12, 13, 20, 21, 28
Geography	5, 16, 17, 18, 19
Economics	3, 8, 14, 15, 26, 27
Political Science	1, 2, 9, 29, 30, 31
Behavioral Science	6, 7, 22, 23, 24, 25, 32

UNIT 1

Comprehending What You Read

Skill at reading starts with comprehending, or understanding, what you read. The lessons in this unit will give you practice using strategies that can increase your reading comprehension. You will get that practice by reading about different topics in social studies, which will help you prepare for the GED.

Nebraska Farmland

Unit 1 Overview

PREPARING TO READ

When you pick a movie at the video store, you take a look at the box. This gives you an idea of what the movie is about. Thinking about the movie prepares you for seeing it.

In the same way, before you read something you can prepare yourself. When you preview something, you look it over before you read it. When you know what you will be reading about, it's easier to understand what you read.

This chapter will show you three ways to prepare for reading: by previewing paragraphs, previewing tables and graphs, and thinking about the topic. You'll practice these skills on passages similar to those on the social studies test of the GED.

Lesson
1

Previewing Paragraphs

A paragraph has a topic, just as a conversation does. A paragraph's topic is what that paragraph is about. If you know what a paragraph is about *before* you read it, it will make more sense when you do read it. By previewing a paragraph you can usually figure out what its topic is.

First Sentence and Words in Special Type

To preview a paragraph, just look it over quickly. Read the first sentence and notice any words that stand out.

Here's some practice at previewing a paragraph.

TRY THIS

Preview the following paragraph. DON'T READ IT. Then choose the best answer to the question below the paragraph.

This book has three main goals. One goal is to help you **develop your reading skills**. You'll see what skills are involved in reading, and you'll practice those skills. A second goal is to **increase your knowledge of social studies**. This book has many social studies readings. While you work on reading skills, you'll be learning about social studies. A third goal is to **prepare you for the GED**. The book has questions like those on the social studies test of the GED. Answering them will give you practice for the GED.

What do you think the topic of the paragraph is?

    (1) the importance of sports
    (2) the goals of this book
    (3) teaching children to read

The paragraph is about the goals of this book, Choice (2). The first sentence says that this book has three goals. Authors often begin paragraphs by saying what they will talk about. That's why it is a good idea to read the first sentence when you preview a paragraph.

When you look for words that stand out in a paragraph, you are scanning. In the paragraph above, the words in dark type stand out. They tell what the three goals are. Together with the first sentence, the words you notice when you scan might help you figure out the topic. These words might even give you some information about the topic.

Repeated Words and Capitalized Words

When you scan, you should also look for words that are repeated or capitalized. If a word comes up several times in a paragraph, it might be important. It might help you figure out what the paragraph is about. A word in the first sentence that is repeated later might be especially important.

Capital letters make the names of people and places easy to spot in paragraphs. One or more of those people and places may be a clue to the topic of a paragraph.

If a word is both repeated and capitalized, it may be the topic of the paragraph.

TRY THIS

Here is another paragraph for you to preview. Read the first sentence. Look for repeated words and the names of people and places. Then answer the questions below the paragraph.

The colony of Pennsylvania was founded, or begun, in 1681. William Penn wanted a place where Quakers could worship freely. They had sometimes been persecuted in England. He therefore asked the king for the right to start a colony in America. Pennsylvania was the eleventh colony started in what is now the United States.

What two important words are repeated in this paragraph?

_____   _____

What six names of people and places are there in the paragraph?

_____   _____

_____   _____

_____   _____

What is the topic of the paragraph?

    (1) Quakers in England
    (2) William Penn
    (3) the founding of the colony Pennsylvania

The words *colony* and *Pennsylvania* are repeated. The capitalized names in the paragraph are *Pennsylvania, William Penn, Quakers, England, America,* and *United States.* (Note that *Pennsylvania* is both repeated and capitalized.) The paragraph is about the founding of the colony of Pennsylvania, Choice (3).

GUILLAUME PENN TRAITE AVEC LES INDIENS

Établissant la Province de Pensilvanie dans l'Amérique Septentrionale en 1681.

William Penn Trading with the Indians

Last Sentence

Sometimes reading the first sentence and noticing certain words in a paragraph may not tell you the topic of the paragraph.

TRY THIS

Preview the following paragraph. Then answer the questions that follow it.

In September 1985, an earthquake struck Mexico. Part of Mexico City was destroyed. Nearly 25,000 people died in the earthquake. In November 1970 a cyclone, or storm, formed in the Bay of Bengal near the country of Bangladesh. The cyclone caused a 20-foot wave of water. The cyclone and wave hit Bangladesh, killing more than 300,000 people. As these examples show, forces of nature can strike cruelly.

What is the first sentence of the paragraph about? _____

What four places are mentioned in the paragraph?

_____   _____

_____   _____

What four important words are repeated in the paragraph?

_____   _____

_____   _____

Survivor of Earthquake in Guatemala in February 1976

The first sentence is about an earthquake in Mexico. The paragraph mentions Mexico, Mexico City, the Bay of Bengal, and Bangladesh. The words *earthquake, cyclone, wave,* and *Bangladesh* are repeated in the paragraph.

The first sentence does not really give you the topic. An earthquake in Mexico is probably not the topic of a paragraph that also mentions a cyclone and Bangladesh.

NOW TRY THIS

Look back at the **Try This** on page 15. Read the last sentence in the paragraph. Then choose the best answer to the following question.

What is the topic of the paragraph?

(1) forces of nature
(2) a cyclone
(3) Bangladesh

The topic, the forces of nature—Choice (1), is mentioned in the last sentence. An earthquake and a cyclone are given as examples of the forces of nature.

Sometimes a writer does not start a paragraph by telling you what it will be about. Sometimes the last sentence sums up the information in a paragraph. For that reason, when you are previewing a paragraph, it is a good idea to read the last sentence.

How to Preview a Paragraph

STEP 1: Read the first sentence.

STEP 2: Scan the paragraph. Be sure to notice:
- words in special type
- repeated words
- capitalized words

STEP 3: Read the last sentence.

STEP 4: Try to figure out what the topic is.

Before you do the following exercise, go back and read the three paragraphs you previewed. They contain interesting information.

Preview—DON'T READ—the following paragraphs. Answer the questions.

Questions 1 and 2 refer to the following paragraph.

      Parents should make rules for their children, explain those rules, and stick to them. Rules help children feel secure. With rules, children know what the results of their behavior will be. Without rules, children may feel unsure or confused. If rules are not explained, children may feel that everything is decided without reason. If rules are not stuck to, children may feel that they can never tell what to expect.

1. What two words are repeated often in this paragraph?

    _____   _____

2. What is the topic of the paragraph?
   (1) children's games
   (2) day care for children
   (3) children's need for rules
   (4) activities for parents and their children

Questions 3 and 4 refer to the following paragraph.

      Benjamin Franklin contributed in many ways to early America. Franklin was a leader. In the 1760s he tried to get England to listen to the complaints of the American colonists. When England didn't listen, Franklin helped move the American people to rebel against England. Franklin was a thinker and a writer. His books were very popular. In 1787, when he was 81, Franklin helped write the Constitution. Franklin was also a scientist. He invented the lightning rod and bifocal eyeglasses. He studied medicine, electricity, and astronomy.

3. Which four words stand out in this paragraph?

    _____   _____   _____   _____

4. Who is the paragraph about? _____

Questions 5 and 6 refer to the following paragraph.

      Computers are having a major effect on jobs. In factories and offices, computers are doing work that people once did. Are computers bad news for workers? "Yes," some people say, "computers have taken jobs away." Other people argue, "No, computers now do many boring jobs. Thanks to computers, people's jobs have become more interesting."

5. What two words are repeated in this paragraph?

    _____   _____

6. Fill in the blanks in the following sentence:

The topic of this paragraph is the effect of _____ on

_____.

Questions 7 and 8 refer to the following paragraph.

William Penn founded Pennsylvania so that Quakers could worship freely. Lord Baltimore founded Maryland as a place where Catholics could practice their religion. Massachusetts was founded by Pilgrims and Puritans. These three colonies and others were founded for religious freedom.

7. What word is repeated in every sentence in the paragraph? _____

8. What is the topic of the paragraph?
   (1) Quakers in Pennsylvania
   (2) why some colonies were founded
   (3) what freedom of religion is

Check your answers on page 211. Then go back and read the four paragraphs you previewed in this exercise. They contain interesting information.

Lesson 2

Previewing Tables and Graphs

Writers sometimes present information in tables and graphs rather than in paragraphs. Tables and graphs are useful when there are many related bits of information to present.

Like a paragraph, a table or graph has a topic. You can find the topic of a table or graph by previewing—that is, by looking it over before you read it.

Tables

A table, or chart, organizes information in columns and rows. Tables are useful for comparing pieces of information.

To preview a table, read its title and column headings. Column headings tell what kinds of information are listed in the body of a table. As part of your previewing, scan the body of the table.

TRY THIS

Preview the following table. DON'T READ IT. Then answer the questions that follow it.

Founding of the Thirteen American Colonies — Title

Colony	Date Founded	Reason Founded
Virginia	1607	economic
Massachusetts	1620	religious freedom
Maryland	1634	economic, religious freedom
Rhode Island	1635	religious freedom
Connecticut	1636	economic
New Hampshire	1638	political, economic
North Carolina	1663	economic
South Carolina	1663	economic
New Jersey	1664	economic
New York	1664	conquered from Dutch
Pennsylvania	1681	religious freedom
Delaware	1682	religious freedom
Georgia	1732	military

Column Headings — Colony

Body — Reason Founded

According to the title, what is the topic of the table?

_____

What three kinds of information are in this table?

(a) _____

(b) _____

(c) _____

The topic of the table is the founding of the thirteen American colonies. The table lists the colonies, the dates they were founded, and the reasons they were founded.

As you scanned the body of the table, you may have noticed other things. For example, you may have noticed that many colonies were founded for economic reasons. As with paragraphs, any information you notice when you preview a table can help you understand it better when you read it.

Previewing a table is faster than previewing a paragraph. The title always tells the topic. The column headings always tell you what kinds of information are in the table. There usually aren't too many words in the body, so there is not a lot to scan.

How to Preview a Table

STEP 1: Read the title to find the topic.

STEP 2: Read the column headings.

STEP 3: Scan the body.

Graphs

Like tables, graphs are useful for comparing pieces of information. Some graphs, like the one that follows, are good for showing trends, or changes over time. Graphs look different from tables, but they're previewed in much the same way. To preview a graph, read its title, its subtitle, and its labels. The labels tell what the numbers along the bottom and the side of a graph represent. Scan the graph itself.

TRY THIS

Preview the following graph. Then answer the questions that follow it.

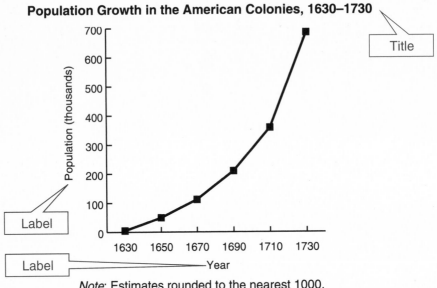

Population Growth in the American Colonies, 1630–1730

Title

Label

Label — Year

Note: Estimates rounded to the nearest 1000.

According to the title, what is the topic of the graph?

_____

What period of time does the graph cover? _____

What do the numbers along the bottom of this graph show? _____

What do the numbers along the side of this graph show? _____

The topic of the graph is the growth of the population in the American colonies. As the title shows, the years covered are 1630 to 1730. A label shows that each number along the bottom of the graph is a year. Another label shows that each number along the side of the graph (standing for thousands) tells the size of the population.

When you scanned the graph, you may have noticed the trend the graph shows: the population grew continually, faster and faster, as the years passed. Whatever you notice when you preview a graph will help you understand the graph better when you look at it closely to find information.

| **How to Preview a Graph** |
| STEP 1: Read the title to find the topic. |
| STEP 2: Read the labels. |
| STEP 3: Scan the graph itself. |

Preview the following table and graph. Answer the questions.

Questions 1 through 4 refer to the following table.

Female Workers in the United States, 1940–1990

Year	Number of Workers	Percent of All Women
1940	12,845,000	25%
1950	18,408,000	34
1960	23,268,000	38
1970	31,580,000	43
1980	45,611,000	52
1990	53,479,000	58

1. What is the topic of the table? _____

2. This table covers the time from _____ to _____.

3. What two parts of the table give the information you need to answer questions 1 and 2? _____ and _____

4. Which two of the following does the table tell you for each year?

  _____ (a) how many female workers there were

  _____ (b) how many male workers there were

  _____ (c) what percent of all women were working women

  _____ (d) what percent of working women had children

Questions 5 through 7 refer to the following graph.

5. What is the topic of the graph?

  _____

6. What ages are covered by the graph? _____

7. On the graph, heights are shown in

  (1) centimeters
  (2) feet
  (3) inches
  (4) meters

Check your answers on page 211.

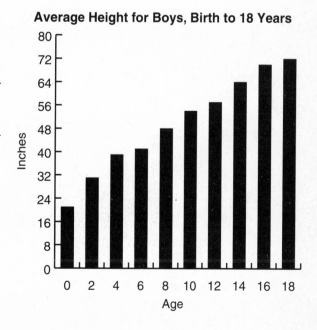

Average Height for Boys, Birth to 18 Years

Thinking About the Topic

You should take one more step after you preview and before you read a paragraph, table, or graph. When you have learned the topic by previewing, think about the topic. Ask yourself two questions:

- What do I already know about this topic?
- What information could this paragraph (or table, or graph) give me about the topic?

To answer these questions, you'll think about the topic. You'll predict what you will read about. That way, you'll be better prepared to read with understanding.

TRY THIS

Preview the following paragraph. Then answer the question that follows it.

Children are influenced in many ways. Parents are an important influence on their children, but they're not the only influence. Children are influenced by other adults, too. A favorite teacher, aunt, or coach might play an important part in a child's life. Children are also influenced by other children, who are often a bigger influence than any adult. Children can even be influenced by the actions of people they don't know, like athletes or actors. Other influences on children are TV, movies, and music.

What is the topic of the paragraph? _____

By reading the first sentence and scanning, you probably saw that the topic is influences on children.

NOW TRY THIS

Ask yourself the following two questions about the topic of the paragraph in the **Try This** on page 22. For each question, give two or more answers.

What do I know about influences on children?

_____

_____

What information could this paragraph give me about influences on children?

(HINT: Words you noticed in scanning might help you answer this question.)

_____

_____

In answering the first question, you might have thought about people who influenced you when you were young. You might have realized that children are influenced by their friends. When you answered the second question, you might have thought that the paragraph could tell you about the various people who influence children. You might have thought you could find out who has the most influence on children. You may not have predicted exactly what the paragraph says, but that doesn't matter. You were thinking about the topic. You prepared yourself to read with better understanding.

Now go back and read the paragraph. See if previewing and thinking about the topic help you when you read. You'll probably find that they do.

EXERCISE 3

Preview the following paragraph. Answer the questions.

Job satisfaction depends on a number of things. Workers feel more satisfied with their jobs when the pay is good. Job satisfaction is higher when there are "extras," such as vacations and health benefits. Studies show that two other things might be even more important than good pay and extras. Workers feel satisfied when they like what they're doing and when their work is appreciated.

1. What is the topic of the paragraph? _____

2. What are two things you already know about this topic?

_____

_____

3. What are two things this paragraph could tell you about the topic?

_____

_____

Check your answers on page 211. Then go back and reread the paragraph. You'll probably find that your thinking about the topic will help you when you read it again.

2 RECOGNIZING STATED MAIN IDEAS

Finding the main idea of a paragraph is the key to understanding how all the ideas in that paragraph fit together. The main idea is the main point a paragraph makes about its topic. Sometimes the main idea, or main point, is stated directly in one of the sentences in a paragraph. If so, the ideas in all the other sentences give details or examples that support or explain the main idea.

Suppose you received an invitation to your cousin's wedding. The wedding would be the main idea. The time and place of the ceremony and reception are the details that support the main idea.

This chapter will show you how to recognize the main idea and supporting details. You will learn how to find the sentence that states the main idea.

Lesson 4 Finding the Main Idea and Supporting Sentences

You know that a paragraph has a topic. In Lesson 1 you found the topics of paragraphs by previewing. Before you can find the main idea of a paragraph, however, you need to read the paragraph. To find the main idea, you need to think about how all the ideas in a paragraph relate to each other.

Finding the main idea of a paragraph takes effort. With practice, it becomes easier.

The Main Idea

The main idea of a paragraph is not the same as the topic. The main idea is the main point the paragraph makes **about** the topic. It is the most important idea in the paragraph.

For example, a paragraph could be about Benjamin Franklin. Its most important idea could be that Benjamin Franklin was a clever inventor. That would be the main idea **about** the topic, Benjamin Franklin.

Before you can find the main idea of a paragraph, you need to know what the paragraph's topic is.

Preview the following paragraph. (Remember: Read the first sentence, scan the paragraph, and read the last sentence.) Then answer the question that follows it.

Different types of maps have different uses. We use **political maps** to see how the world is divided into countries, states, and cities. We use **road maps** to figure out how to get where we're going. We use **weather maps** to understand weather changes. There are many other kinds of maps, each with its own use.

What is the topic of the paragraph?

_____

Hurricane David, September 3, 1979

The topic of the paragraph is maps or different types of maps. (The first sentence mentions different types of maps. Every sentence has the word *maps* in it.)

A paragraph's main idea is often stated in one of the sentences in the paragraph. To find the main idea sentence in the paragraph about maps, you need to read the paragraph. Go back and read the paragraph now. Look for the sentence that states the paragraph's main point about different types of maps.

NOW TRY THIS

These four sentences come from the paragraph. Which one states the main point the paragraph makes **about** maps?
   (1) Different types of maps have different uses.
   (2) We use **political maps** to see how the world is divided into countries, states, and cities.
   (3) We use **road maps** to figure out how to get where we're going.
   (4) We use **weather maps** to understand weather changes.

You are right if you picked Choice (1). The paragraph's main idea about maps is that different types of maps have different uses. The sentences in Choices (2), (3), and (4) support the main idea. Each one explains the use of a certain type of map.

In the paragraph about maps, the main idea is stated in the first sentence. The main idea is often, but not always, stated in the first sentence of a paragraph.

Supporting Sentences

A paragraph's main idea does not usually stand alone. It is supported by details or examples. When the main idea is stated in one sentence, the other sentences in the paragraph are called supporting sentences.

TRY THIS

Pretend that you have already previewed the following paragraph. You have found that it is about kinds of vegetation (trees and plants). Now read the paragraph and answer the questions that follow it. (The sentences in the paragraph are numbered.)

(1) The kind of vegetation an area has depends mainly on the temperature and rainfall in that area. (2) For example, warm, wet areas have thick rainforests full of trees and heavy vines. (3) Hot, dry areas, on the other hand, have only a few sturdy plants that do not need much water.

Which sentence states the main idea about kinds of vegetation? ____

In this paragraph, the two supporting sentences give examples. Which sentences are those? ____ and ____

Sentence (1) states the main idea: the kind of vegetation an area has depends on temperature and rainfall. Sentences (2) and (3) are the supporting sentences. They tell about the kinds of vegetation that grow in two areas with different temperatures and amounts of rainfall. Notice that one of the supporting sentences even begins with the words *For example*.

NOW TRY THIS

Read the following paragraph about the Constitution. Then answer the questions that follow it.

(1) The Constitution, written in 1787, set up the government of the United States. (2) It says that the government will have three branches: a congress, a president, and a supreme court. (3) It explains the separate powers and duties of each. (4) It also explains that power will be divided between the national government and the states.

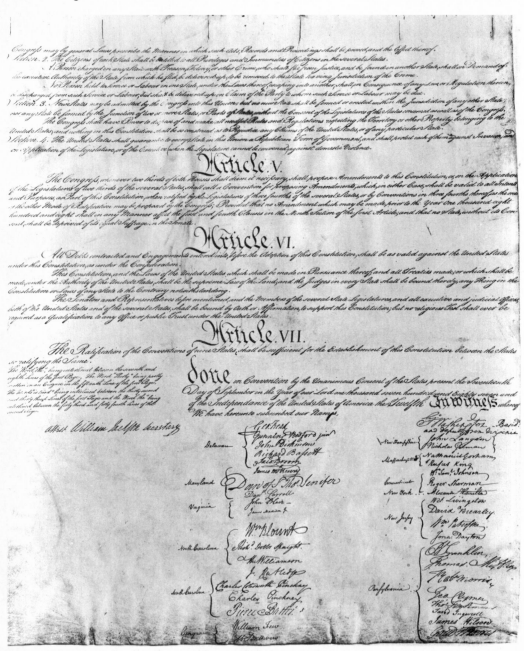

Portion of the Constitution of the United States

Which sentence states the main idea about the Constitution?_____

In this paragraph, the three supporting sentences give details. Which
sentences are those?   ____, ____ and ____

Sentence (1) states the main, or most important, idea: the Constitution set up the government of the United States. Sentences (2), (3), and (4) are the supporting sentences. They give some details about what the Constitution says.

EXERCISE 4

Preview and read each paragraph. Answer the questions.

Questions 1 and 2 refer to the following paragraph.

In the 1760s, England made many laws the colonists didn't like. Some laws required the colonists to pay taxes. The Stamp Act is an example. Other laws limited the colonists' movements. For example, one law said colonists could not settle west of the Appalachian Mountains. Still other laws forced the colonists to do certain things. For example, the Quartering Act required them to feed and house soldiers from England.

1. What is the topic of the paragraph? _____

2. These sentences come from the paragraph. Tell which one states the main idea. Tell which ones are supporting sentences.

   _____ (a) In the 1760s, England made many laws the colonists didn't like.
   _____ (b) Some laws required the colonists to pay taxes.
   _____ (c) Other laws limited the colonists' movements.
   _____ (d) Still other laws forced the colonists to do certain things.

Questions 3 and 4 refer to the following paragraph.

The unemployment rate for teenagers is high. In 1986, the unemployment rate for 16- to 19-year-olds was 18 percent. This means that out of every 100 teenagers who looked for jobs, 18 were unable to find one. (For adults that year, the rate was a much lower 7 percent.) The unemployment rate for teenagers in minority groups is especially high. In 1986 it was 36 percent.

3. What is the topic of the paragraph? _____

4. These sentences come from the paragraph. Tell which one states the main idea. Tell which ones are supporting sentences.

_____ (a) The unemployment rate for teenagers is high.

_____ (b) In 1986 the unemployment rate for 16- to 19-year-olds was 18 percent.

_____ (c) The unemployment rate for teenagers in minority groups is especially high.

_____ (d) In 1986 it was 36 percent.

Questions 5 and 6 refer to the following paragraph.

A young person's teenage years are filled with problems and challenges. One problem is that a teenager must make many important decisions. Should he or she go on with school? What kind of school should he or she attend? Should he or she look for a job? What kind of job? Another problem is that a teenager must take on new responsibilities. These problems are also challenges. Teenagers have the challenge of shaping their own futures.

5. What is the topic of this paragraph? _____

6. These sentences come from the paragraph. Tell which one states the main idea. Tell which ones are supporting sentences.

_____ (a) A young person's teenage years are filled with problems and challenges.

_____ (b) One problem is that a teenager must make many important decisions.

_____ (c) These problems are also challenges.

_____ (d) Teenagers have the challenge of shaping their own futures.

Check your answers on page 211.

Lesson 5

Finding the Sentence That States the Main Idea

So far in this chapter you've seen paragraphs with main ideas stated in the first sentence. In some paragraphs, the main idea is stated in a sentence other than the first sentence.

TRY THIS

Read the following paragraph about forces of nature, repeated from page 15. Then answer the question that follows it.

In September 1985, an earthquake struck Mexico. Part of Mexico City was destroyed. Nearly 25,000 people died in the earthquake. In November 1970 a cyclone, or storm, formed in the Bay of Bengal near the country of Bangladesh. The cyclone caused a 20-foot wave of water. The cyclone and wave hit Bangladesh, killing more than 300,000 people. As these examples show, forces of nature can strike cruelly.

In this paragraph, the main idea about the forces of nature is not stated in the first sentence. Which sentence does state the main idea?

_____

The last sentence states the main idea. The main idea is that forces of nature can strike cruelly. The other sentences give examples that support the main idea.

Most of the sentences in a paragraph are supporting sentences. Therefore, when you are looking for the main idea, ask yourself these questions: Does this sentence state the main point about the topic, or does it give an example or a detail?

NOW TRY THIS

Preview and read the following paragraph. Answer the questions that follow it.

Labor unions have fought for greater safety in the workplace. Unions have worked for a shorter work week and higher wages for employees. They have bargained with employers for benefits like sick pay and health insurance. In short, unions have fought to improve the lives of workers.

What is the topic of the paragraph? _____

Which sentence in the paragraph states the main idea?

_____

The topic is labor unions. (The word *unions* is repeated throughout the paragraph.) The main idea is that unions have fought to improve the lives of workers. This idea is stated in the last sentence of the paragraph. All the other sentences give examples that support the main idea. They mention aspects of workers' lives that unions have tried to improve.

The main idea sentence is most often the first sentence in a paragraph. It is also common to find the main idea stated in the last sentence. Or, the main idea sentence may be somewhere else.

Preview and read the following paragraph. Answer the questions that follow it.

When the United States became a country, only white men who owned property were allowed to vote. Over the years, the vote was extended to more and more groups of people. By the 1830s, white men without property were allowed to vote. Beginning in 1870, African-American men were given the vote. In 1920 the vote was extended to women. In 1971 the voting age was lowered from 21 to 18.

What is the topic of the paragraph? _____

Which of these sentences from the paragraph states the main idea?

    (1) When the United States became a country, only white men who owned property were allowed to vote.

    (2) Over the years, the vote was extended to more and more groups of people.

    (3) Beginning in 1870, African-American men were given the vote.

    (4) In 1971 the voting age was lowered from 21 to 18.

The topic is the vote. The main idea is that the vote was extended to more and more groups over the years. Therefore, Choice (2) is the right answer. Choices (3) and (4) are examples that support the main idea. They mention groups who gained the vote. Choice (1), the first sentence in the paragraph, gives background information you need in order to understand the main idea.

How to Find the Main Idea in a Paragraph

STEP 1:   With the topic in mind, read the paragraph.

STEP 1:   Look for the sentence that states the paragraph's main point about the topic. Look at the sentences in this order:
- the first sentence
- the last sentence
- the other sentences

STEP 3:   When you think you have found the main idea sentence, check by asking yourself this question: Do the other sentences in the paragraph support the main idea by giving examples or details?

EXERCISE 5

Preview and read each paragraph. Answer the questions. (Remember: A paragraph's main idea may be stated in any sentence.)

Questions 1 and 2 refer to the following paragraph.

The continent of Antarctica is very cold and dry. Its land is covered with ice and lacks vegetation. Antarctica is an icy desert.

Antartica: Ross Sea Ice Shelf near Little America Five

1. What is the topic of the paragraph? _____

2. Which sentence in the paragraph states the main idea?
   (1) the first sentence
   (2) the second sentence
   (3) the last sentence

Questions 3 and 4 refer to the following paragraph.

The American Revolution began with events in Massachusetts. The British General Thomas Gage knew the colonists were storing weapons in Concord. He knew two of the colonists' leaders, John Hancock and Samuel Adams, were hiding in Lexington. Gage ordered his men to find and arrest Hancock and Adams and to seize the weapons. Colonist spies learned of the general's plan and sent out a warning. By the time the British soldiers reached Lexington, Hancock and Adams had escaped. The colonists in Lexington fought the British. Badly outnumbered, the colonists lost that first battle.

3. What is the topic of the paragraph? _____

4. These sentences come from the paragraph. Tell which one states the main idea. Tell which ones are supporting sentences.

_____ (a) The American Revolution began with events in Massachusetts.

_____ (b) Gage ordered his men to find and arrest Hancock and Adams and to seize the weapons.

_____ (c) The colonists in Lexington fought the British.

_____ (d) Badly outnumbered, the colonists lost that first battle.

Questions 5 and 6 refer to the following paragraph.

Jobs can be divided into three general categories. Goods-producing jobs are jobs with companies that make products, or goods. Construction jobs and jobs in factories are examples. Service-producing jobs are jobs with employers that provide people with services. Jobs with banks, insurance companies, stores, and government agencies are examples. Farming jobs are the third type of jobs.

A Construction Site in New York City

5. What is the topic of the paragraph? _____

6. There are six sentences in the paragraph. Which one states the main idea?

_____

Questions 7 and 8 refer to the following paragraph.

In a recent year, one out of every 10,000 teenagers committed suicide. This was double the number of suicides of ten years earlier. The rate of suicides among teenagers is climbing fast.

7. What is the topic of the paragraph? _____

8. Which sentence states the main idea about the topic?
   (1) the first sentence
   (2) the second sentence
   (3) the last sentence

Questions 9 and 10 refer to the following paragraph.

Psychologists say there are several common warning signs before a teenage suicide attempt. One is a sudden drop in school attendance or grades. Another is extreme unhappiness over the breakup of a romantic relationship. Total avoidance of friends is a third sign.

9. What is the topic of the paragraph? _____

10. Which sentence states the main idea about the topic?
    (1) the first sentence
    (2) the second sentence
    (3) the third sentence
    (4) the last sentence

Questions 11 and 12 refer to the following paragraph.

One of the eight Americans to die in the Battle of Lexington was Prince Estabrook, a slave. Peter Salem, a freed slave, killed the British commander Major Pitcairn at the Battle of Bunker Hill. Two African-Americans, Oliver Cromwell and Prince Whipple, were with General George Washington when he made his famous crossing of the Delaware River. James Armistead, a slave, was a double agent. Pretending to spy for the British, he gathered important information for the American generals. An African-American officer named Middleton led an all African-American unit from Massachusetts. These and thousands of other African-American men had important roles in the American Revolution.

11. What is the topic of this paragraph? _____

12. Which of these sentences from the paragraph states the main idea?
    (1) One of the eight Americans to die in the Battle of Lexington was Prince Estabrook, a slave.
    (2) An African-American officer named Middleton led an all African-American unit from Massachusetts.
    (3) These and thousands of other African-American men had important roles in the American Revolution.

Question 13 refers to the following paragraph.

The vote was extended by *amendments*, or changes, added to the Constitution. The right of African-Americans to vote is stated in the Fifteenth Amendment. The right of women to vote is stated in the Nineteenth Amendment.

13. Which sentence states the main idea of the paragraph?
    (1) the first sentence
    (2) the second sentence
    (3) the last sentence

Question 14 refers to the following paragraph.

The number of jobs there are depends partly on how the economy of the country and of the region is doing. When the economy is doing well, businesses need many workers. When the economy is doing poorly, businesses don't hire, and may lay off, workers.

14. Which sentence states the main idea of the paragraph?
    (1) the first sentence
    (2) the second sentence
    (3) the last sentence

Question 15 refers to the following paragraph.

The U.S. Constitution is now 200 years old. It is the oldest written constitution in the world. It has been amended several times to keep it up to date. Even though it is old, the Constitution still works.

15. Which sentence states the main idea of the paragraph?
    (1) the first sentence
    (2) the second sentence
    (3) the third sentence
    (4) the last sentence

Check your answers on page 211.

Chapter

3 UNDERSTANDING THE DETAILS

If you live in Chicago and are driving to New Orleans, you know you have to travel south. But you would have a clearer understanding of your route if you knew which highways to take and which states and cities you will pass through.

Similarly, to understand a paragraph, it's not enough to know the main idea. You also need to understand the details. The main idea will give you a general sense of the paragraph. The details will provide a more specific understanding of the topic.

Don't forget, the main ideas and the details are related. They are both about the topic. The details support and explain the main idea. Understanding details helps you find the main idea. Finding the main idea helps you understand the details.

In this chapter you will practice finding and understanding details in paragraphs, tables, graphs, and maps.

Lesson 6

Reading for Details

In a paragraph, the examples and explanations that make a main idea clear are made up of details. Noticing the details as you read a paragraph deepens your understanding of its main idea.

TRY THIS

Read the following paragraph and answer the questions that follow.

Humans can live on only a small part of the earth's surface. More than 70 percent of the earth's surface is covered by water. Therefore, less than 30 percent of the earth is land. Much of this land cannot be lived on. Its climate may be too cold or its soil, too poor. No one lives in Antarctica, for example. Yet Antarctica takes up a lot of the earth's land. It takes up more land than Europe does.

What is the main idea of the paragraph?

_____

About how much of the earth's surface does water take up?
   (a) 5 percent
   (b) 30 percent
   (c) 70 percent

Which of the following statements about Antarctica is true?

    (a) Antarctica is large but has no people.
    (b) Antarctica is large and has many people.
    (c) Antarctica is very small and has no people.
    (d) Antarctica is very small but has many people.

The main idea of the paragraph is stated in the first sentence: *Humans can live on only a small part of the earth's surface.* By itself, this sentence might not be fully clear. But the rest of the paragraph explains and supports the idea. First it says that most of the earth is covered with water. Then it says that a lot of the land isn't fit to live on. Antarctica is given as an example.

The details about oceans and Antarctica help you make sense of the main idea. The main idea helps you notice and make sense of the details. You notice that 70 percent of the earth is covered with water, because this detail fits with the main idea. For the same reason you notice that Antarctica is large but has no people.

The answer to the second question is (c). The answer to the third is (a). You probably had to go back to the paragraph to find or check the answers. This often happens. Understanding the fit between main idea and detail makes answers easy to find and check.

NOW TRY THIS

Read the following paragraph and answer the questions that follow. Look for the main idea. Keep it in mind as you read the details.

The Walt Disney Company tries to make its workers happy so its customers will also be happy. When people leave Disney World, their impressions are not just about Mickey Mouse and rides. The feelings they have also depend on how the workers treated them. Happy workers are more likely to be polite and helpful to people. Workers will be happy, the Disney Company believes, if they feel like part of the company. When workers start at Disney, they are given special training. They learn all about Disney World and Disney movies. They learn that they are an important part of the company.

Mickey Mouse Welcomes Guests to Walt Disney's Magic Kingdom

Which sentence gives the main idea of the paragraph?

_____

When people leave Disney World, they remember the attractions and rides. What else do they remember?_____

_____

How does the Disney Company help workers learn to be polite to guests?

(a) It pays workers lots of money.
(b) It watches the workers very closely.
(c) It makes workers feel like they're part of the company.

The main idea is in the first sentence: Disney tries to make its workers happy in order to make its guests happy.

The answer to the second question is that guests recall how workers treated them. The answer to the third question is (c). Disney makes workers happy by treating them like part of the company.

Both of the details asked for in the questions are related to the main idea. If, when you read, you fit details to the main idea, you'll find detail questions easy to answer.

EXERCISE 6

Preview and read each paragraph. Answer the questions. (Remember: If a question asks about a detail you don't recall, scan the paragraph to find it.)

Questions 1 through 3 refer to the following paragraph.

Early in the Revolutionary War, it looked as though England might have an easy victory over the Americans. England was a major military power with a large, well-trained army. In 1776 England sent a 30,000-man force to New York. It easily defeated General George Washington's small, poorly trained American army there. The Americans would have been completely destroyed, but fog allowed them to escape. England's army occupied New York City.

1. Which sentence states the main idea of the paragraph?

(1) the first sentence
(2) the second sentence
(3) the last sentence

2. How many men did England send to New York in 1776? _____

3. Which two of the following statements about the American army in New York in 1776 are true?

(a) George Washington was its general.
(b) It was large and well trained.
(c) It was defeated by the English.
(d) It was totally destroyed by the English.

Question 4 refers to the following paragraph.

George Washington led his army to an important victory late in 1776. Trenton, New Jersey, was held by a group of Hessians, German soldiers hired by England. Washington decided to attack them the day after Christmas when they would be having parties. He crossed the Delaware River with his troops in a snowstorm, surprised the Hessians, and defeated them. That victory boosted the morale of the American troops.

4. Which two of the following statements about the Hessians are true?
   (a) They were German soldiers.
   (b) They were hired by the Americans.
   (c) George Washington's army defeated them at Trenton.

Questions 5 and 6 refer to the following paragraph.

After the Battle of Saratoga, France gave the Americans support that helped them win independence from England. The Americans had defeated a large English force in Saratoga, New York, in October 1777. Until then, France had lent the Americans money and provided them with weapons. The Battle of Saratoga convinced the French that the Americans could succeed in their revolution. After Saratoga, France recognized American independence and became America's ally. The French army and navy helped the Americans win the last important battle of the Revolutionary War at Yorktown in 1781. In 1783 England recognized American independence by signing the Treaty of Paris.

5. The following sentences come from the paragraph. Which one gives an example of the support France gave the Americans?
   (1) After the Battle of Saratoga, France gave the Americans support that helped them win independence from England.
   (2) The Americans had defeated a large English force in Saratoga, New York, in October 1777.
   (3) The French army and navy helped the Americans win the last important battle of the Revolutionary War at Yorktown in 1781.

6. Before the Battle of Saratoga, France had
   (1) been an ally of England
   (2) supplied money and weapons to the Americans
   (3) recognized American independence

Question 7 refers to the following paragraph.

People often find retirement to be unsatisfactory at first. Usually they are tired of working and look forward to retiring. There are many things they want to see and do. Yet when retirement comes, it is a shock. They may feel lonely at home. Time may pass slowly. Even though they now have time to do things, they may not have the money. Within a year of retiring, though, most people are no longer unhappy. Some find new hobbies or work. Others form closer ties to their families.

7. The following sentences come from the paragraph. Which two give examples that show that retirement is not pleasant at first?

    (a) Usually they are tired of working and look forward to retiring.

    (b) They may feel lonely at home.

    (c) Even though they now have time to do things, they may not have the money.

    (d) Within a year of retiring, though, most people are no longer unhappy.

Check your answers on page 212.

Lesson 7

Seeing How Details Are Organized

In a paragraph, the details are usually organized by one pattern or another. If you can see how the details in a paragraph are organized, you'll understand the paragraph better. Usually there are clue words or phrases that can help you figure out what pattern of organization is used.

Sequence

In some paragraphs, details are organized by time order, or sequence. You first read about the thing that happened earliest, then about the next thing that happened, and so on. This is often true of paragraphs that tell about events in history.

TRY THIS

Read the following paragraph. Look for the clue words and phrases that let you know that the details are organized in sequence. Answer the questions that follow the paragraph.

As time passed, England made more and more laws that the American colonists resented. The Proclamation of 1763 told the colonists that they could not settle west of the Appalachian Mountains. In 1765 England passed the Stamp Act, a tax on legal documents and newspapers. In the same year the Quartering Act made the colonists provide food and housing for English soldiers. The Townshend Acts of 1767 placed taxes on certain goods imported by the colonists: paper, glass, paint, and tea. Such laws increased colonists' desire for independence from England.

What are the clues that show that the details are organized by sequence?

_____ _____

_____ _____

_____

In what order did England make these laws?

_____ the Stamp Act

_____ the Townshend Acts

_____ the Proclamation of 1763

Two kinds of clues show organization by sequence. The following dates appear in order in the paragraph: *1763, 1765,* and *1767.* The phrase *In the same year* also indicates time order. England made these laws in this order: (1) the Proclamation of 1763, (2) the Stamp Act (1765), and (3) the Townshend Acts (1767).

To find the order of a series of events with a sequence organization, you just need to notice their order in the paragraph.

Classification

Some paragraphs organize details by type. They classify details into groups. Organization by classification is common when a paragraph gives details about two or more things.

TRY THIS

Read the following paragraph. Look for the clue phrases that let you know that the details are organized by classification. Answer the questions that follow the paragraph.

Workers are often divided into two groups. Blue-collar workers make up one group of workers. They are paid by the hour. They usually work with their hands and wear work clothes. The other group is made up of white-collar workers. Most are paid an annual salary. Some, like doctors and lawyers, are paid fees by their clients. Their jobs may require higher education. They often wear business dress.

What are the clue phrases that show that the details are organized by classification?

_____   _____

_____   _____

How are blue-collar workers paid? _____

How are white-collar workers paid? _____

These phrases show that the details are organized by classification: *two groups, one group,* and *The other group.* Blue-collar workers are paid by the hour; white-collar workers are paid annual salaries or fees.

Notice that the first sentence in the paragraph introduces the two groups. Next you read all the details about one group. Then you read the details about the other group. With a classification organization, to find a detail about one group you just need to look in the part of the paragraph where that group is described.

Comparison and Contrast

The details in some paragraphs are organized to show how things are alike. Such paragraphs make comparisons between two or more things. Other paragraphs show how things contrast, or are different. Some paragraphs both compare and contrast.

TRY THIS

Read the following paragraph. Look for the clue words and phrases that show that the contrast between two things is explained. Answer the questions that follow the paragraph.

Weather and climate are different things. Although the weather in New York may be cold and snowy on a winter day, this does not mean that New York has a cold climate. On the contrary, the average temperature in New York is 52°F. Weather refers to conditions on a certain day. Climate, on the other hand, refers to conditions over a long period of time.

What are the clue words and phrases that show that the details contrast two things?

_____   _____

_____   _____

What two things are contrasted in the paragraph?

_____ and _____

These words and phrases show that the paragraph contrasts two things: *different things*, *Although*, *On the contrary*, and *on the other hand*. The two things contrasted are weather and climate.

Notice that the first sentence says that climate and weather are different. The rest of the sentences give examples and explanations of the differences.

In a paragraph that compares two things, you might find clue words and phrases like these: *the same*, *in the same way*, and *likewise*.

Cause and Effect

Some paragraphs describe a series of causes and effects. In a sense, the details are organized to show how one thing leads to another.

TRY THIS

Read the following paragraph. Look for the clue words that let you know that the details are organized as a series of causes and effects. Answer the questions that follow the paragraph.

Mountains cause weather. By causing weather, they in effect create forests and deserts. When moist air blows onto a mountain range, it is forced upward and becomes cooler. Water droplets form and drop on the mountains as rain or snow. The rain or snow can be so extensive that forests result. After the air reaches the top of the mountains, it slides down the other side. Because the now-dry air warms up as it descends, it picks up moisture from the land. Deserts are the result.

What are the clue words that show a cause-and-effect organization of details in the paragraph?

_____   _____

_____   _____

Here are three events described in the paragraph. Tell what the effect of each is.

Cause	Effect
moist air rises	_____
moist air cools	_____
dry air warms up	_____

These words show that the details in the paragraph are organized by cause and effect: *in effect, result, because, the result.*

As moist air rises, it cools. When moist air cools, it drops its moisture as rain or snow. When dry air warms up, it absorbs moisture from the land.

Not every sentence in the paragraph has a clue word. Some sentences make a cause-effect relationship clear without clue words.

How to Figure Out How Details Are Organized

As you read, ask yourself these questions:
- Are the details in time order?
- Are the details classified into groups?
- Do the details compare or contrast things?
- Do the details explain causes and effects?

Read each paragraph. Note how details are organized in each to help you understand what you're reading. Then answer the questions that follow each.

Questions 1 through 5 refer to the following paragraph.

Middle age has its down side. In middle age, it's harder to keep in physical shape. You realize you're getting older. You may feel less positive about life. In other ways, middle age has its benefits. It can bring a feeling of "having arrived." You can feel settled and satisfied with what you've accomplished. For many people, the best thing about middle age is that their children are grown and managing on their own.

1. Write the sentence that introduces the part of the paragraph about the bad side of middle age. _____

2. What three bad points about middle age does the paragraph mention?

   _____
   _____
   _____
   _____

3. Write the sentence that introduces the part of the paragraph about the good side of middle age. _____

4. What three good points about middle age does the paragraph mention?

   _____
   _____
   _____

5. The details in this paragraph are organized by
   (1) sequence
   (2) classification
   (3) comparison and/or contrast
   (4) cause and effect

Questions 6 through 10 refer to the following paragraph.

For a child, learning language takes a long time. There are some quick bursts in learning and some periods during which progress is slow. A child begins to speak sometime around his or her first birthday. By eighteen months, most children can say between 10 and 20 words, including *mama* and *dada*. At age two a child uses one or two words to mean a whole sentence. "Cookie" can mean "I want a cookie" or "My cookie broke." By three, children know about 900 words and can use them in three- and four-word sentences.

6. At about what age does a child begin to speak? _____

7. By about what age can a child say as many as 20 words? _____

8. At age two, how does a child express his or her thoughts? _____

9. How old is a child when he or she can say about 900 words? _____

10. The details in this paragraph are organized by

    (1) sequence
    (2) classification
    (3) comparison and/or contrast
    (4) cause and effect

Questions 11 through 13 refer to the following paragraph.

      People lose jobs for two main reasons. One reason has to do with the economy. When business is slow, a company may not be able to keep all its employees. It may lay off people. The other reason has to do with job performance. When an employee doesn't handle his duties well, he or she may be fired.

11. What phrases give clues to the way the paragraph is organized?

_____   _____   _____

12. What two reasons does the paragraph give for people losing their jobs?

_____

_____

13. The details in this paragraph are organized by

    (1) sequence
    (2) classification
    (3) comparison and/or contrast

Check your answers on page 212.

Lesson 8

Finding Details in Tables

To find details in a table, you need to know what kind of information the table shows and how that information is organized.

    As you learned in Lesson 2, you can find out what a table shows by previewing it. To preview a table, you read the title and the column headings and scan the body.

TRY THIS

Preview the following table. Then answer the questions that follow it.

Unemployment Rates by Job Type, 1975 and 1987

Job Type	1975	1987
Construction	18%	13%
Farming	10%	11%
Manufacturing	11%	6%
Mining	4%	10%
Sales	7%	5%

Note: The unemployment rate is the number of workers without jobs for every 100 workers.

The topic of the table is _____

rates for different jobs in the years _____ and _____.

The three column headings in the table are _____,

_____, and _____.

How many job types are listed in the table? _____

As the title shows, the topic of the table is unemployment rates in 1975 and 1987. The three column headings are *Job Type, 1975*, and *1987*. The table lists five job types.

Look back at the table. It has a special feature, a footnote. The footnote is the sentence at the very bottom of the table. It tells something about the table. In this case the footnote explains what *unemployment rate* means.

A table may contain an asterisk (*). If you find an asterisk, look for a footnote that also begins with an asterisk.

To find a piece of information in a table, you read down a column to the row that has the detail you want.

NOW TRY THIS

Use the table to answer these questions:

What was the unemployment rate for mining jobs in 1975? _____%

Out of every 100 mining workers, how many were unemployed in 1975? _____

The unemployment rate for mining jobs in 1975 was 4 percent. That means that for every 100 workers in mining in 1975, 4 were unemployed.

To find the percent, first look in the *Job Type* column to find *Mining*. Then run your finger down the *1975* column until you come to the row that has *Mining* in it. You find the figure *4%*. The footnote explains what that figure means in terms of people.

Tables are useful for comparing pieces of information.

NOW TRY THIS

Look back at the table again to find the answer to the following questions.

In which job type shown was unemployment highest in 1975?

_____

Was unemployment in manufacturing higher in 1975 or in 1987?

_____

In 1975 unemployment was highest in construction. In manufacturing, unemployment was higher in 1975 than in 1987.

To find the answer to the first question, find the highest percent in the *1975* column: *18%*. Then look across the same row to the *Job Type* column where you find the word *Construction*. To find the answer to the second question, compare the two percents in the *Manufacturing* row: *11%* and *6%*. Look at the column heading for the column with the higher percent: *1975*.

EXERCISE 8

Preview each table. Then find the details in each table that answer the questions about it.

Questions 1 through 5 refer to the following table.

Average Weekly Earnings by Job and Sex

Job	For Males	For Females
Manager	$623	$405
Salesperson	$454	$243
Mechanic	$422	$409
Clerk	$413	$291
Driver	$375	$296
Farmer	$222	$184

Note: Figures are for 1986.

1. What does the footnote to the table explain? _____

2. What were the average weekly earnings for male clerks? _____

3. What were the average weekly earnings for female clerks? _____

4. What were the average weekly earnings for female mechanics? _____

5. On average, who earned more, male drivers or female drivers? _____

Questions 6 through 9 refer to the following table.

Major Mining Locations and Uses of Some Metals

Metals	Locations	Uses
Aluminum	Australia, France, Guyana, Jamaica, Russia, Sierra Leone, Surinam	Airplanes, foil, wire, heating equipment
Iron	Australia, Brazil, Canada, China, France, Russia, US	Machines, cars, pipes, ships
Silver	Canada, Chile, Mexico, Russia, US	Silverware, dental fillings, jewelry
Uranium	Australia, Canada, France, South Africa, Spain, Russia, US, Zaire	Nuclear energy

6. What are two uses for iron? _____ and _____

7. Uranium is used in making _____

8. In how many major locations is silver mined? _____

9. Is the United States a major mining location for aluminum? _____

Check your answers on page 213.

Lesson 9

Finding Details in Graphs

To find details in a graph, you need to know what kind of information the graph shows and how that information is represented. This applies to any of the three main types of graphs: line graphs, bar graphs, and circle graphs.

Line Graphs

A line graph uses a line to represent data. Line graphs are especially useful for showing trends, or changes over time.

In Lesson 2 you previewed line graphs. Remember that to preview a line graph, you read the title and the labels and scan the graph itself.

Preview the following line graph. Then answer the questions that follow it.

Average Life Expectancy in the United States, 1900–1980

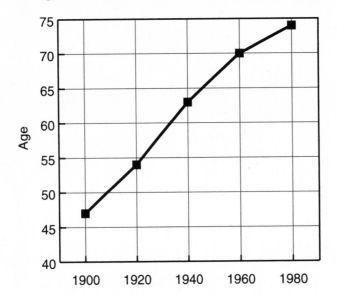

What is the topic of the graph?_____

What do the numbers along the bottom of the graph represent?_____

What do the numbers along the side of the graph represent?_____

The topic of the graph is average life expectancy in the United States for the years 1900 to 1980. (Life expectancy means the average age people live to.) The numbers along the bottom of the graph are years; those along the side are ages—the average ages people live to.

The details a line graph shows are represented by the line. Each point, or spot, on the line represents one piece of information. To understand that information, you look at the position of a point on the line in relation to the numbers along the bottom and side of the graph.

NOW TRY THIS

In the line graph, find the detail that answers this question:

What was the average life expectancy in 1960? _____

In 1960 the average life expectancy was 70 years. To read that piece of information, find the line that goes straight up from the year *1960*. Notice at which point that line hits the slanted line of the graph. From that point, look straight across to the left to find what age the point is even with. (You may want to use a ruler.) The point is even with the *70*.

Sometimes you have to estimate to get a piece of information from a line graph.

NOW TRY THIS

Look at the line graph again. Find the answer to this question:

About what was the life expectancy in 1900? _____

In 1900 the life expectancy was about 47. Notice where the line that goes up from 1900 hits the slanted line of the graph. When you look left, you see that the age is between 45 and 50. It seems to be at about 47.

You can tell what trend a line graph shows by noticing which way the line slants.

NOW TRY THIS

Look at the line graph one more time. Find the answer to this question:

Is life expectancy increasing or decreasing? _____

The line on the graph slants upward. That indicates that life expectancy is increasing. The line runs from the left (1900) toward the present. 1980 is the most recent date shown. At the same time, the line goes up from lower ages to higher ages—from about 47 to about 74. Life expectancy has become longer and longer as time has gone by.

Bar Graphs

The main difference between bar graphs and line graphs is in the way the data are shown. As their name suggests, bar graphs represent data with bars.

Bar graphs are laid out like line graphs. A bar graph has a title at the top and labels along the bottom and side. You can preview a bar graph just as you do a line graph. You also read a bar graph about the same way you read a line graph.

TRY THIS

Preview the following bar graph. Then answer the questions that follow it.

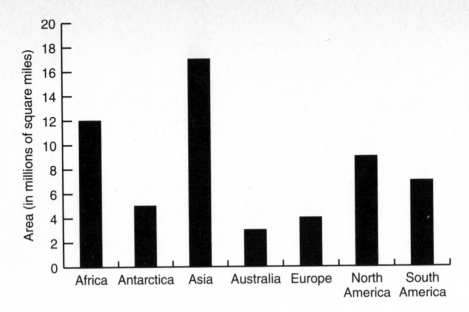

Sizes of the Continents

What is the topic of the graph?_____

The numbers along the side of the graph show area. What does the

number 8 mean? _____

About how large is Africa? _____

About how large is North America?_____

The topic of the graph is the sizes of the continents. The numbers along the side of the graph show areas in millions of square miles. Therefore, the number *8* means 8 million square miles. Africa's area is about 12 million square miles, and North America's is about 9 million square miles.

Because the lengths of bars are different, bar graphs are useful for showing comparisons.

NOW TRY THIS

Compare the bars in the bar graph to find the answers to the following questions.

Which continent is the largest? _____

Which continent is the smallest _____

North America is about half as large as which continent? _____

Asia is the largest continent: Its bar is the tallest of all the bars on the graph. Australia, with the shortest bar, is the smallest continent. The bar that stands for the size of North America is about half as long as the one for Asia, which shows that North America is about half as large as Asia.

Circle Graphs

Circle graphs are laid out differently from line graphs and bar graphs. As with other graphs, to preview a circle graph you read its title and labels.

TRY THIS

Preview the following circle graph. Then answer the question that follows it.

The Earth's Land Area: Portion per Continent

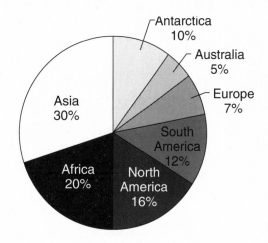

The circle stands for all—100 percent—of the land on the earth. What does each section of the circle stand for?

Each section of the circle stands for one continent, or the land area of one continent.

In a circle graph, the whole circle stands for 100 percent, or all, of something. Each section of the circle stands for a portion, or part, of that thing. Sometimes the sections are labeled with percents.

NOW TRY THIS

Look back at the circle graph. Find the information that completes each of the following statements.

Asia has _____ percent of all the land on the earth.

South America has _____ percent of all the land on the earth.

Asia has 30 percent of all the land on the earth. South America has 12 percent. The size of a section in a circle graph shows how much of the whole thing the portion is. For that reason, circle graphs are useful for comparing the sizes of the parts of something.

NOW TRY THIS

Look once again at the circle graph. Find the answers to the following questions.

Two continents take up half, or 50 percent, of the land area on the earth. Which two are those? _____ and

_____

The other half of the earth's land area is divided among the other five continents. In order of size, largest first, those five continents are

(a) _____   (b) _____

(c) _____   (d) _____

(e) _____

The two continents that take up half the land on the earth are Asia and Africa. In order of size, the other five continents are (a) North America, (b) South America, (c) Antarctica, (d) Europe, and (e) Australia.

EXERCISE 9

Preview each graph. Then find the details you need to answer the questions about each.

Questions 1 through 4 refer to the following line graph.

Number of Unemployed Workers in the United States, 1940–1980

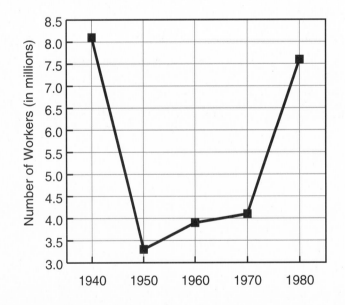

1. About how many workers were unemployed in 1980? _____

2. About how many workers were unemployed in 1960? _____

3. During which ten-year period did the number of unemployed workers go down?
   (1) 1940–1950
   (2) 1950–1960
   (3) 1960–1970
   (4) 1970–1980

4. From 1940 to 1980, the number of unemployed workers was lowest in _____ and highest in _____ .

Questions 5 through 8 refer to the following bar graph.

Number of Workers in the United States, 1900–1980

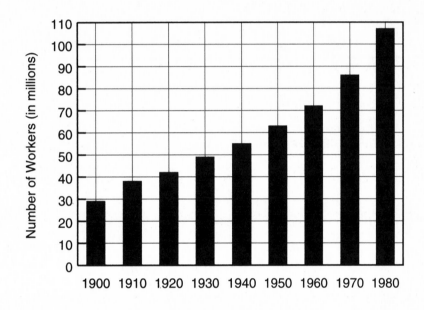

5. About how many workers were there in 1900? _____

6. About how many workers were there in 1980? _____

7. In which of the years shown were there slightly more than 60 million workers? _____

8. There were about twice as many workers in 1980 as in
   (1) 1970
   (2) 1940
   (3) 1910

Questions 9 through 12 refer to the following circle graph.

World Population: Portion per Continent

9. On which continent do most of the people in the world live?
   (1) South America
   (2) Africa
   (3) Asia

10. What percent of the world's population lives in North America?

    _____ percent

11. Which continent is not shown on the graph?_____

12. Which two continents have populations that are about the same size?
    (1) Africa and North America
    (2) North America and South America
    (3) Australia and Europe

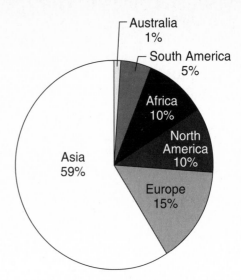

Note: Antarctica is not shown because it has no permanent population.

Check your answers on page 213.

Lesson 10

Finding Details in Maps

To find the details in a map, you need to know what kinds of information the map shows and what the symbols on the map mean. Maps fall into two main groups: political maps and special-purpose maps. Both types are commonly used in social studies.

Political Maps

Political maps show the boundaries of countries and states, and sometimes counties, cities, and towns. To know what information a certain political map shows, you need to preview it, much as you preview a graph.

To preview a map, just look at its title and key and scan the map itself. The key explains what the symbols, patterns, or colors on a map mean.

TRY THIS

Preview this map of the United States as it once was. Then answer the questions that follow it.

The United States in 1783

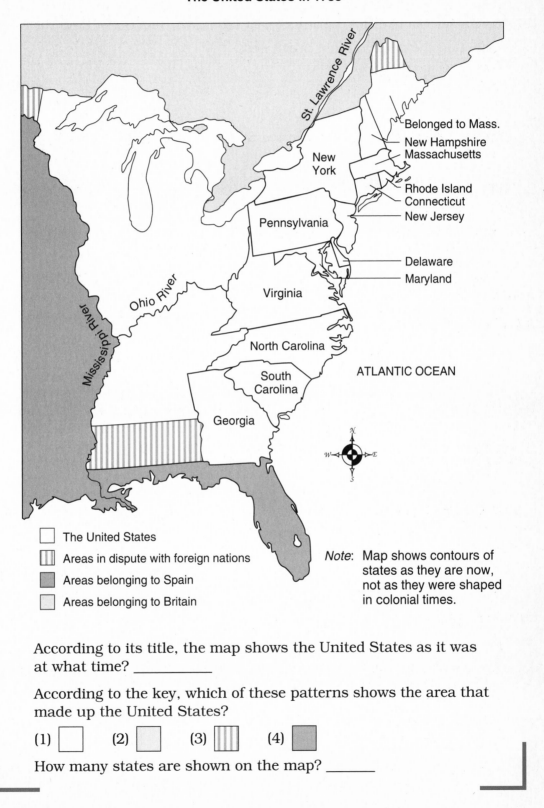

According to its title, the map shows the United States as it was at what time? _____

According to the key, which of these patterns shows the area that made up the United States?

(1) ☐   (2) ▨   (3) ▥   (4) ▨

How many states are shown on the map? _____

The map shows the United States in 1783. The key shows that pattern (1) covers the area that was the United States. The map shows thirteen states. (Did you notice that Massachusetts was in two parts in 1783? Did you notice that much of the area that made up the United States in 1783 was not divided into states then?)

Most maps are drawn so that north is toward the top of the map. Usually they have a symbol like this $\stackrel{N}{\lambda}$ or this $\cdot \diamondsuit \cdot$ that shows directions. Find the direction symbol on the map you just previewed.

NOW TRY THIS

Look again at the map of the United States. Use it to answer these questions:

Which state was farthest north in 1783? _____

Which state was farthest south in 1783? _____

Which river shown on the map was the western border of the United States?_____

Which border of the United States did the Atlantic Ocean form: northern, eastern, or southern?_____

Since north is toward the top of the map, the state farthest north is the one closest to the top: Massachusetts. The state farthest south is the one closest to the bottom of the map: Georgia. The western border of the United States is on the left side of the country. It was the Mississippi River. Since the Atlantic Ocean is to the right of the United States, it formed the eastern border of the country.

Special-Purpose Maps

Special-purpose maps typically show only one kind of information, such as how much rain falls per year in a certain area. By previewing, you can find out what a special-purpose map shows. Once you know that, you will be able to understand the details on the map.

TRY THIS

Here is a special-purpose map that shows annual rainfall in the United States. The key shows that darker patterns mean higher rainfall. Use the map to answer the questions that follow it.

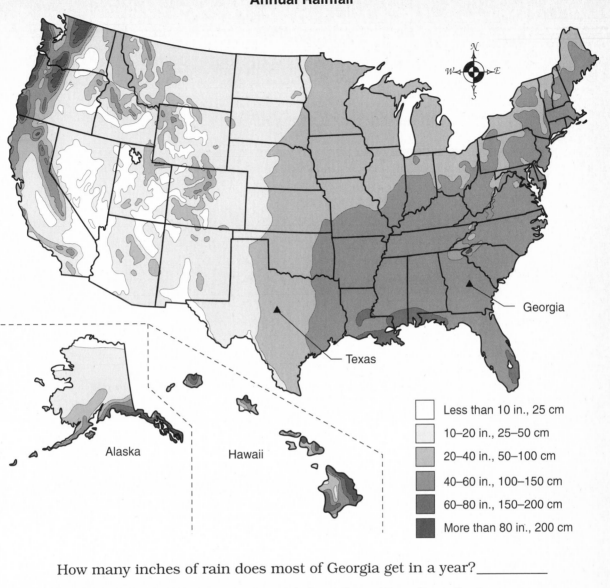

How many inches of rain does most of Georgia get in a year?_____

The areas in the United States with less than 10 inches of rain a year are in which part of the country: eastern, western, northern

or southern? _____

Which part of Texas gets the most rain: eastern, central, or

western? _____

Most of Georgia is covered with this pattern ▮, which means that it gets 40–60 inches of rain a year. This pattern ☐ stands for less than 10 inches of rain a year. The areas with that pattern are all in the western part of the country. This pattern ▮ in Texas, compared to the others, shows that the eastern part of the state gets the most rain.

Did you notice that two states, Alaska and Hawaii, are shown in boxes at the bottom of the map? The map is not big enough to show them in their actual locations, so they are shown in insets, or boxes.

Preview each map. Then find the details in each that answer the questions about it.

Questions 1 through 5 refer to the following map.

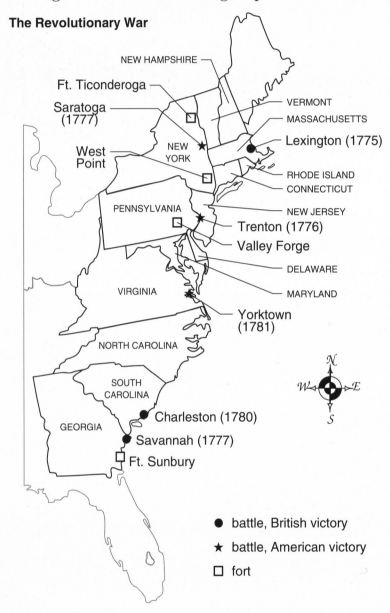

The Revolutionary War

1. Which battle is the earliest one shown on the map? _____

2. Which side won the Battle of Savannah? _____

3. What two forts were located in New York? _____ and
   _____

4. Which is the last battle shown on the map? _____

5. In what state was Fort Sunbury located? _____

Questions 6 through 9 refer to the following map.

Average Yearly Wages by State, 1987

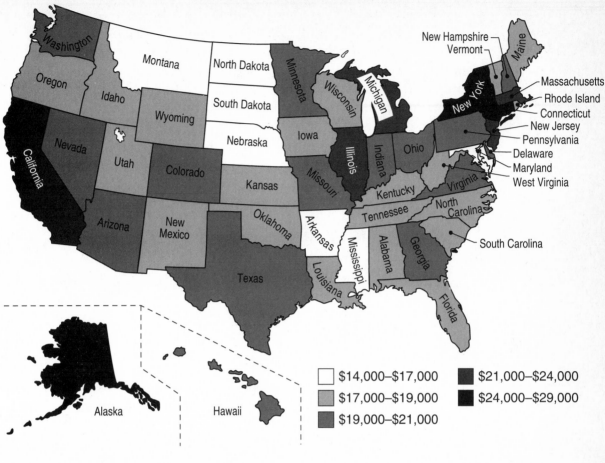

6. In which of the following states was the average yearly wage in 1987 between $21,000 and $24,000?

   (1) Kentucky
   (2) Oregon
   (3) California

7. Which state had a higher average yearly wage in 1987, Texas or

   Tennessee? _____

8. The average yearly wage in 1987 in Pennsylvania was in what category?

   $_____ to $_____

9. Which three states had the highest average yearly wages in 1987?

   _____, _____, and _____.

Check your answers on page 214.

On the next 10 pages you will find twenty short readings in the five areas of social studies: history, geography, economics, political science, and behavioral science. They will help you prepare for the Social Studies Test of the GED in three ways. You can use them to

- refresh what you already know about social studies
- expand your general knowledge of social studies
- practice your reading skills

HISTORY READINGS

BRITISH SETTLEMENT OF AMERICA

British settlement of America began with Jamestown, Virginia, in 1607. Over the next 150 years, further British settlement greatly increased the number of colonies and people in America. By 1750 there were thirteen colonies. These colonies stretched from Georgia to what is now Maine and had more than 1.5 million inhabitants. People had come to the colonies for many reasons. Some wanted the freedom to follow their own religions. Others came to escape poverty; they wanted a chance for a new life. Some had been jailed as debtors. Others were forced to come: almost one-fourth of the population were slaves brought from Africa against their will.

1. Which of the following is the topic of the paragraph?
   (1) Jamestown, Virginia
   (2) British settlement of America
   (3) the search for religious freedom
   (4) the beginnings of slavery in America

2. How many colonies were there in 1750?

   _____

3. About how many people were in the colonies by 1750? _____

4. State two reasons people came to the colonies._____

   _____

DIFFERENCES AMONG THE COLONIES

Because of differences in location, soil, and climate, the American colonies produced different goods. The colonies can be thought of in three groups. The New England colonies were Massachusetts, New Hampshire, Connecticut, and Rhode Island. Their climate was somewhat cold, and their soil was not very good. They had rich forests and good harbors, so many of the people worked as shipbuilders, sailors, or merchants. The middle colonies were New York, Pennsylvania, New Jersey, and Delaware. Their soil and climate were suitable for farming, and many small farms grew crops such as grain. The southern colonies were Maryland, Virginia, North Carolina, South Carolina, and Georgia. Because of their rich soil and warm climate, they had large plantations that grew cotton, rice, and tobacco.

5. These sentences come from the paragraph. Tell which one states the main idea.
   (1) Because of differences in location, soil, and climate, the American colonies produced different goods.
   (2) They had rich forests and good harbors, so many of the people worked as shipbuilders, sailors, or merchants.
   (3) Because of their rich soil and warm climate, they had large plantations that grew cotton, rice, and tobacco.

6. How are the details in this paragraph organized?
   (1) in sequence
   (2) by classification
   (3) to describe a series of causes and effects

7. What were the three groups of colonies?
   _____, _____, and _____

8. List the four middle colonies.

   _____ _____

   _____ _____

9. Which type of colony had many small farms?_____

10. Which type of colony had large plantations?_____

DISCONTENT WITH BRITISH RULE

Over the years the colonists became unhappy with British rule. They objected to taxes they had to pay to Britain. The colonists argued that since they weren't represented in the British government, they shouldn't have to pay taxes. Further, the colonists objected to laws that forced them to sell certain goods only to Britain. They also objected to laws that forced them to buy certain goods from Britain. They wanted to trade with other countries, too, and to make more goods for themselves. In addition, the colonists had developed a sense of themselves as Americans. They didn't want to be ruled by a faraway country.

11. The following sentences come from the paragraph. Tell which one states the main idea and which ones are supporting sentences.

    _____ (a) Over the years the colonists became unhappy with British rule.
    _____ (b) They objected to taxes they had to pay to Britain.
    _____ (c) They didn't want to be ruled by a faraway country.

12. The colonists objected to paying taxes to Britain because
    (1) they were unhappy with British rule
    (2) they weren't represented in British government
    (3) they wanted to trade with other countries

13. Give one reason, besides taxes, that the colonists were unhappy with British rule.

    _____

    _____

BEGINNINGS OF THE UNITED STATES

The United States came about as a result of two struggles. The first struggle was the American Revolution. The fighting began in 1775 in Lexington. It ended eight years later with the Treaty of Paris. In the Treaty of Paris, Britain gave the colonies their independence. The second struggle was not a war. It was the effort to create a government that would work. The government that had been set up by the Articles of Confederation was too weak to do much. In 1787, to make the government stronger, new rules were written. Those rules—the Constitution—gave the government the basic shape it has today.

14. Which of these sentences from the paragraph expresses the main idea?
    (1) The United States came about as a result of two struggles.
    (2) In the Treaty of Paris, Britain gave the colonies their independence.
    (3) The second struggle was not a war.

15. In what year did fighting begin in the American Revolution? _____

16. In what year was the United States Constitution written?_____

GEOGRAPHY READINGS

Geography is the study of the earth. It looks not only at the earth itself but also at the relationship between the earth and human beings. Geographers are interested in how the earth affects people. They know that the work people do, the clothes they wear, and the kinds of houses they build are all affected by where people live. Geographers are also interested in how people affect the earth. When people dig mines, build dams, or discard waste, they affect the earth. Geographers must learn about the earth before they can study the relationship between the earth and people.

17. What two things does geography study?

    (a) _____

    (b) _____

18. Give an example of the way the earth affects people.

    _____

19. Give an example of the way people affect the earth.

    _____

CONTINENTS AND OCEANS

Millions of years ago, all the land on earth was one large land mass. There was just one large ocean. Very slowly, over a long period of time, the mass of land split up and the pieces of it moved away from each other. Since then, different parts of the ocean have separated the pieces of land from each other. Today nearly all the land on earth is divided among the seven continents. (Some small land areas—islands—are not part of the continents.) Even though most of the water on earth is still part of one large ocean, geographers think of it as four oceans: the Atlantic, Pacific, Indian, and Arctic oceans. The Pacific is the largest and deepest ocean. By itself, it is larger than all the continents combined.

20. Today there are seven continents, but at one time all the land on earth

    (1) was split into millions of pieces
    (2) formed one large ocean
    (3) was part of one large mass

21. What separates the continents from each other? _____

22. Which ocean, by itself, is larger than all seven continents? _____

WEATHERING

Although we're seldom aware of it, the earth's surface is always changing. Mountains, hills, plains, and coastlines are slowly being reshaped. Weathering is the process by which the forces of weather break rocks down into smaller and smaller pieces. Sand, for example, is nothing more than weathered rock that has broken into tiny particles. Weathered rock is carried from one place to another by wind and water. Weathering can turn mountains into hills, but it takes centuries and centuries for that to happen.

23. These sentences come from the paragraph. Which one states the main idea?

    (1) Although we're seldom aware of it, the earth's surface is always changing.
    (2) Mountains, hills, plains, and coastlines are slowly being reshaped.
    (3) Weathering can turn mountains into hills, but it takes centuries and centuries for that to happen.

24. What is the name of the process that causes rocks to break down? _____

25. Which two of the following move weathered rock from one place to another?

    (a) water
    (b) wind
    (c) sand
    (d) mountains

CLIMATE REGIONS

The earth has different climate regions. The climate in an area depends, in part, on its latitude, or how far it is from the equator. (See the climate map below.) Because the sun hits the area near the equator almost directly, that area has a warm climate. It is called the tropical region. The climate near the North and South Poles is very cold. The sun's rays do not hit those areas directly. They are called the polar regions. Between the tropical region and the polar regions are the warm and cold regions. They have less-extreme temperatures, even though their summers may be hot and winters cold.

26. Which of the following sentences from the paragraph states the main idea?

    (1) The earth has different climate regions.
    (2) The climate in an area depends, in part, on its latitude, or how far it is from the equator.
    (3) The climate near the North and South Poles is very cold.

27. Tell where these climate regions are located on the earth:

Climate Region	Location
tropical region	_____
warm and cold regions	_____
polar regions	_____

28. (a) Which climate region is the warmest?

    _____

    (b) Why is it so warm in that region?

    _____

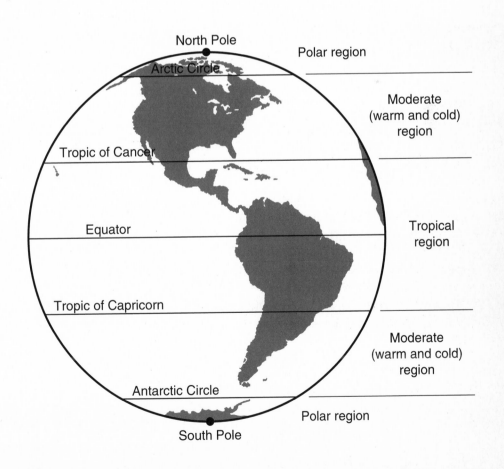

ECONOMICS READINGS

PEOPLE AND THE ECONOMY

Most people in the United States contribute to the country's economy in three ways. First, they contribute as workers. That is, they help to create goods and provide services as they earn money to support themselves and their families. Second, they contribute as consumers by spending some of the money they earn on goods and services. Thus they help keep businesses alive and growing. Finally, they contribute as taxpayers. They pay part of the money they earn to the government. The government uses that money to provide various goods and services to the community.

29. In how many ways do most people in the United States contribute to the economy?

    _____

30. When a person buys things, he or she contributes to the economy as a

    (1) worker
    (2) consumer
    (3) taxpayer

31. As a taxpayer, a person helps the government provide goods and services to

    (1) himself or herself
    (2) businesses
    (3) the community

SUPPLY AND DEMAND IN THE LABOR MARKET

All workers are part of the labor market. That is, they sell their labor. Some workers are able to get a better price for their labor, or higher wages, than others. This can be explained, in part, by the law of supply and demand. If workers' skills are those an employer needs very much, the employer will pay those workers higher wages. In other words, the greater the demand, the higher the price. Likewise, if workers have skills few others have, an employer will pay those workers higher wages. Or, the smaller the supply, the higher the price. On the other hand, employers pay lower wages to workers whose skills are not much in demand. They also pay lower wages to workers with skills that many people have.

32. What do workers sell on the labor market?

    _____

33. In which two of the following cases would workers' wages be higher?

    _____ (a) The workers' skills are rare—not many people have them.
    _____ (b) The employer needs the workers' skills only a little.
    _____ (c) The employer needs the workers' skills a lot.
    _____ (d) The workers' skills are common—many people have them.

34. Which of the following means about the same thing as the last sentence in the paragraph?

    (1) The smaller the demand, the lower the price.
    (2) The greater the demand, the higher the price.
    (3) The smaller the supply, the higher the price.
    (4) The greater the supply, the lower the price.

EFFECT OF SUPPLY AND DEMAND ON WAGES: THREE EXAMPLES

The following examples show different ways supply and demand can affect wages.

- Example 1: The economy is doing well. Businesses are growing; new ones are opening up. There is a greater demand for workers. Wages go up.

- Example 2: A large company in a certain town decides to shut down. It lays off its workers. There is now a smaller demand for workers in that town. With more people looking for work, there is a greater supply of workers there. Wages go down.

- Example 3: Many people can type, but fewer know word processing. When a typist learns word processing, that worker gains skills that are in smaller supply than a typist's. With a new job in word processing, that former typist's wages will go up.

35. When the economy is doing well, wages
    (1) go up
    (2) stay the same
    (3) go down

36. When a company closes, wages in that area
    (1) go up
    (2) stay the same
    (3) go down

37. When a worker learns a skill that not many others know, that worker's wages
    (1) go up
    (2) stay the same
    (3) go down

THE LABOR MARKET OF THE FUTURE

As we move toward the year 2000, several changes will occur in the labor market. These are some of the predictions economists make:

- The supply of workers will be greater because more women and young people will enter the labor market.
- The overall demand for workers will grow. There will be about 20 million more jobs in 2000 than there were in the mid-1980s. Also, retiring workers will need to be replaced.
- The demand for labor will increase more in some jobs than in others. For example, there will be little growth in the demand for factory workers. There will be a lot of growth in the demand for workers in service-producing jobs.
- The demand will increase most for workers with post–high school education and job training.

38. Economists predict that by 2000 there will be more workers from which two groups in the labor market?

    _____ and

    _____

39. Compared to the recent past, the demand for labor in the year 2000 will be
    (1) greater
    (2) about the same
    (3) smaller

40. By 2000, there will be a greater demand for workers whose backgrounds include what kinds of schooling?

    _____ and

    _____

POLITICAL SCIENCE READINGS

GOVERNMENT POWER BEFORE THE CONSTITUTION

By the late 1700s, Americans had lived under two governments: one too strong, and the other too weak. When Americans were colonists, the British government had ruled them with far too much power, they thought. They had had no voice in making the laws that controlled their lives. After the Revolution, the Americans had formed a central government that was not powerful enough. With the Articles of Confederation as the law, each state did pretty much what it wanted to do. There was no president, and the only central government was a weak Congress. To form a central government that had more power, but not too much, the Americans adopted the Constitution as their law.

41. Which of the following sentences from the paragraph states the main idea?

    (1) By the late 1700s, Americans had lived under two governments: one too strong, and the other too weak.
    (2) When Americans were colonists, the British government had ruled them with far too much power, they thought.
    (3) After the Revolution, the Americans had formed a central government that was not powerful enough.

42. The Americans thought the government was too strong

    (1) when they were colonists
    (2) after the Revolution
    (3) both when they were colonists and after the Revolution

43. With the Articles of Confederation,

    (1) there was no Congress
    (2) there were no states
    (3) there was no president

GOVERNMENT POWER AFTER THE CONSTITUTION

After the Revolution and before the Constitution, there was no United States as we think of it today. The thirteen colonies had become thirteen independent states. They had joined together, but not as a union. The following table compares the government at that time to the stronger central government that came later after the Constitution was adopted.

American Government: The Articles of Confederation Compared to the Constitution

	Articles of Confederation (1781–1789)	Constitution (1789–present)
States	Independent; loosely tied as a league	United as one nation
Powers	Most with individual states, almost none with central government	More with the central government, some still with the states
Congress	Had little power	Had much more power
Leaders	None	President and vice-president
Courts	Only in states	Central and state courts

44. Compared to the Articles of Confederation, the Constitution made the central government

    (1) weaker
    (2) no weaker or stronger
    (3) stronger

45. For each of the following comments, tell whether it applies to government under the Articles of Confederation or under the Constitution.

_____ (a) No central courts

_____ (b) Powers in both the central government and the states

_____ (c) Weak Congress

_____ (d) President as leader

THE CONSTITUTION AND THE DIVISION OF POWERS

Federalism is the form of government that divides powers between a central government and states. A federal system of government was set up in the United States by the Constitution. The Constitution defines which powers belong to the central government. It tells which powers belong to the states. It also explains which powers are shared by the central government and the states. For example, only the central government can print money. On the other hand, only the states can make laws to control trade within their own boundaries. Both the central government and the states can collect taxes.

46. With a federal system of government,
    (1) the central government has all the powers
    (2) the states have all the powers
    (3) both the central government and the states have powers

47. How did federalism come to be the form of government the United States has?___

_____

48. According to the Constitution, the central government and the states share the power to
    (1) print money
    (2) tax people
    (3) control trade within a state

THE CONSTITUTION AND THE SEPARATION OF POWERS

The Constitution set up the central government so that it would have three branches. It separates the powers of the central government among those branches. The executive branch includes the president and his or her advisors. One of the president's powers is to be in charge of relationships with other countries. The legislative branch is Congress, which has the power to make laws. The judicial branch is made up of the Supreme Court and other courts. One of the powers of the judicial branch is to decide whether laws agree with the Constitution.

49. The Constitution separates powers among
    (1) the states
    (2) the branches of the central government
    (3) the central government and the states

50. Tell which branch of the central government each of the following belongs to:

	Branch
the President	_____
Congress	_____
the Supreme Court	_____

51. Which branch of government makes laws?

_____

BEHAVIORAL SCIENCE READINGS

TYPES OF CHANGE DURING HUMAN DEVELOPMENT

During the human life span—from infancy through old age—all people develop in much the same way. We go through certain stages and experience changes. Some changes are physical. When we are children, our bodies grow. They become adult bodies when we are teenagers. When we are older, our bodies begin to age. Other changes are cognitive, or mental. Most children, for example, say their first word when they're about a year old and speak in full sentences by age three. Still other changes are psychological and social. This means that our feelings, relationships, and activities change throughout our lives. Our needs—what we must have and what we want to get out of life—change as we get older.

52. The stages of human development
    (1) are different for each person
    (2) are about the same for all people
    (3) occur during infancy

53. The paragraph mentions three kinds of changes people experience as they grow older. What are they?

    _____

    _____

    _____

54. Learning to talk is an example of what kind of change?

    _____

CHILDREN'S NEEDS

What needs do we have as children? According to many psychologists, young children's greatest need is for security, a feeling of safety. Even babies need to feel that the world is safe. They gain this feeling through close contact with their parents. As they get older, children develop new needs. They need to feel confident and independent. That is, they need to feel that they are able to do things well on their own. They need to feel good about themselves and their abilities. Parents can encourage these feelings by giving their children both rules and freedom.

55. What does a young child have the greatest need for? _____

56. As children get older, how do they need to feel? _____

    and _____.

57. When a parent gives a child both rules and freedom, the parent helps that child meet his or her need for
    (1) close contact with the parent
    (2) a feeling of trust
    (3) confidence and independence

ADOLESCENTS' NEEDS

Adolescence refers to the teenage years. Adolescents are no longer children, but they're not yet adults. Many adolescents still live with their parents. Soon, however, they will be on their own. Adolescents' biggest need is to develop a strong sense of identity. That is, they need to figure out who they are and what they want to do with their lives. This doesn't mean deciding what kind of work they will do, although that may be part of it. Instead it means sorting out their values—finding what's right and what's wrong for them. It means coming to have more understanding of themselves.

58. Which of the following sentences from the paragraph states the main idea of the paragraph?
    (1) *Adolescence* refers to the teenage years.
    (2) Many adolescents still live with their parents.
    (3) Adolescents' biggest need is to develop a strong sense of identity.
    (4) It means coming to have more understanding of themselves.

59. In what age group are adolescents?

_____

60. To develop a strong sense of identity, adolescents need to
    (1) be on their own
    (2) make career plans
    (3) sort out their values

ADULTS' NEEDS

People's needs continue to change as adults. During young adulthood (the 20s and 30s), people's strongest need is to develop close relationships with others. Friends are important. During this stage many people marry and start families. During the stage called middle adulthood (from 40 to 65), people focus on contributing something to the world. Their most important need is for a feeling of accomplishment. Many people earn that feeling from their jobs or in some other way, such as in community work. In late adulthood (after age 65), people's strongest needs are tied to the fact that their lives are closing. They need to feel satisfied with how they've lived their lives. They also need to continue to enjoy life even as they face the idea of death.

61. How are the details in this paragraph organized?
    (1) to describe a series of causes and effects
    (2) to make a comparison
    (3) by classification
    (4) to show a contrast

62. Which of the following is the strongest need for people in their 20s and 30s?
    (1) developing relationships
    (2) contributing to the world
    (3) feeling satisfied with their lives

63. From what do many people in middle adulthood get the sense of accomplishment they need?_____

64. After age 65, what are people's needs related to?_____

Check your answers on page 214.

A Newly Married Couple

SOCIAL STUDIES READINGS 1 SKILLS CHART

To review the readings skills covered by the items in Social Studies Readings 1, study the following parts of Unit 1.

Unit 1	Comprehending What You Read	Item Number
Chapter 1	**Preparing to Read**	
Lesson 1	Previewing Paragraphs	1
Chapter 2	**Recognizing Stated Main Ideas**	
Lesson 4	Finding the Main Idea and Supporting Sentences	5, 11, 23, 41, 58
Lesson 5	Finding the Sentence That States the Main Idea	14, 26
Chapter 3	**Understanding the Details**	
Lesson 6	Reading for Details	2, 3, 7, 8, 9, 10, 12, 13, 15, 16, 17, 18, 19, 20, 21, 22, 24, 28, 29, 30, 31, 32, 34, 35, 36, 37, 38, 39, 40, 42, 43, 44, 46, 47, 48, 49, 50, 51, 52, 53, 54, 55, 56, 57, 59, 60, 62, 63, 64
Lesson 7	Seeing How Details Are Organized	4, 6, 25, 33, 61
Lesson 8	Finding Details in Tables	45
Lesson 10	Finding Details in Maps	27

This section will give you practice answering questions like those on the GED. The Social Studies Test of the GED has 64 multiple-choice questions. Each question has five choices. The 10 questions in this Practice are all multiple choice, like the ones on the GED.

As you do this Practice, use the reading skills you've studied in this unit:

- Before you read a paragraph or graph, preview it.
- Preview the questions, too. That way you will have an idea about what information you will need to answer them.
- Read the paragraph or look at the graph. As you read a paragraph, look for the information you need to answer the questions. In a graph, look for the details you need.

Directions: Choose the one best answer to each item.

Items 1 through 3 are based on the following information.

Businesses are having problems finding and keeping good workers. When they do find workers, businesses' problems may not be over. First, workers tend to leave jobs before long. Second, some workers lack skills they need, so they don't perform well enough. To fight these problems, businesses are trying some new ideas. One is to have day-care centers at work. Such centers make it possible to attract mothers of young children. Another new idea is to provide job-related education for workers. Many companies find that workers who take courses tend to stay and to perform better.

1. The paragraph is about the problems that
   (1) businesses have selling their products
   (2) businesses have finding and keeping good workers
   (3) mothers with children have finding jobs
   (4) students who drop out of school have keeping jobs
   (5) workers have taking night courses

2. Some companies have day-care centers in order to
   (1) improve workers' skills
   (2) provide education for workers
   (3) help workers perform better
   (4) attract mothers of young children as workers
   (5) prepare children to work for the company

3. Workers who take courses provided by their company usually
   (1) leave their jobs before long
   (2) have young children
   (3) perform better
   (4) are mothers
   (5) put their children in day-care centers

Items 4 through 6 are based on the following information.

A recent study found that 20 percent of the world's population has serious health problems. In some African and Asian countries, the rate is as high as 40 percent. Poverty is the cause of many health problems. Poor people often have poor living conditions and little or no medical care. They often cannot afford to eat well. For these reasons, poor people easily become ill. Poor countries, where health problems are greatest, often cannot afford to spend much money on health care. In such countries it is common for disease to spread rapidly.

4. According to the passage, serious health problems affect 40 percent of

   (1) all people
   (2) poor people
   (3) the people in poor countries
   (4) the people in some African and Asian countries
   (5) people who do not eat well

5. Which of the following sentences from the paragraph states the main idea?

   (1) A recent study found that 20 percent of the world's population has serious health problems.
   (2) In some African and Asian countries, the rate is as high as 40 percent.
   (3) Poverty is the cause of many health problems.
   (4) Poor people often have poor living conditions and little or no medical care.
   (5) Poor countries, where health problems are greatest, often cannot afford to spend much money on health care.

6. The paragraph mentions several things that contribute to health problems. One thing it does not mention is

   (1) poor living conditions
   (2) lack of medical care
   (3) poor diet
   (4) lack of health education
   (5) lack of money

Items 7 through 10 are based on the following graph.

Percent of People Who Vote, by Age

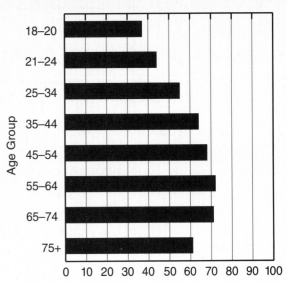

7. For which age group is the percent of people who vote highest?

   (1) 18–20
   (2) 25–34
   (3) 45–54
   (4) 55–64
   (5) 75+

8. For which age group is the percent of people who vote lowest?

   (1) 18–20
   (2) 25–34
   (3) 45–54
   (4) 55–64
   (5) 75+

9. About what percent of people who are 35 to 44 vote?

   (1) 40 percent
   (2) 45 percent
   (3) 55 percent
   (4) 65 percent
   (5) 70 percent

10. In general, the percent of people who vote increases with age, but it falls beginning with age

   (1) 35
   (2) 45
   (3) 55
   (4) 65
   (5) 75

Check your answers on page 216.

GED PRACTICE 1 SKILLS CHART

To review the readings skills covered by the items in GED Practice 1, study the following parts of Unit 1.

Unit 1	Comprehending What You Read	Item Number
Chapter 2	Recognizing Main Ideas	
Lesson 4	Finding the Main Idea and the Main Idea	1, 5
Chapter 3	Understanding the Details	
Lesson 6	Reading for Details	2, 3, 4, 6
Lesson 9	Finding Details in Graphs	7, 8, 9, 10

GED PRACTICE 1 CONTENT CHART

The following chart shows the area of social studies to which each item in GED Practice 1 refers.

Area of Social Studies	Item Number
Geography	4, 5, 6
Economics	1, 2, 3
Political Science	7, 8, 9, 10

UNIT 2

Inferring as You Read

In everyday life you make inferences all the time. For example, if you come home from work and smell something delicious, you infer that someone is cooking. You figure this out without entering the kitchen. Similarly, when you read you make inferences. Inferring means that you understand what is meant even when it is not actually stated. You use clues to understand what's not said.

Washington, D.C.

Unit 2 Overview
Chapter 1   Inferring Word Meanings
Chapter 2   Inferring Details
Chapter 3   Inferring Unstated Main Ideas
_____

Social Studies Readings 2
GED Practice 2

1 INFERRING WORD MEANINGS

When you read, if you don't understand the words in a passage, you might not understand the passage. One solution is to look up words in a dictionary. But you won't always have a dictionary on hand. Also, looking a word up might take your attention away from what you're reading.

There is another—sometimes better—solution: using a word's context to infer, or figure out, its meaning. Context means surroundings. A word's context includes the words and sentences that surround it.

As you read this chapter, you will improve your ability to infer meanings from context, recognize definitions and synonyms, infer meanings from examples and contrasts, and infer meanings from the general context. You'll use these skills to read passages like those on the social studies test of the GED.

Lesson 11

Understanding Meanings from Context

When you read a word you don't understand, looking at its context can often give you good clues about the word's meaning. You may be able to guess the word's meaning without using a dictionary.

TRY THIS

To see how useful context is, read the following passages.

After talking to his advisers, the senator decided to run again.

What does *run* mean in this sentence?
   (1) move quickly along the ground
   (2) manage an organization
   (3) campaign to be elected

In the American Civil War over 750,000 _____ were killed.

What word is missing from the above sentence?

People tend to think of women as being more empathic than men. For this reason many people feel more comfortable telling their problems to women than to men.

The paragraph above contains the word *empathic*. What does it mean?

   (1) easily angered
   (2) understanding and sympathetic
   (3) without compassion

Run has many meanings, but its context here tells you that Choice (3) has the right meaning for the sentence about the senator's decision.

The word missing from the sentence about the Civil War is *men* or *soldiers*. Of all the words in the English language, only a few fit in this context.

You can guess from its context that *empathic* means "understanding and sympathetic" (Choice 2). Most people would prefer to confide in an understanding and sympathetic person rather than in a person who is easily angered or a person who has no compassion.

Within a passage, some words are more important than others. If a word seems important to your understanding of a passage, try to figure out its meaning. Usually the more important a word is in a passage, the more context clues there will be. You will probably not have to figure out the meaning of *every* word you don't understand.

EXERCISE 11

Read the following passage. Try to figure out the meanings of the underlined words by using their contexts.

In the years after the Revolution, slavery seemed to be headed toward gradual extinction. One by one the northern states prohibited slavery. By 1808 slaves could no longer be brought to the United States. Later, an event revitalized slavery. This event was the invention of the cotton gin, a machine that separates cotton fiber, or threads, from cotton seeds. With the gin it was possible to prepare large amounts of cotton for sale. Many hands were needed to grow so much cotton. The South became dependent on cotton—and on slavery.

1. The paragraph says that at one point slavery seemed *headed toward gradual extinction.* This means that slavery was slowly

   (1) going out of existence
   (2) becoming more important
   (3) bringing the country nearer to war

2. What does *prohibited* mean?

   (1) allowed
   (2) refused to permit
   (3) encouraged

3. What does *revitalized* mean?

   (1) made by machine   (3) figured out
   (2) gave new life   (4) got rid of

Check your answers on page 217.

Recognizing Definitions and Synonyms

Definitions and synonyms are special kinds of context clues.

Definitions

A definition is a statement of the meaning of a word. For example, the following sentence gives a definition for *political science*: Political science is the study of government.

TRY THIS

Read each passage. Try to figure out the meanings of the underlined terms by using their contexts.

Many businesses in the United States have only one owner. A business with only one owner is a <u>single proprietorship</u>.

What is the best definition of *single proprietorship*?
    (1) a business in the United States
    (2) a business with only one owner
    (3) a business with two or more owners

Our Congress is <u>bicameral</u>. In other words, it has two chambers, the Senate and the House of Representatives.

What does *bicameral* mean?
    (1) having two chambers
    (2) congressional
    (3) representative

<u>Senators</u>—members of the Senate—are elected to six-year terms.

What are senators? _____

In the 1800s when the country was still fairly small, Americans believed in <u>Manifest Destiny</u>. That is, people thought that the United States was meant to expand its territory.

What is the definition of *Manifest Destiny*? _____

The best definition of *single proprietorship* is in Choice (2). The second sentence in the passage contains the definition.

Bicameral means "having two chambers," Choice (1). The definition is signaled by the phrase *In other words*.

A senator is a member of the Senate. In this case, dashes (—) signal the definition of the word.

Manifest Destiny was the belief that the United States was meant to grow in territory. The words *that is* signal the definition.

Synonyms

A synonym is a word that means almost the same thing as another word. In the following sentence the word *diary* is a synonym for *journal*: Columbus kept a journal, or diary. *Diary* and *journal* mean almost the same thing in this sentence.

TRY THIS

Read each passage. Try to figure out the meanings of the underlined terms from their contexts.

Everyone belongs to one or the other <u>gender</u>, or sex. Everyone is either male or female.

What word means the same thing as *gender*? _____

Psychologists have collected much <u>data</u>, or information, about how gender affects our lives.

What word is a synonym for *data*? _____

Sex means the same thing as *gender*. *Information* is a synonym for *data*. In both passages, the synonyms are signaled by a comma and the word *or*.

When a word appears with a definition or a synonym, you don't have to figure anything out. You just have to recognize the definition or synonym.

How to Recognize a Word's Definition or Synonym

STEP 1: Look for signals like *in other words*, *that is*, a comma with *or*, and dashes.

STEP 2: See if the definition or synonym makes sense.

EXERCISE 12

Read the following passage. Try to figure out the meanings of the underlined words by looking for their definitions or synonyms.

Businesses are owned in three different ways. A single proprietorship is a business that has only one owner. A <u>partnership</u> is a business that has two or more owners. A corporation's ownership is divided into <u>shares</u>, or parts. Anyone who buys shares in a corporation is a part owner. A corporation may have millions of part owners, called <u>shareholders</u>.

Few businesses are corporations. Corporations are usually large. They take in the bulk of <u>business revenue</u>, or money earned by businesses.

1. What is a partnership?
   (1) a business owned by only one person
   (2) a business owned by two or more people
   (3) a business divided into shares and owned by many people

2. What is a share?_____

3. What is a part owner of a corporation called? _____

4. What does *business revenue* mean? _____

Check your answers on page 217.

Using Examples and Contrasts

Examples and contrasts are less clear than definitions and synonyms as context clues. They are still useful in helping you figure out a word's meaning.

Examples

If examples of a word are given, you can often figure out the word's meaning.

TRY THIS

Read each passage. See whether the examples in each help you figure out the meanings of the underlined words.

The earth's <u>terrain</u> includes mountains, hills, and plains.

What does *terrain* refer to?
   (1) land types
   (2) mineral wealth
   (3) climate extremes

In the 1840s the United States followed a policy of <u>expansionism</u>. It annexed Texas in 1845. An 1846 agreement with Britain allowed the United States to claim a large area north of California. By fighting a war with Mexico from 1846 to 1848, the United States gained a large area that included California and New Mexico.

Expansionism was a policy of gaining
   (1) businesses
   (2) territory
   (3) money

Terrain refers to land types. Mountains, hills, and plains are examples of land types.

Expansionism was the U. S. policy for increasing the size of its territory. The paragraph gives three examples of how the United States expanded its size. (Did you notice that *expansionism* is related to *expand*? Sometimes you can figure out an unfamiliar word by relating it to other words you know.)

Westward Expansion by Oxen-Drawn Wagon Trains

Examples, like definitions, are sometimes signaled by words or phrases, such as *for example*, *like*, *including*, and *such as*.

Contrasts

Contrasts occur when things are different from or opposite to each other. Sometimes you can tell from a word's context that it means the opposite of another word. Such contrasts are context clues. You can use contrast clues to figure out the meaning of the word you don't know.

Use contrast clues to help you figure out the meanings of the under-lined words in the following two passages.

Today the United States lacks minerals such as tin and mercury. In the past these minerals were <u>abundant</u>.

Abundant means

    (1) gone
    (2) plentiful
    (3) useful

In the 1850s violence was common in the U.S. territory of Kansas. Fights often broke out between those who favored slavery and those who were <u>abolitionists</u>.

Abolitionists were people who

    (1) opposed slavery
    (2) abolished territories
    (3) owned land

    Abundant means "plentiful," or "existing in large amounts"—Choice (2). The two sentences in the passage make a contrast between the situation now and that in the past. The words *Today* and *In the past* signal this contrast.

    Abolitionists were people who opposed slavery—Choice(1). They wanted to abolish it. The clue is that abolitionists fought against people who favored slavery. There is no word that signals the contrast, but the sense of the sentence shows that *abolitionists* contrasts with *those who favored slavery*.

    Words that signal contrast include *although, but, even though, even so, however, in contrast, instead, on the other hand,* and *or*.

    Examples and contrasts—unlike definitions and synonyms—don't give you a word's meaning. With examples and contrasts you have to figure out a word's meaning by using the clues they provide.

How to Use Examples and Contrasts to Figure Out a Word's Meaning

STEP 1:   Look for signals of examples, such as *for example, like, including,* and *such as*.

STEP 2:   Look for signals that show contrasts, such as *although, but, even though, even so, however, in contrast, instead, on the other hand,* and *or*.

STEP 3:   See if the meaning you've figured out makes sense.

Read the following passages and answer the questions about the underlined words in them.

Questions 1 and 2 refer to the following paragraph.

Psychologists—scientists who study human behavior—have found several differences between men and women. Men appear to be more aggressive, that is, more likely to act in violent ways. Men also appear to be more socially dominant. For example, they are more likely to express opinions in groups and to be leaders. Women appear to be more empathic—better able to sympathize with others—and more nurturing—better able to care for others. Why do these differences exist? Are these differences innate, or do boys and girls learn different behaviors as they grow up?

1. What does *socially dominant* mean?
   (1) needing other people's company
   (2) using power in a group
   (3) sympathizing with others

2. An *innate* difference is a difference you
   (1) are born with
   (2) learn through experience
   (3) lead groups with

Question 3 refers to the following paragraph.

There are 435 members in the House of Representatives. The number of representatives from each state depends on the state's population. States with few people have few representatives. In contrast, populous states have many representatives.

3. Populous states have
   (1) few people
   (2) many people
   (3) few representatives

Questions 4 and 5 refer to the following paragraph.

When the Civil War began, many people thought it would be a short war. They thought it might end within a few months and cost few lives. Instead, the Civil War was a protracted struggle with many casualties.

4. What does *protracted* mean?
   (1) short
   (2) long
   (3) useless

5. What does *casualties* in this paragraph mean?_____

Check your answers on page 217.

Using the General Context

Sometimes there are no specific clues to a word's meaning. Words you don't know might appear without definitions, synonyms, examples, or contrasts. Nevertheless, you can still use the word's context to figure out its meaning.

When there are specific clues, the work you do is similar to the work you do when you use an example or a contrast to guess a word's meaning. The only difference is that hints about a word's meaning can come from anywhere in the general context. You need a strategy for using the context—for getting meaning from the surrounding words and sentences.

A strategy for using general context to figure out word meaning follows.

When you're reading a sentence and you see a word you don't know, finish reading the sentence. Then think about what other words could replace the one you don't know. Use your experience to make a thoughtful guess about the meaning of the unfamiliar word.

As you resume reading, see if your guess about the word's meaning makes sense. The context following the word will probably do one of three things. (1) It can show you that your guess was right. (2) It can help you make a more exact guess. (3) It can show you that your guess was wrong and that you should make a new guess. The more you read of the context, the better your guess about the word's meaning will be.

TRY THIS

Read the following paragraph. Its sentences are numbered. Use the strategy described above to figure out the meaning of the underlined word, which appears twice in the paragraph.

(1) In the United States the economies of the North and the South had <u>diverged</u> by the middle of the nineteenth century. (2) The North manufactured goods in factories; the South grew crops, especially cotton. (3) As the two economies <u>diverged</u>, so did their societies. (4) Life in a northern city had became different from life on a southern plantation.

What does *diverged* mean?
  (1) became wealthy quickly
  (2) ran into problems
  (3) moved in different directions

Interior of the Great Weaving Room, Fall River, Massachusetts, in the 1800s

Diverged means "moved in different directions"—Choice (3). The first sentence does not give you enough information to guess the meaning of *diverged*. Based on the first sentence only, *diverged* could have any of the meanings in Choices (1), (2), or (3).

Sentence (2) tells you how the economies of the North and South had become different. Sentence (3) says that the societies had diverged, too. Sentence (4) says that life in the North and South had become different.

Sentences (2) and (4) provide strong hints about the meaning of *diverged* because they are both about differences between the North and the South. If you reread the paragraph with the meaning *moved in different directions* in mind, you can see that this definition for *diverged* makes sense.

How to Use the General Context to Figure Out a Word's Meaning

STEP 1: After reading the sentence in which the word appears, guess its meaning.

STEP 2: As you keep reading, see if your guess makes sense.

STEP 3: If the meaning you've guessed doesn't make sense, go back and change your guess.

The only way to become good at this strategy for using the general context is to practice. Exercise 14 gives you some practice.

Read the following passages and answer the questions about the underlined words in them.

Questions 1 and 2 refer to the following paragraph.

In the first half of the nineteenth century, the United States grew rapidly. As the country grew, the issue of slavery kept <u>reemerging</u>. Should slavery be allowed in the new territories or should it be barred? The northern states had one viewpoint. The southern states had another. Time after time, Congress came up with <u>compromises</u>. But these compromises didn't please either side.

1. What does *reemerging* mean?

   (1) appearing again and again
   (2) being hidden over and over
   (3) leading to more and more violence

2. What are *compromises*?

   (1) different viewpoints on an issue
   (2) ways to maintain slavery
   (3) agreements that allow two sides to settle their differences

Questions 3 and 4 refer to the following paragraph.

Businesses differ greatly from one another. They may be large or small. They may have one owner or many owners. Yet all businesses have the same basic <u>objective</u>. That objective is to make a profit. A profit is made if revenues—money taken in—<u>exceed</u> costs—money spent.

3. What does *objective* mean?

   (1) profit
   (2) goal
   (3) cost

4. *Exceed* means

   (1) is greater than
   (2) is less than
   (3) is the same as

Questions 5 and 6 refer to the following paragraph.

Some sweaters are knit by hand. Most, however, are made by machine. The <u>production</u> of sweaters, like the production of many other goods, has been <u>mechanized</u>. With a machine, it takes much less time to make a sweater. Sweaters can now be mass-produced; that is, they can be produced in large quantities.

5. Fill in the blank in the following sentence:

Production is "the process of _____."

6. Mechanized production requires
   (1) sweaters
   (2) machines
   (3) quantities

Questions 7 through 9 refer to the following paragraphs.

A bill is a <u>proposed</u> law that has been introduced in Congress. There are many steps before a bill becomes law.

A bill can be introduced in the House or the Senate. It must be approved by the <u>relevant</u> committee. Suppose a bill to help farmers is introduced in the House. It would have to be approved by the House Committee on Agriculture. If the committee approves the bill, the entire House discusses the bill and then votes on it. If the bill is approved by the entire House, it goes to the Senate for further discussion and a vote. After both the House and the Senate approve a bill, it goes to the president. If the president doesn't veto it, it becomes a law.

Because there are so many steps, chances are a bill will be <u>modified</u> before it becomes a law. Thus, a law that is finally passed may not look much like the bill that was first introduced.

7. What does *proposed* mean?
   (1) popular
   (2) suggested
   (3) new

8. What does *relevant* mean?
   (1) important
   (2) related
   (3) agriculture

9. What does modified mean? _____

Check your answers on page 217.

Chapter

2 INFERRING DETAILS

Inferences about word meanings, which you practiced in Chapter 1, are only one kind of inference. You make an inference whenever you understand something that is suggested but not actually stated.

For example, suppose a woman you just met says, "I'll never get used to living in New York." From this statement you can make inferences about the woman. You can infer that she now lives in New York. You can also infer that she is from somewhere else. A person who has lived in New York all her life wouldn't talk about getting used to it. Based on the woman's statement alone, you could not infer that she is from outside the United States. Her statement doesn't give you enough information to infer where she is from.

Just as you make inferences during conversation, you make inferences when you read. In fact, you must make inferences to understand what you read fully. In this chapter you will practice making inferences from written material and from graphic material.

Lesson 15

Making Inferences from Written Material

To make an inference, you must have evidence. Inferences must be firmly based on what you read.

Sometimes an inference can be based on as little as a single word.

TRY THIS

Read the following sentence and answer the question that follows.

Congress's main function is to legislate, or makes laws.

Which one of the following can you infer about Congress?
   (1) It is more powerful than the president.
   (2) It has various functions.
   (3) It spends all its time making laws.

The correct answer is Choice (2). The word *main* provides the clue for this inference. Since passing laws is Congress's *main* function, Congress must have other functions. You can infer that Congress has various functions.

The inference in Choice (3) cannot be correct if Choice (2) is correct. There is not enough information in the sentence to make the inference in Choice (1).

A single sentence in a paragraph can also be the basis for an inference. Most inferences, though, are based on information from more than one sentence. Understanding—including understanding through inferences—involves putting meanings from different sentences together. Whenever you read, you continually make inferences.

TRY THIS

Read the following passage and answer the questions that follow it.

Problems between the North and the South grew during the 1850s. In 1860 there was a presidential election. The two regions voted for different candidates. The winner was Abraham Lincoln, the Republican candidate.

For many Southerners this was the last straw. Within months seven states had seceded from the Union. They were no longer part of the United States. They joined together to form the Confederate States of America, or the Confederacy.

From what region did Lincoln's support come? _____

From what region were the states that seceded? _____

Lincoln's support came from the North. The passage states that the two regions voted for different candidates. The beginning of the second paragraph says that for many Southerners, Lincoln's election was the last straw. Since Southerners were unhappy about Lincoln's election, you can infer that his support came from the North.

You can use this same information to infer that the states that seceded were from the South.

NOW TRY THIS

Read the following passage and answer the questions that follow.

Sometimes before sending a bill to the president, Congress adds one or more riders. A rider is a measure that has nothing to do with the bill to which it is added. For example, a rider to help farmers might be added to a bill providing money for weapons.

Usually a rider is a measure the president doesn't like. Congress is afraid that if the rider went to the president as a separate bill, the president would veto it and it would not become law. So Congress attaches the rider to a bill the president likes. Congress knows that the president will sign that bill. When the bill is signed, the rider, as part of the bill, becomes law.

You can infer from the passage that the president has the power to

(1) give money to the army
(2) write laws
(3) accept or turn down proposed laws

Can the president veto a *part* of a bill? _____

The answer to the first question is Choice (3). The paragraph indicates that the president may either veto or sign bills. Therefore, the president's power is to accept or turn down proposed laws.

From the discussion about riders, you can infer that the president cannot veto a part of a bill. If the president could veto a part of a bill, riders would serve no purpose.

When reading, you may be able to make inferences not only about facts but also about the writer's opinions or beliefs.

TRY THIS

As you read the following paragraph, look for the writer's opinion about a bill to increase the minimum wage. (The minimum wage is the lowest hourly wage that can be paid to employees.) Answer the question that follows the paragraph.

(1) I believe that everyone should have a fair chance. (2) All people should have a chance to earn enough money to support themselves and their families. (3) If this law is passed, many employers will be required to pay more to their employees. (4) Employers won't be able to afford to hire more employees. (5) As a result many potential employees will not be hired.

Does the writer support or oppose the proposal to increase the minimum wage? _____

The writer opposes the increase in the minimum wage. The writer believes the increase would result in fewer workers being hired.

To infer the writer's opinion, you need to read the entire paragraph. Sentences (1) and (2) seem to imply that an increase in the minimum wage would help people support themselves better. Sentence (3) describes an effect of the law. Sentences (4) and (5) force you to change your inference about the writer's opinion.

If you look back at Sentences (1) and (2) now, you interpret them differently. The writer feels that the increase would keep some people from being able to earn any money.

This example makes an important point that applies to all inferences: As you read, you will sometimes need to change your inferences. An inference that makes sense at first may not fit with information you read later. When this happens, change your inference.

When you infer an opinion, be sure to infer *the writer's* opinion. Don't confuse your opinion with the writer's. As with all inferences, inferences of opinions must be backed by evidence from the passage.

How to Make Inferences from Written Material

STEP 1: As you read each sentence in a passage, think about what the information suggests.

STEP 2: Check that an inference you make is based on evidence in the passage and on knowledge you have.

STEP 3: As you keep reading, see if your inference continues to make sense.

STEP 4: If the inference you've made stops making sense, change it.

EXERCISE 15

Read the following passages and answer the questions about them.

Question 1 refers to the following paragraph.

Some countries are rich in natural resources like minerals. Others are poor. Natural resources are the products of processes that have occurred in and on the earth over millions of years. Large countries usually have many natural resources. It's not surprising that the United States has more minerals than most other countries.

1. What can you infer about the United States?
   (1) It has minerals found nowhere else in the world.
   (2) It covers more land area than most other countries.
   (3) It has more people than any other country.

Question 2 refers to the following paragraph.

In the Sierra Madre, a mountain range in Mexico, the soil is good for farming. Yet there is not much usable land. Large farms are possible only in the flat valleys of the region.

2. Why is so much of the land in the Sierra Madre not usable?
   (1) It has poor soil.
   (2) It is too steep.
   (3) It is too rocky.

Questions 3 through 6 refer to the following passage.

According to some historians the Civil War nearly ended differently. In 1864 the Civil War was in its fourth year. For the North 1864 was an election year. President Abraham Lincoln, a Republican, was running for reelection. His opponents, the Democrats, promised that they would make peace their first priority.

The war had brought many deaths and no real victory. Peace had come to seem more important to many Northerners than keeping the

Union together. Then, in September 1864, General Sherman took Atlanta, one of the South's most important cities. Its surrender was a major victory for the North. This victory greatly affected the outcome of the election. The results of the election in turn affected the outcome of the war.

Sherman and His Generals, 1865

Left to right (*seated*): J.A. Logan, W.T. Sherman, H.W. Slocum, and F. Blair; (*standing*): O.O. Howard, W.B. Hazen, Jefferson C. Davis, J.A. Mower

3. For which side did General Sherman fight in the Civil War? _____

4. What can you infer was Lincoln's opinion about continuing the war?

   (1) He preferred immediate peace to more deaths in battle.
   (2) He preferred continuing the war because he thought a northern victory was possible.
   (3) He had no opinion about whether to continue the war or not.

5. Which party can you infer won the election of 1864?_____

6. The first sentence says *According to some historians the Civil War nearly ended differently.* In the context of the paragraph, what does this probably mean?

   (1) The South might have become powerful enough to beat the North.
   (2) The North might have given up trying to win the war and made peace with the South.
   (3) The North and the South, weakened by war, might have been conquered by other countries.

Questions 7 through 9 refer to the following paragraph.

Today many women work outside the home. Yet women still earn less than men. On average, women earn only 68 cents for every dollar that men earn. Moreover, in many cases outside work adds a burden for women. When married women were asked about housework, 82 percent said they did most or all of it. Women have made progress. Their situation is better than in the past. Yet it is clear that they still have a distance to go.

7. Put a check next to each inference you can make based on the passage.

____ (a) In the past, men earned more than women.
____ (b) In the past, fewer women worked outside the home.
____ (c) In the past, men and women shared the housework equally.
____ (d) Women today feel angry about the amount of housework they do.
____ (e) Women feel their lives might have been much happier in the past.

8. The writer

(1) is in favor of women working outside the home
(2) is not in favor of women working outside the home
(3) seems to have no opinion about women working outside the home

9. Does the writer think that women are in the best possible situation today? Give your reason for your answer.

Questions 10 through 12 refer to the following passage.

We now travel on highways, by rail, and even through the air. Yet for most of human history, people depended largely on rivers.

In terms of usefulness, not all rivers are equal. This is shown by the rivers of Central and South America.

Central America has many rivers, but they are too short to be useful for travel. The Amazon, the second-longest river in the world, flows through Brazil. It isn't traveled much because it is located in the Amazon rainforest, where very few people live. The Rio de la Plata system is also in South America. Until recent times this system was important for moving people and goods.

10. You can infer that rivers of the Rio de la Plata system

(1) are not short
(2) are polluted
(3) are dangerous

11. You can infer that the area through which the Rio de la Plata system passes

(1) has many mountains   (3) has many people
(2) has few people   (4) is flat

12. The passage indicates that the Rio de la Plata system has become less important. Based on the passage, you can infer that many things that once were moved on these rivers

(1) are now moved on the Amazon
(2) are now moved in other ways—for example, by trucks and airplanes
(3) are no longer moved

Question 13 refers to the following paragraph.

Suppose that parents have a son and a daughter. When the daughter cries the parents comfort her. When the son cries they say, "Come on, now. Big boys don't cry." For her birthday the daughter gets a doll. For his the son gets a toy gun. The children see on the TV that in commercials and programs, men and women behave differently. The men in a beer commercial have little in common with the mother in the cereal commercial who tries to decide what cereal is best for her family. These experiences encourage differences in behavior between boys and girls.

13. You can infer that the writer's opinion is that behavior differences between boys and girls are mainly

(1) inborn
(2) learned
(3) caused by watching television

Check your answers on page 218.

Making Inferences from Graphic Material

Written material and graphic material work quite differently. Written material *discusses* information; graphic material *shows* information.

Graphs

Graphics suggest much more than they directly state. In other words, you can make many inferences when you look at graph.

Take a moment to make sure you remember how to read graphs. You may want to look back at Lesson 9, which begins on page 49.

TRY THIS

Look carefully at the bar graph on the top of page 97 and then answer the questions below. Notice that there are three bars for each region of the world. The key below the graph explains the meaning of each bar.

Which region of the world is the most populous? _____

About how much of the world's energy does Asia produce?

(1) 15 percent   (3) 40 percent
(2) 20 percent   (4) 55 percent

Asia produces more energy

(1) than it consumes
(2) than it produces

The World Energy Picture

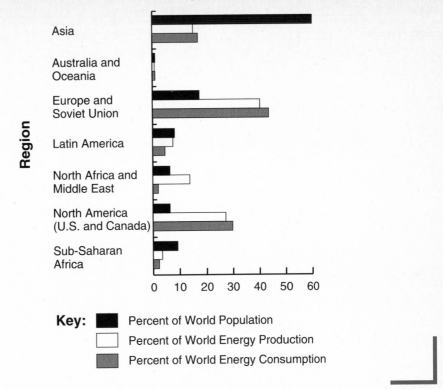

Key: Percent of World Population
Percent of World Energy Production
Percent of World Energy Consumption

Asia is the most populous region of the world. Asia's top bar, which shows its population, is much longer than any other population bar on the graph. It shows that Asia has about 55 percent of the world's population.

Asia's middle bar stands for energy production. Its length shows that Asia produces about 15 percent of the world's energy—Choice (1).

Asia consumes more energy than it produces—Choice (2). Asia's bottom bar shows energy consumption. It is slightly longer than the production bar just above it.

NOW TRY THIS

Look at the energy graph again. Answer the following inference questions about it.

Is the amount of energy consumed related to the size of the population that consumes it?

(1) Yes, the more people a region has, the more energy it consumes.
(2) No, there is no relationship between energy consumption and population size.

Which three regions of the world probably don't need to get energy from other regions?

_____ _____ _____

The answer to the first inference question is Choice (2). The following two examples, among others, support that inference. Asia has about 55 percent of the world's population but consumes less than 20 percent of its energy. North America has less than 10 percent of the world's population but consumes nearly 30 percent of its energy.

The energy production bar for each of the following regions of the world is longer than its consumption bar: Latin America, North Africa and the Middle East, and Sub-Saharan Africa. Those regions produce more energy than they consume, so they probably don't need to import energy sources.

Inferences from a graph are usually based on comparisons among the parts of the graph. To answer the first inference question, you had to compare the lengths of each region's population and energy-consumption bars. To answer the second inference question, you had to compare the lengths of each region's energy-production and -consumption bars. (Seeing the relationships among the parts of a graph requires analysis, a skill you will study further in Unit 3.)

Cartoons

A cartoon is a humorous drawing that makes a point about a serious issue. A newspaper often has a cartoon on its editorial page, the page that presents opinions and views. Cartoons comment on current events and on our society.

Cartoons are graphic material of a special sort. They can be understood only by making inferences. If you look at a cartoon without making inferences, the cartoon won't make any sense.

TRY THIS

To see why cartoons require inferences, look at this cartoon about nuclear power plants—places where nuclear energy is made. Something is wrong in the cartoon. What detail in the cartoon would you not find in a real nuclear power plant?

_____

_____

from *Herblock on All Fronts* (New American Library, 1980)

You would not find a rabbit's foot as the "solution" for emergencies in a real nuclear plant. A rabbit's foot is simply a good luck charm. It would not be useful in a nuclear emergency.

This cartoon, like many, uses humorous exaggeration to make a point.

TRY THIS

Look at the nuclear plant cartoon again. Which of the following points does the cartoon make?

(1) Nuclear plants use too many complicated devices.
(2) Nuclear plants have too few workers.
(3) Nuclear plants don't have perfect plans to cover all emergencies.
(4) Nuclear plants discourage businesses from using other sources of energy.

The cartoon's point is that nuclear plants don't always have perfect plans for emergencies. You can infer this from the detail that stands out: the rabbit's foot for emergencies. The cartoonist expresses an opinion by exaggerating: in nuclear emergencies that we can't control, our only hope may be to rub a rabbit's foot.

Cartoons often use people or other figures to stand for groups or even ideas.

TRY THIS

Look at this cartoon. A fat man has just finished a big dinner. His wife is responding to what he has just asked. Her words are above the cartoon. Which of the following points does the cartoon make?

(1) The man in the picture is overweight and needs to diet.
(2) Americans consume energy with too little concern for future energy needs.
(3) Too much of the energy Americans consume comes from nuclear power.
(4) U.S. factories are polluting the environment.

"WHAT DO YOU MEAN, 'WHAT'S FOR TOMORROW?'"

from *Herblock on All Fronts* (New American Library, 1980)

The cartoon's point is stated in Choice (3). Choice (1) ignores the important clues to the cartoon's meaning. The man, with "U.S. Energy Consumption" on his shirt, stands for the way the United States uses energy. The man (the United States) has eaten a huge meal (has consumed a lot of energy) and wants to know what tomorrow's meal will be. The wife, standing in front of an empty cupboard that represents depleted energy resources, knows there won't be anything for tomorrow because the man has eaten everything today.

Choices (3) and (4) are wrong because nothing in the cartoon suggests anything about nuclear power or pollution.

How to Infer the Meaning of a Cartoon

STEP 1: Remember that the meaning of a cartoon is never given directly. You must infer its meaning.

STEP 2: Notice the clues provided in the cartoon, such as the labels on figures and the details that stand out.

STEP 3: Make sure that the meaning you infer is suggested by the clues in the cartoon.

EXERCISE 16

Look at the following graphics and answer the questions about them.

Question 1 refers to this cartoon.

1. What is the cartoon's point about laws to restrict and control the sale of handguns?
   (1) The laws aim at the right target; they greatly reduce crime in America.
   (2) The laws aim at the wrong target; it's more important to control submachine guns.
   (3) The laws are too strong; people who need handguns can't buy them.
   (4) The laws are too weak; they aren't effective in limiting handguns.

from *Herblock on All Fronts*
(New American Library, 1980)

©1975 HERBLOCK

Question 2 refers to the following graph.

Annual Earnings, Japan's Major Car Makers

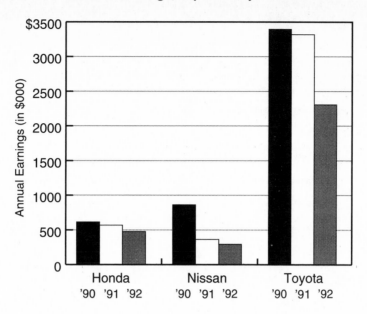

2. Which of the following can you infer from the graph?
   (1) Nissan's 1990 profit was higher than Honda's 1990 profit.
   (2) As a whole, Japan's major car makers earned more than U.S. car makers from 1990 to 1992.
   (3) Japan's major car makers sold fewer cars in 1992 than in 1990.
   (4) Toyotas are priced higher than Hondas and Nissans.

Check your answers on page 219.

Chapter

3 INFERRING UNSTATED MAIN IDEAS

In Unit 1 you saw that the sentences in a paragraph are about a topic. They develop a main idea—the most important point—about the topic and give details to support the main idea. The main idea is often directly stated in one of the sentences in the paragraph.

Sometimes the main idea of a paragraph is not directly stated. You must infer it. In this chapter you will work with both paragraphs and passages that have unstated main ideas.

Lesson 17

Inferring the Main Idea of a Paragraph

As you learned in Lesson 1, when you preview a paragraph you read its first sentence, which often gives the main idea. You scan the rest of the paragraph and read the last sentence. You try to figure out what the topic of the paragraph is. You may even find its main idea. Whatever you learn about a paragraph by previewing helps you when you start to read it.

When you read, you pick up where previewing left off. If you think the first sentence states the main idea, you see whether the other sentences in the paragraph support it. Sometimes you may know what the paragraph's topic is but not know its main idea. Then, as you read, you look for the main idea.

Looking for the main idea is not an activity separate from other reading activities. It's something you do as a part of reading. As you read you think about how the different statements about the topic relate to each other. You try to find which of the statements is the main point and which are the supporting points.

Sometimes when you read a paragraph you may not find a sentence that expresses the main idea, even though you have a sense of what the main idea is.

TRY THIS

None of the sentences in the following paragraph directly states its main idea. See if you can figure out what the main idea of the paragraph is. Then answer the question that follows the paragraph.

Has the U.S. president's involvement in making the country's laws increased? The first president was George Washington. He was president from 1789 to 1797. In his entire eight years as president, Washington took positions on five bills and vetoed three. Ronald Reagan also served for eight years, from 1980 to 1988. In his first four years alone, he expressed opinions on 341 bills and vetoed 39 bills.

Which of the following is the main idea of the paragraph?
(1) Ronald Reagan served almost two hundred years after George Washington.
(2) George Washington was not very involved in making our country's laws.
(3) Over the years the president's involvement in lawmaking has increased.
(4) Compared to the early days of the United States, government today is quite different.
(5) Over the years there has been little change in the president's involvement in lawmaking.

The main idea is stated in Choice (3). All the sentences in the paragraph relate to this main idea. The first sentence asks whether the president's involvement in lawmaking has increased. Taken together, the other sentences show that the president's involvement has increased. They show that George Washington was less involved than Ronald Reagan in lawmaking. You can also infer that this is the main idea of the paragraph. It is a general idea that all the sentences relate to.

Neither Choice (1) nor Choice (2) can be the main idea. They express supporting details. Choice (4) is too general. It is about government in general, not just the president's role in lawmaking. Choice (5) cannot be the main idea because the statements in the paragraph do not support it.

NOW TRY THIS

Read this paragraph and decide which of the statements that follow it expresses its main idea.

When Europeans first settled in Australia, they discovered the land was too poor for farming. The settlers couldn't earn enough money from their crops. They had to find another source of income. Some settlers had brought sheep that could live in a hot climate. By experimenting, they were able to breed sheep with high-quality wool. The settlers were able to make a living by selling this wool. Today Australia is the world's leading producer of wool.

Which of the following is the main idea of the paragraph?
(1) Australia cannot depend on crops for income because its soil isn't rich enough.
(2) After Australians found they could earn a good income by raising sheep, Australia became the world leader in wool production.
(3) Australians experimented with sheep and developed types that are especially useful.

The main idea is expressed in Choice (2). The paragraph tells first about the settlers' economic problem, then about how they solved it, and last that Australia became the world leader in wool production as a result.

Choices (1) and (3) are statements that support the paragraph's main idea. Thus, neither of them can be the main idea.

In this example, you can find the main idea by summarizing the paragraph in your mind. No one sentence in the paragraph expresses the main idea. Instead, the main idea is developed throughout the paragraph. By summarizing the paragraph, as Choice (2) does, you express its main idea.

How to Infer the Unstated Main Idea of a Paragraph

STEP 1: Preview the paragraph and find its topic.

STEP 2: Read the paragraph. Note how the statements in the paragraph relate to each other.

STEP 3: If you do not find the main idea stated in the paragraph, state in your mind what you think it is.

STEP 4: Ask yourself these questions about the statement you made in STEP 3:

- Is it the most important point of the paragraph?
- Is it general enough to cover all points in the paragraph?
- Is it specific enough to relate to the paragraph?
- Does it summarize the paragraph?

STEP 5: If your first inference is wrong, reread the paragraph and try again.

EXERCISE 17

Read each of the following paragraphs and select the statement that best expresses the main idea of each.

Question 1 refers to the following paragraph.

In wars before the American Civil War, the smoothbore musket had been used. It was not very accurate and was almost useless from a distance. Soldiers charged in large groups and fought the enemy up close. In the Civil War new rifled muskets were used. These weapons were much more accurate, even from a distance. Because army commanders still ordered their soldiers to charge in large groups, the charging soldiers could be cut down from a distance by defenders. Thus, in a single day at the battle of Fredericksburg, 13,000 Union soldiers were killed or wounded.

1. Which statement best expresses the main idea of the paragraph?
   (1) A rifled musket is more accurate than a smoothbore musket.
   (2) Because some Civil War battles were fought using old strategies with new weapons, there were many battle casualties.
   (3) The battle of Fredericksburg was among the bloodiest of the Civil War, especially for the Union side.

Question 2 refers to the following paragraph.

To find out whether women experience more emotion than men, psychologists tried an experiment. They showed women and men some pictures of babies, sad events, and other things that might stir up emotions. They tested each person's heart rate as the pictures were shown because they knew that when people experience emotions, their heart rate goes up. The women, much more than the men, expressed emotions when they saw the pictures, but the women's heart rates were no higher than the men's.

2. Which of the following best expresses the main idea of the paragraph?
   (1) Heart rate is a scientific measurement of emotion.
   (2) In our society women are often considered more emotional than men.
   (3) Scientific experiments show that women express emotion more than men but seem not to experience more emotion than men.
   (4) Happy sights and sad sights can stir up people's emotions.

Question 3 refers to the following paragraph.

To what extent do the president and Congress agree on issues and work well together? The answer depends on many things, but the most important is often party affiliation. In 1965 a Democrat, Lyndon Johnson, was president. That year there were twice as many Democrats as Republicans in Congress. Johnson was very successful in getting his programs through Congress. In 1976 Congress again had twice as many Democrats as Republicans. Then, however, a Republican, Gerald Ford, was president. Ford was considerably less successful in getting his programs through Congress.

3. Which of the following best summarizes the paragraph and expresses its main idea?
   (1) Congress and the president tend to work together well when many congresspeople are from the same political party as the president.
   (2) Lyndon Johnson was far more successful than Gerald Ford at working with Congress.
   (3) Democratic presidents tend to do better than Republican presidents at getting Congress to accept their programs.
   (4) The United States has two main political parties, the Republican party and the Democratic party.

Check your answers on page 219.

Lesson 18

Inferring the Main Idea of a Paragraph in a Passage

In Lesson 17 you worked with paragraphs that stood alone. Usually, though, paragraphs appear in a context. The main idea of a paragraph often depends in part on the paragraphs around it.

TRY THIS

Read the paragraph below and decide which of the statements that follow it expresses its main idea.

In a recent experiment people were shown a video of a baby playing with a jack-in-the-box. The jack-in-the-box popped out, and the baby reacted. The people had been lied to about the baby's name. Half of the people had been told the baby's name was David. Most of them thought that the baby reacted to the jack-in-the-box with anger. The other half of the people had been told the baby's name was Diana. Most of them thought that the baby reacted with fear.

Which of the following best expresses the main idea of the paragraph?

(1) In an experiment, people interpreted a baby's reaction as anger if they thought the baby was a boy, but as fear if they thought the baby was a girl.

(2) In a recent experiment, people were lied to about a baby's name, so that some would think the baby a boy and others would think the baby a girl.

(3) Young children react to sudden movements, like a jack-in-the-box popping out of a box.

The sentence in Choice (1) is the best statement of the paragraph's main idea. Choice (2) states only a supporting fact from the paragraph. Choice (3) states an inference that can be drawn from the second sentence in the paragraph.

NOW TRY THIS

Read the following passage. It includes the paragraph you just read. Decide which of the statements following the passage states that paragraph's main idea.

Psychologists sometimes lie to people who participate in their experiments. They lie in order to get at the truth.

Psychologist Stanley Milgrim wanted to know if people would obey orders to hurt another person. People always say they wouldn't obey such orders. Yet in an experiment, Milgrim found that many people did obey orders to give strong electrical shocks to a person. Actually, the shocks weren't real. The people giving these "shocks," however, didn't know it until after the experiment. During the experiment many people, although they obeyed, felt very upset.

After Milgrim's experiment psychologists decided to limit strictly the use of lies in experiments. Lies could not be used if they might upset or frighten a person. Lies in experiments today—as, indeed, in most experiments in the past—are harmless. The more usual use of lies should be clear from the following example.

In a recent experiment people were shown a video of a baby playing with a jack-in-the-box. The jack-in-the-box popped out, and the baby reacted. The people had been lied to about the baby's name. Half of the people had been told the baby's name was David. Most of them thought that the baby reacted to the jack-in-the-box with anger. The other half of the people had been told the baby's name was Diana. Most of them thought that the baby reacted with fear.

Which of the following best expresses the main idea of the last paragraph?

    (1) In an experiment, people interpreted a baby's reaction as anger if they thought the baby was a boy but as fear if they thought the baby was a girl.

    (2) In a recent experiment, people were lied to about a baby's name, so that some would think the baby a boy and others would think the baby a girl.

    (3) Young children react to sudden movements, like a jack-in-the-box popping out.

The main idea of this paragraph when it appears in the passage is Choice (2). The passage is about the use of lies in experiments. In the passage, the jack-in-the-box experiment is discussed to show how the lies psychologists use today are usually harmless.

As you have seen, the same paragraph can have a different main idea depending on the context in which it occurs.

EXERCISE 18

Read the paragraph and the passage that follows it. Answer the questions.

The Great Plains of the United States had good soil and large herds of buffalo. Native American tribes of the Great Plains used the buffalo as their main resource—for food, clothing, and shelter. They moved from place to place to follow the buffalo herds.

1. What is the main idea of the paragraph?

    (1) Tribes of the Great Plains relied on the buffalo for their necessities.

    (2) The buffalo helped to determine the Great Plains tribes' way of life.

    (3) The tribes of the Great Plains migrated with the buffalo herds they hunted.

The Great Plains of the United States had good soil and large herds of buffalo. Native American tribes of the Great Plains used the buffalo as their main resource—for food, clothing, and shelter. They moved from place to place to follow the buffalo herds.

The white settlers of the Great Plains weren't interested in the buffalo. In fact, they killed the buffalo off and in the process destroyed the tribes' way of life. Instead, the settlers were interested in the soil resources of the Great Plains. They used these resources to support a farming and ranching way of life.

2. What is the main idea of the first paragraph?

    (1) Tribes of the Great Plains relied on the buffalo for their necessities.

    (2) The buffalo helped to determine the Great Plains tribes' way of life.

    (3) The tribes of the Great Plains migrated with the buffalo herds they hunted.

Check your answers on page 219.

Lesson 19

Inferring the Main Idea of a Passage

Lesson 18 makes an important point: when you read, you shouldn't focus on each paragraph alone. Instead, you should think about all the paragraphs in the passage together. You should look for the main idea of the whole passage.

The main idea of a passage is the main thing that it says about its topic. Because an entire passage is connected with one topic, its main idea should not be hard to figure out. With practice, you will probably find it easy to find the main idea of a passage. In the meantime you can use the following strategy for finding the main ideas of passages.

You infer the main idea of a paragraph by looking at the ideas in its sentences. In the same way, you can infer the main idea of a passage by looking at the main ideas in its paragraphs. The main idea of a passage may not be stated even though the main ideas of some of its paragraphs may be stated. Sometimes it helps to start with the main idea of the passage. By summarizing the main ideas of the paragraphs, you get the main idea of the passage.

TRY THIS

Read the following passage. Find the main idea in each paragraph. Then infer the main idea of the whole passage.

The past 40 years have seen fast growth for fast-food businesses. The first fast-food restaurants were opened in the 1950s. Today fast-food restaurants dot every highway and town in America.

The fast-food business grew rapidly because of changes in American life. In particular, more women went to work full time. They had less time to prepare meals. In general, the pace of life got quicker. People liked the idea of eating a quick meal without spending much money.

Competition has increased so much recently that fast-food businesses have fallen on hard times. People today have many fast-food options to choose from. Fast-food restaurants must compete against one another as well as against the frozen-food counters in supermarkets that also offer quick, cheap meals. With so much competition, small chains— and perhaps some of the big ones—may be forced to close.

For each paragraph, write the sentence that states its main idea.
(*Hint*: Each paragraph's main idea is directly stated.)

Paragraph 1: _____

Paragraph 2: _____

Paragraph 3: _____

Now write a sentence that expresses the main idea of the entire passage.
The sentence should summarize the main idea of the three paragraphs.

_____

The main idea of Paragraph 1 is in its first sentence: The past 40 years have seen fast growth for fast-food businesses. The main idea of Paragraph 2 is also in its first sentence: Fast-food business grew rapidly because of changes in American life. The first sentence of Paragraph 3 states its main idea: Competition has increased so much recently that fast-food businesses have fallen on hard times.

These three ideas could be summarized to state the main idea of the passage: For 40 years fast-food businesses grew rapidly because of changes in American life, but increased competition has brought them hard times.

There are other ways to state the main idea. Your main idea statement doesn't have to match the one here, but it should include the main ideas of all three paragraphs.

NOW TRY THIS

Read the following passage and decide which of the statements that follow it expresses its main idea.

The Civil War produced many important changes in American life. No change was greater or more important than the abolition of slavery.

The first step toward abolition was taken in 1863 by the Emancipation Proclamation. In this proclamation Lincoln declared that slaves in the Confederate states were free. Of course, the proclamation didn't have much effect until the North won the war. Further, it didn't free slaves in the slave-holding states that had not seceded.

The second, and final, step was taken in 1865, when the Thirteenth Amendment was passed. This amendment to the Constitution said that slavery was prohibited throughout the United States.

Which of the following best expresses the main idea of the passage?
  (1) As a result of the Civil War, American life changed in many significant ways.
  (2) The most important change in American life brought by the Civil War was the abolition of slavery through the Emancipation Proclamation and the Thirteenth Amendment.
  (3) In 1865 the addition of the Thirteenth Amendment to the Constitution abolished slavery.
  (4) The Emancipation Proclamation freed slaves in the Confederate states but did not end slavery throughout the United States.

The main idea is best expressed by Choice (2). This sentence summarizes the main ideas of all three paragraphs in the passage.

Choice (1) is too general. The passage is not about many changes; it discusses only one change. Choices (3) and (4) each relate to only one paragraph of the passage.

How to Infer the Main Idea of a Passage

STEP 1: Find the main idea of each paragraph in the passage.

STEP 2: Summarize these main ideas to get the main idea of the passage.

STEP 3: Ask yourself these questions about the statement you made in STEP 2:

- Is it general enough to be the main idea of the passage?
- Is it specific enough to relate to the passage?
- Does it summarize the main ideas of the paragraphs?

STEP 4: If your first inference is wrong, reread the passage and try again.

EXERCISE 19

Read each passage and select the statement that best expresses its main idea.

Question 1 refers to the following passage.

When there is competition among companies, the consumer does well. Companies try to offer lower prices than their competitors. They try to provide high-quality products and services because they want the consumer to buy from them.

If a certain product or service is provided by only one company, that company has a monopoly. When a company has a monopoly, consumers are hurt. A company that has a monopoly can charge high prices and might not offer top-quality products. The company can get away with these things because the consumer has no other choice.

1. Which of the following expresses the main idea of the passage?
   (1) Some companies offer higher-quality products and services than others.
   (2) Consumers prefer to pay low prices for high-quality products and services.
   (3) A company has a monopoly if it is the only one that provides a certain product or service.
   (4) Consumers benefit by competition among companies and are hurt when a company has a monopoly.

Question 2 refers to the following passage.

A bill can be introduced in either the House or the Senate. It must first be approved by the relevant House or Senate committee. If approved by the committee, the bill is discussed by the entire membership of the body in which it was introduced. If it is again approved, the bill goes to the other side of Congress for approval.

At each stage the bill may change a little. The bill that Congress sends to the president may not look much like the bill that was first introduced.

2. What is the main idea of this passage?
   (1) The president has the power to approve or reject bills that Congress passes.
   (2) Bills may originate in either the House of Representatives or the Senate.
   (3) Because there are so many steps in passing bills, most are modified before Congress passes them to the president.

Check your answers on page 219.

On the next 11 pages you will find sixteen short readings in the five areas of social studies: history, geography, economics, political science, and behavioral science. They are there to help you prepare for the Social Studies Test of the GED in three ways. You can use them to

- refresh what you already know about social studies
- expand your general knowledge of social studies
- practice the reading skills you have studied in Units 1 and 2

HISTORY READINGS

FACTORS CONTRIBUTING TO THE CIVIL WAR

The first half of the 1800s was a period of expansion for the United States. In 1800 the United States extended only as far west as the Mississippi River. By 1853 it extended all the way to the Pacific Ocean.

The first half of the 1800s was also a period of growing sectionalism. That is, people began to place more importance on their region than on the United States as a whole. They thought of themselves as Southerners, Northerners, or Westerners, rather than as Americans.

The regions themselves—especially the South and the North—had become more diverse. The South had developed an agricultural economy and society. It was mainly rural and had large plantations that depended on slaves. The North had become increasingly industrial. Cities and factories had become more and more important. Slavery was prohibited in the northern states.

As the United States grew, members of Congress argued whether slavery should be allowed in new territories. Congress could not reach a lasting agreement. In 1861 seven southern states seceded, or separated, from the United States. They seceded following the election of Abraham Lincoln to the presidency. Their secession set the stage for the Civil War.

1. What does *sectionalism* mean in the second paragraph?
   - (1) the decision to separate from the nation
   - (2) focusing on the interests of one's own part of the nation rather than on the nation as a whole
   - (3) a nation's policy of increasing its territory
   - (4) the belief that slavery should be allowed in some sections of the country

2. Which of the following sentences from the third paragraph in the passage expresses its main idea?
   - (1) The regions themselves—especially the South and the North—had become more diverse.
   - (2) The South had developed an agricultural economy and society.
   - (3) Slavery was prohibited in the northern states.

3. Which of the following best expresses the main idea of the passage?
   - (1) The first half of the 1800s was a period of great change for the United States.
   - (2) The election of Abraham Lincoln led to the South's secession, which set the stage for the Civil War.
   - (3) Territorial expansion, increasing sectionalism and diversity, and disagreement over slavery in new territories set the stage for the Civil War.

Events in the early months of 1861 made war inevitable. The Southern states formed their own nation, the Confederacy. They adopted a constitution and elected a president and a congress. Both the Confederacy and the Union sought volunteers. In April the Confederates captured Fort Sumter, a U.S. fort off the South Carolina coast. The war had begun.

On the surface the North seemed to have all the advantages. It had more than twice as many states and people as the South. It also had two-thirds of the country's railroads, three-quarters of its financial resources, and nine-tenths of its industry. Railroads, money, and factories were all crucial to the war effort.

The South, on the other hand, had outstanding generals—men like Robert E. Lee and "Stonewall" Jackson. The South also had the easier task. It had only to hold off its enemy, whereas the North had to invade and conquer.

Although both sides were at first confident the war would be short, it lasted four years. Bull Run, Antietam, Gettysburg, Shiloh, Vicksburg—these and other battles took the lives of thousands. The number of deaths in the Civil War exceeded the total deaths in all other wars the United States has fought in.

4. What is the meaning of *inevitable* in the first sentence?

   (1) unavoidable   (3) unpopular
   (2) unlikely   (4) destructive

5. What kind of volunteers did the North and South seek? (See the first paragraph.)_____

6. What is the main idea of the second paragraph?

   (1) To win a war, it is necessary to have financial and industrial resources.
   (2) The North had most of the country's resources that were important for fighting a war.
   (3) The North had more states and more people than the South.

Southern military successes encouraged General Lee to invade the North in 1863. His plans were upset by the battle of Gettysburg, Pennsylvania, which became a turning point in the war. Around the same time, Lincoln finally found capable generals, especially Ulysses S. Grant and William Sherman. Even so, the Confederate army persevered. A Northern victory did not seem assured until July 1864, when Sherman took Atlanta. In April 1865, Lee surrendered to Grant at Appomattox Court House, Virginia.

The task of recovery from the war was a difficult one. It was made even more so by the assassination of Lincoln less than a week after Lee's surrender. Large areas of the South had been destroyed by war. The region's economy had to be rebuilt. Plans were needed for readmitting Southern states back into the Union. The 3.5 million slaves who had been freed also had to be brought into the life of the nation.

The Civil War ended slavery. It also, with the passage of the Fourteenth and Fifteenth Amendments, made citizens of African-Americans and gave African-American men the right to vote.

The Civil War had other important effects. In two major ways it made the United States more like it is today. First, it strengthened the national government. Because of the Civil War, the idea that states could leave the national government disappeared. Further, the Civil War caused the national government to use two of its powers for the first time: collecting income taxes and drafting an army. Second, the Civil War encouraged the development of industry, since new factories were needed to supply the military. At the start of the war the United States had been mainly an agricultural country. By the war's end the United States had taken major steps toward becoming a modern, industrial nation.

7. Which side won the battle of Gettysburg?

_____

8. What does the first paragraph suggest
   was a weakness of the North in the early
   years of the war?

   (1) a lack of good military leadership
   (2) losing the battle of Gettysburg
   (3) the abilities of Generals Grant and
       Sherman

9. What is the meaning of *persevered* in the
   first paragraph?

   (1) kept going despite difficulties
   (2) conquered large amounts of land
   (3) lacked the spirit to fight

10. Name three changes that the Civil War
    helped bring about.

    a. _____

    b. _____

    c. _____

Mining Crew Drifting for Gold below Discovery Point,
Deadwood, Dakota Territory, circa 1876

HOW THE PHYSICAL ENVIRONMENT AFFECTS CULTURES

People's physical environment influences the way they live. Climate, terrain, and the availability of natural resources all influence people's lives. For example, people who live in the polar climate dress differently than people who live in jungles.

Environment is not the only factor that influences how people live. It may not even be the main factor. People's culture—their religion, language, customs, beliefs, and technologies—affect their way of life, too. (*Technologies* refers to the tools and systems people use in their work and other activities.)

Their environment offers possibilities to the people of any culture and sets limits for them. For example, in the West the environment contains coal, gas, oil, copper, iron, tin, zinc, and many other resources. Use of these resources has enabled the West to develop the modern technologies on which its life depends. But because the supply of natural resources is limited, the West must always look for new technologies so as not to exhaust its natural resources.

11. All of the following are elements of culture EXCEPT
    (1) language
    (2) religion
    (3) land formations
    (4) customs
    (5) beliefs

12. Which of the following expresses the main idea of the passage?
    (1) Culture is the main factor in determining how people live.
    (2) Both their physical environment and their culture affect how people live.
    (3) Their environment offers the people of any culture possibilities and sets limits for them.

THE INDUSTRIAL REVOLUTION AND THE ENVIRONMENT

The Industrial Revolution changed the relationship between people and their environment. The Industrial Revolution refers to a period of great change in technology. It began late in the 18th century when people discovered that coal could be used for energy. This discovery made it possible to develop machine technologies to replace many processes that were done by hand. Mechanization allowed people to produce much more than before.

Changes brought by the Industrial Revolution have allowed people to overcome many of the limits set by their environment. In the past, for example, cities were usually built near water because water provided the means for transportation. Now, because there are modern roads and air travel, cities can be located anywhere. To give another example, it was once difficult to grow crops where land became dry or flooded easily. Modern methods of irrigation and flood control have made such land more useful. The list of possible examples is long.

Before the Industrial Revolution people had little effect on their environment. Since the Industrial Revolution people have significantly changed the environment. Some of these changes have been deliberate; others have not. Some have had dangerous consequences. For example, cars, which permit us to move around freely, pollute our air. Air pollution has immediate and long-term dangers. Factories make goods that allow us to live better. They, too, pollute the air and water on which we depend.

Since the Industrial Revolution our way of life has depended increasingly on heavy use of natural resources. Most natural resources are nonrenewable; they cannot be replaced. We therefore must use the environment's resources wisely.

The Industrial Revolution allowed us to overcome certain environmental limitations. It also made us more dependent on environmental resources. Since we will always depend on our physical environment, we must be cautious about the way we treat it.

13. Which of the following is NOT an effect of the Industrial Revolution?

    (1) Mechanization allows us to produce more goods than before.
    (2) We use more natural resources than before.
    (3) We are affected by our environment.
    (4) We have a greater effect on our environment than before.

14. What is the meaning of *irrigation* near the end of the second paragraph?

    (1) farming with modern equipment
    (2) supplying water to land
    (3) going from one place to another
    (4) controlling floods with dams

15. What is one example the passage gives to show how the Industrial Revolution helped people overcome the limits of their environment?

    _____

16. What is one example the passage gives to show how the Industrial Revolution has caused harm to the environment?

    _____

17. What is a *nonrenewable* natural resource?

    _____

18. Which of the following *best* expresses the main idea of the passage?

    (1) Modern transportation has changed the way people live.
    (2) One effect of the Industrial Revolution has been harm to the environment.
    (3) The Industrial Revolution increased both people's effect and dependence on their environment.

ECONOMICS READINGS

THE U.S. ECONOMIC SYSTEM

The United States has a capitalist economic system. In a capitalist system, businesses are privately owned and operate competitively to make a profit. Government does not interfere much in a capitalist system.

Capitalism is a free enterprise system. That means that businesses are free to produce whatever products and services they wish and to charge customers whatever they wish. Of course, businesses compete with one another to attract customers. The result of this competition is often high-quality products and services at prices customers find reasonable.

19. In a capitalist economic system

    (1) the government owns all businesses
    (2) businesses are privately owned
    (3) the government owns some but not all businesses

20. According to the passage, customers benefit from a free enterprise system because

    (1) all products and services produced are of high quality
    (2) most products and services are reasonably priced
    (3) all similar products and services cost the same

THE PROFIT MOTIVE

By lowering prices, businesses attract more customers. Businesses will lower their prices only to a certain point, however. This is explained by the profit motive.

Businesses are in business to make a profit. If a business lowered its prices too far, its income would be lower than or equal to its costs. The business would not make a profit. Therefore, businesses keep prices low enough to attract customers but high enough to yield a profit.

Customers benefit from the profit motive because the desire for profits encourages businesses to improve products and services. Yet customers benefit from the profit motive only in situations where there is competition. If a company is the only one that produces a product customers need, they must buy from that company. The company can charge a high price because there is no competition. The customer suffers.

21. A business makes a profit when its income

    (1) is higher than its costs
    (2) is lower than its costs
    (3) is equal to its costs

22. Why might a business not make a profit if its prices are too high?

_____

23. The profit motive benefits customers

    (1) all the time
    (2) when there is competition
    (3) when there is no competition
    (4) at no time

THE ROLE OF THE GOVERNMENT IN THE U.S. ECONOMIC SYSTEM

The government does not interfere with businesses in a free enterprise system unless there is evidence that the consumer may be hurt by certain business practices. When it feels that consumers need protection, the government makes and enforces laws, such as those that ensure product safety and that forbid false advertising.

Since businesses are motivated by profit in a free enterprise system, they seldom supply products and services that would bring in small profits. The government steps in and supplies products such as low-cost housing and services such as public libraries.

Because the government has a limited role in the U.S. economic system, that system is not purely capitalistic. It is basically a capitalist system, though, since businesses are privately owned and supply consumers with the products and services that allow businesses to make profits.

24. What does *ensure* near the end of the first paragraph mean?

    (1) discourage
    (2) advertise
    (3) guarantee

25. The government's role in the U.S. economic system includes each of the following EXCEPT

    (1) protecting consumers against unsafe products
    (2) protecting consumers against false advertising
    (3) providing products and services not provided by private businesses
    (4) telling businesses what products and services to provide consumers

26. The main idea of the passage is that the U.S. economic system is basically capitalistic

    (1) because businesses are privately owned and make profits
    (2) because businesses do not supply products and services that do not bring in profits
    (3) even though the government controls certain business practices and provides some products and services

THE BRANCHES OF THE FEDERAL GOVERNMENT

The American federal, or national, government has three branches: the legislative, the executive, and the judicial branches. The Constitution established these three branches so that there would be a separation of powers. That is, power would be divided and not concentrated in one person or group. In this way tyranny would be prevented.

The legislative branch makes the laws. The executive branch carries out the laws. The judicial branch decides whether the laws made can be supported by the Constitution.

27. *Tyranny* means
    (1) government with a separation of powers
    (2) government divided against itself
    (3) harsh government by one ruler or group with too much power

28. Write what you think is the main idea of the second paragraph in the passage.

THE LEGISLATIVE BRANCH

The legislature, or Congress, is divided into the Senate and the House of Representatives. The people of each state elect their senators and representatives. In Congress there are two senators from each state; the number of representatives from each depends on the state's population.

Congresspeople choose leaders from among themselves to serve on committees. These committees play important roles in the legislative process, the process of making laws.

The legislative process is a complex one with many steps, as the diagram below shows. At any point during the process, the bill may be changed or even killed.

29. Compared to more-populous states, less-populous states have
    (1) more senators
    (2) fewer senators
    (3) more representatives
    (4) fewer representatives

The Route of a Bill through Congress

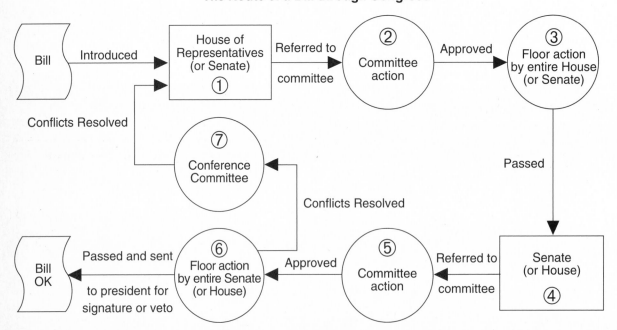

Note: Any bill *except* a money bill may start in the Senate.

30. Which of the following can be inferred from the diagram on page 118?

(1) Bills are introduced directly to committees in either part of Congress.
(2) A representative can introduce a bill to spend $2 billion on housing.
(3) Only the president can introduce a bill to Congress.

THE EXECUTIVE BRANCH

As head of the executive branch, the president carries out the laws the legislative branch makes. The president has the help of many government agencies, such as the Department of the Treasury, the Department of Agriculture, and the Department of Transportation. Each agency deals with matters that fall in its area. The heads of these agencies are appointed by the president. They form the president's cabinet, or group of advisers.

In addition to carrying out laws, the president has a number of other important functions. As leader of the country, the president meets with the leaders of other countries. The president is commander-in-chief of the military, an important function in times of war. As party leader the president supports candidates from his or her party and helps decide the party's stand on issues.

31. Who makes up the cabinet?

_____

32. List three functions of the president that do not involve carrying out laws.

(a) _____

(b) _____

(c) _____

THE JUDICIAL BRANCH

The judicial branch consists of the federal courts. There are three levels of federal courts: district courts, appeals courts, and the Supreme Court. The Supreme Court is the nation's highest and most powerful court.

Federal courts hear cases that relate to U.S. laws and to the Constitution. They also hear cases that involve people from different states.

Federal court cases usually start out in district courts, the lowest level of the federal court system. If a district court's decision is appealed, the case is heard in an appeals court. A few important cases go all the way to the Supreme Court.

The nine Supreme Court justices are appointed by the president and serve for life. The Supreme Court makes final decisions about whether laws can be supported by the Constitution. If the Supreme Court rules a law unconstitutional, the law cannot stand.

33. When a court's decision is appealed, a case is

(1) referred to a higher court for further consideration
(2) settled to the satisfaction of all concerned
(3) dropped even though it hasn't been settled

34. What is the meaning of *unconstitutional* in the last sentence?

_____

35. The Supreme Court is the most-powerful federal court because

(1) it is made up of nine justices
(2) the president appoints its members
(3) it makes final decisions about whether laws are constitutional

BEHAVIORAL SCIENCE READINGS

ORIGINS OF GENDER DIFFERENCES

Our gender—our maleness or our femaleness—is basic to how we think of ourselves and how we interact with others. For this reason gender is an important topic in the behavioral sciences, such as psychology, which study behavior.

One question behavioral scientists ask is why there are gender differences in behavior. Are differences in behavior biological and innate? That is, are they an inborn part of being male or female? Or do these differences have a social explanation? That is, are they differences that we learn as children from people around us?

36. What does *innate* in the second paragraph mean?
    (1) inborn
    (2) learned
    (3) unimportant

37. Which sentence in the second paragraph states the paragraph's main idea?

SCIENTISTS STUDY GENDER DIFFERENCES

Behavioral scientists try to find out what male-female differences there are and what explains them. One way they do this is to study how men and women behave in different parts of the world. Different countries have different cultures. That is, they have different beliefs, customs, and ways of living. People follow their culture's ideas about appropriate behavior. One thing behavioral scientists can study is whether women express emotion more than men in all cultures or just in some cultures.

38. What is one way behavioral scientists study gender differences?

39. Suppose scientists found that in some cultures women express emotions more than men but in others men express emotions more. Based on the passage, you can infer that this difference between men and women is
    (1) cultural
    (2) innate
    (3) unimportant

RESULTS OF RESEARCH ON GENDER DIFFERENCES

Lab experiments that study gender differences seem to show that some differences are biological and that others are cultural. For example, it seems that expressing emotion is a cultural difference, and that being aggressive is at least partly biological.

In experiments on emotion, scientific measures showed that women did not react with more emotion than men. In experiments on aggression, scientists found that men tended to be more aggressive than women. For instance, men were more willing to give another person what they thought were strong electrical shocks.

Studies that have looked at various cultures also show that there are sometimes biological and sometimes cultural explanations for differences in men's and women's behaviors. In the United States women are more likely to express emotions than men. In Iran men are more likely to express emotion. Yet in almost all cultures men are more socially dominant than women. They are more likely to lead in groups, more likely to contribute to discussions, and so forth.

40. Which of the following best expresses the main idea of the passage?

(1) In the United States women express emotions more than men, but in Iran the opposite is true.

(2) Both lab experiments and studies of different cultures show that male-female differences in expressing emotion are cultural, not biological.

(3) Both lab experiments and studies of different cultures show that some gender differences in behavior are cultural and others are biological.

41. One gender difference in behavior that seems to have a cultural explanation is

(1) aggression

(2) social dominance

(3) expressing emotion

THEORIES ABOUT GENDER DIFFERENCES

Scientists' conclusions about behavioral differences between men and women are tentative. New evidence may force new conclusions. At this point it seems that (a) there are behavioral differences between men and women, but not as many as people think, and (b) some of these differences are biological and others are cultural.

Some differences are likely to be both biological and cultural. Differences in aggressiveness is an example. Testosterone is a hormone that men have in larger amounts than women. Scientists have found a relationship between testosterone levels and levels of aggression. Therefore, differences in aggressiveness probably have a biological cause. Yet cultural factors, such as a society's disapproval of aggressive behavior, can influence a person's behavior. Thus, a man who is innately aggressive may not behave aggressively because of cultural influences.

That some gender differences probably have both biological and cultural causes doesn't surprise scientists. Time and again behavioral scientists have found that what we are is the product of both our biology and our environment.

Scientists stress that gender differences shouldn't be exaggerated because the differences are only tendencies. Many women are more socially dominant than many men. Many men are more emotional than many women. Scientists also note that as people get older, gender differences diminish. Males and females may behave quite differently as teenagers, but twenty years later differences in their behavior are not as obvious.

42. What is the meaning of *tentative* in the first paragraph?

(1) definite

(2) not final

(3) evident

43. The root of gender differences in aggressive behavior seems now to be

(1) biological

(2) social

(3) both biological and social

44. What is the meaning of *diminish* near the end of the last paragraph?

_____

Check your answers on page 219.

SOCIAL STUDIES READINGS 2 SKILLS CHART

To review the readings skills covered by the items in Social Studies Readings 2, study the following parts of Units 1 and 2.

		Item Number
Unit 1	Comprehending What You Read	
Chapter 2	Recognizing Stated Main Ideas	
Lesson 5	Finding the Sentence That States the Main Idea	2, 37
Chapter 3	Understanding the Details	
Lesson 6	Reading for Details	10, 13, 23, 31, 35, 38
Lesson 7	Seeing How Details Are Organized	11, 15, 16, 32
Unit 2	Inferring as You Read	
Chapter 1	Inferring Word Meanings	
Lesson 11	Understanding Meanings from Context	5, 42
Lesson 12	Recognizing Definitions and Synonyms	1, 17, 19, 36
Lesson 13	Using Examples and Contrasts	9, 44
Lesson 14	Using the General Context	4, 14, 24, 27, 34
Chapter 2	Inferring Details	
Lesson 15	Making Inferences from Written Material	7, 8, 20, 21, 22, 25 29, 33, 39, 41, 43
Lesson 16	Making Inferences from Graphic Material	30
Chapter 3	Inferring Unstated Main Ideas	
Lesson 17	Inferring the Main Idea of a Paragraph	28
Lesson 18	Inferring the Main Idea of a Paragraph in a Passage	6
Lesson 19	Inferring the Main Idea of a Passage	3, 12, 18, 26, 40

This section will give you practice answering questions like those on the GED. The ten questions in this Practice are all multiple choice, like the ones on the GED.

As you do this Practice, use the reading skills you've studied in Units 1 and 2.

- Preview each passage or graph before you read it. Preview the questions, too.
- Read each passage to look for its main idea and note the details it contains.
- If you don't understand a word, try to infer its meaning from its context.
- Make inferences about things not stated directly in passages.

Directions: Choose the one best answer to each item.

Items 1 through 4 refer to the following passage.

In October 1989 President Bush and Congress agreed to increase the minimum wage to $4.25 per hour over a two-year period. From 1981 to 1989, the minimum wage had been $3.35 per hour. Nevertheless, the prices of products and services increased significantly during those eight years.

Here's how the agreement on the increase came about:

- Some members of the House wanted to increase the minimum wage to $5.25 per hour over three years. Bush proposed an increase to $4.25 over three years. He also proposed a "training wage"—a lower minimum wage for new workers.

- In May 1989 Congress passed a minimum-wage increase to $4.55 per hour over three years. Bush vetoed this bill. Congresspeople who supported the bill did not have enough votes to override the veto so the bill could become law.

- Congress and the president worked out a compromise. The final bill contained a training wage, but only for teenagers who were new workers. It raised the minimum less than Congress had wanted but more quickly than the president had proposed.

1. The passage says that the minimum wage stayed the same from 1981 to 1989 even though the prices of products and services increased. What can you infer from this?
   (1) There were fewer workers earning the minimum wage in 1989 than in 1981.
   (2) Workers who earned the minimum wage could buy less in 1989 than in 1981.
   (3) From 1981 through 1989 American workers lost jobs to workers in other countries.
   (4) The minimum wage increases whenever the price of goods increases.
   (5) From 1981 to 1989 the income of workers who earned the minimum wage increased significantly.

2. You can infer from the passage that when the president vetoes a bill,
   (1) there is no way that bill can become a law
   (2) Congress can reconsider the bill only when there is a new president
   (3) the bill becomes a law anyway if enough congresspeople vote for it a second time
   (4) he or she writes a new version which then becomes law
   (5) Congress can appeal the veto to the Supreme Court

3. Which of the following was part of the bill Congress and the president compromised on?

    (1) an increase to $5.25 per hour
    (2) a lower-than-minimum wage for all new workers
    (3) a training wage for teenagers who are new workers
    (4) an increase in the hourly wage that matched the increase in the cost of living since 1981
    (5) funding for programs to train new workers

4. The passage shows that in the American political system

    (1) politicians always respond to the demands of the voters
    (2) the president is more powerful than Congress
    (3) Congress is more powerful than the president
    (4) Congress focuses on national issues more than the president
    (5) the branches of government can work together to solve problems

Item 5 refers to the following paragraph.

To its millions of fans, football is a sport. To the owners of its 28 teams, football is a business. The owners make a profit if their income is greater than their costs. Most of the owners' income comes from selling the right to broadcast games to TV networks. Most of their costs are players' salaries. Owners complain that in recent years they have actually lost money because salaries have risen so much.

5. You can infer that owners' income from TV networks in recent years

    (1) has gone up more than players' salaries
    (2) has not gone up as much as players' salaries
    (3) has gone down
    (4) has gone up
    (5) has stayed the same

Items 6 and 7 refer to the following graph.

U.S. Use of Natural Resources for Energy

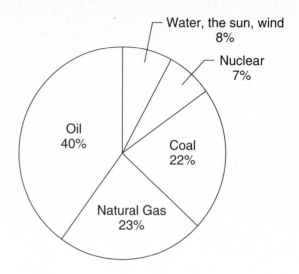

6. Which of the following natural sources of energy is the one the United States relies on most?

    (1) water
    (2) the sun
    (3) wind
    (4) coal
    (5) oil

7. Coal, natural gas, and oil are nonrenewable natural resources. Water, the sun, and wind are renewable natural resources. Using this information and information from the graph, you can infer that for its energy needs the United States is dependent

    (1) mostly on nonrenewable resources
    (2) mostly on renewable resources
    (3) equally on nonrenewable and renewable resources
    (4) more on renewable resources than nonrenewable resources
    (5) mostly on imported nonrenewable resources

Items 8 and 9 refer to the following paragraph.

Politicians in recent elections have taken to negative campaigning. A news reporter summed up the 1989 campaign as follows: "From Virginia to Alabama to California, candidates were calling one another liars and crooks with remarkable enthusiasm." Even though negative campaigning has become popular, many people question whether it works.

The candidates for governor of one state each ran TV commercials calling the other a liar. "It's not worth voting for anyone," said a voter who had seen the commercials.

8. Negative campaigning is an attempt to gain political office by

   (1) an unsuccessful politician
   (2) by attacking the opposition
   (3) by a little-known candidate
   (4) by advertising on TV
   (5) by focusing on important issues

9. Which of the following is the main idea of the passage?

   (1) The two-party system needs to be changed.
   (2) Many dishonest people go into politics.
   (3) After a negative campaign, voters may have a bad opinion of candidates.
   (4) Candidates' campaign efforts sometimes come to nothing because many citizens don't vote.
   (5) Negative campaigning is a successful strategy for politicians.

Item 10 refers to the buildup of supplies of military weapons. The figure on the left is Uncle Sam, who stands for the U.S. government.

Auth © 1987 The Philadelphia Inquirer
Reprinted with permission of UNIVERSAL PRESS SYNDICATE. *All rights reserved.*

10. Which of the following is the point of the cartoon?

    (1) The United States should spend less money on the military.
    (2) The United States should limit the number of Japanese cars brought into the country.
    (3) The United States should continue its buildup of weapons.
    (4) American car companies should work with Japanese companies to develop better cars.
    (5) The U.S. government should collect more money in taxes.

Check your answers on page 223.

GED PRACTICE 2 SKILLS CHART

To review the readings skills covered by the items in GED Practice 1, study the following parts of Units 1 and 2.

		Item Number
Unit 1	Comprehending What You Read	
Chapter 3	Understanding the Details	
Lesson 6	Reading for Details	3
Lesson 9	Finding Details in Graphs	6
Unit 2	Inferring as You Read	
Chapter 1	Inferring Word Meanings	
Lesson 14	Using the General Context	8
Chapter 2	Inferring Details	
Lesson 15	Making Inferences from Written Material	1, 2, 5
Lesson 16	Making Inferences from Graphic Material	7, 10
Chapter 3	Inferring Unstated Main Ideas	
Lesson 19	Inferring the Main Idea of a Passage	4, 9

GED PRACTICE 2 CONTENT CHART

The following chart shows which area of social studies each item in GED Practice 2 refers to.

Area of Social Studies	Item Number
Geography	6, 7
Economics	5, 10
Political Science	1, 2, 3, 4, 8, 9

UNIT 3

Thinking Critically as You Read

Anyone who has held a job knows how important critical thinking skills are. When you work, you apply your knowledge and experience to new situations. You think about what you're doing, and you make judgments about the work and the people around you.

When you read, you use similar critical thinking skills. You may not be aware of it, but you apply knowledge to understand new facts and ideas. You think about the relationships among ideas. You also evaluate, or make judgments about, what you are reading.

Pearl Harbor, December 7, 1941

Unit 3 Overview

Chapter 1   Applying What You Read
Chapter 2   Analyzing What You Read
Chapter 3   Evaluating What You Read

Social Studies Readings 3
GED Practice 3

1 APPLYING WHAT YOU READ

Arithmetic is a kind of knowledge you use every day. When you get paid, shop for groceries, or pay the rent or mortgage, you apply, or use, your knowledge of arithmetic in new situations. Similarly, you often apply information you gain by reading to new situations or in new contexts.

In this chapter you will practice applying information from written and graphic material. You will also learn to apply information to categories.

Lesson 20

Applying Information from Written Material

To apply information means to use it. Applying information often means using general ideas in specific situations. Writers often give specific examples to help readers understand the ideas they are explaining.

TRY THIS

Read the following passage. Look for examples that illustrate the topic of the paragraph. Then answer the questions.

As children grow, they learn how to behave with other people. They also learn the values of the people around them. This kind of learning is called socialization.

Parents begin children's socialization. They teach children how to behave and what to believe by setting examples, by rewarding or punishing behaviors, and by enforcing rules. For example, to reward a child a parent may praise him or her for sharing a toy with another child. As a result, the child learns that sharing is good behavior.

As children's worlds expand, people other than their parents help their socialization. Brothers, sisters, schoolmates, teachers, friends, and even television characters teach children how to behave and what to believe.

What is socialization?
  (1) the process of learning how to behave and what to believe
  (2) a system of rewards and punishments used to teach children
  (3) the people who teach children how to behave

Which of the following is the example of socialization given in the paragraph?
  (1) Parents start a child's socialization.
  (2) A parent praises a child for sharing a toy.
  (3) Children learn behaviors and values.

The answer to the first question is Choice (1). The first paragraph in the passage defines socialization.

The answer to the second question is Choice (2). The second paragraph contains this example that illustrates socialization. Choices (1) and (3) do not give examples of socialization.

In the passage the writer applied a general idea by describing a specific example. You can do the same thing.

NOW TRY THIS

Reread the passage about socialization. Then use the information in it to answer the following question.

A father wanted his three-year-old to learn to get along with other children, so he
  (1) gave the child her own room
  (2) bought the child educational toys
  (3) sent the child to preschool

Choice (3) is the best answer. Learning to get along with other children is part of the process of socialization. The passage indicates that schoolmates and teachers contribute to a child's socialization. Therefore, sending the child to preschool, where she will have to get along with schoolmates and teachers, is an example of socialization. It applies the concept of socialization in a specific situation.

The other two choices do not describe opportunities for the child to be with other people.

Sometimes writers explain concepts only in general terms and leave it to you to apply them to specific situations.

Read the following passage and answer the question.

Prices depend on the law of supply and demand. This law states two things. First, consumers will pay a high price when they demand, or want, a product or when little of the product is available. Second, consumers pay a low price for a product when few people demand it or when there is more than enough of the product available.

Which of the following is an example of the law of supply and demand?

    (1) A store cut its prices by 20 percent during a sale.
    (2) A real diamond costs more than a manmade diamond.
    (3) Prices have been rising steadily over the last four decades.

Choice (2) illustrates one part of the law of supply and demand: *Consumers will pay a high price . . . when little of the product is available.* Real diamonds are scarce compared to manmade diamonds.

Choices (1) and (3) do not illustrate any part of the law of supply and demand, which explains only why some things cost more than others. Choices (1) and (3) describe situations in which all prices change.

To choose the right answer, you had to use both the information in the passage and your own knowledge and experience. You had to apply what you read about the law of supply and demand to what you know about sales, diamonds, and inflation. Then you could figure out which example illustrated part of the law of supply and demand.

How to Apply Knowledge You Gain by Reading

STEP 1: Think about the main ideas in a passage.

STEP 2: See if the passage contains examples that apply those ideas.

STEP 3: Ask yourself: What does this remind me of? What situations do these ideas relate to?

EXERCISE 20

Read the following passages. Use the information in each together with your own knowledge and experience to answer the questions.

Questions 1 through 3 refer to the following paragraph.

Each of the three branches of the U.S. government has its own powers. Each also has ways to check, or limit, the powers of the others. For example, Congress can pass a bill, but if the president vetoes it the bill does not become law. Once the president signs a bill into law, the Supreme Court can rule that the law is unconstitutional and cannot remain a law. In these ways the president and the Supreme Court can check the powers of Congress.

1. Which of the following is an example of Congress checking the president's powers?

    (1) The vice-president votes in the Senate to break a tie.
    (2) The president exercises an executive power by signing a treaty, but the Senate votes it down.
    (3) Congress passes a bill it knows the president doesn't like.

2. Which of the following is an example of the president checking the powers of the courts?

    (1) Some judges are appointed by the president to serve for life.
    (2) Some judges are elected by popular vote.
    (3) The president's appointments of Supreme Court judges must be confirmed by Congress.

3. When the president vetoes a bill, a two-thirds majority vote in Congress overrides the veto and the bill becomes law. This is an example of

    (1) the president checking Congress's powers
    (2) Congress checking the president's powers
    (3) the president and Congress checking the Supreme Court's powers

Question 4 refers to the following paragraph.

The kind of shelter a group of people builds depends on where they live. It also depends on the resources, or materials, found in that place. People in Mali in Africa use mud to build everything from homes to temples. Native Americans and Spanish settlers in Mexico built lodgings of adobe bricks made with clay. The Plains tribes used buffalo skins for their teepees. In many parts of Europe people used rocks from the hillsides to make homes.

4. Which of the following is an example of the use of local resources for building shelters?

(1) The Japanese buy U.S. lumber for building.

(2) Inuit people build igloos from snow and ice.

(3) Steel skyscrapers mark the skylines of major cities all over the world.

Question 5 is based on the following passage.

The Statue of Liberty was built in 1876. The following is part of the poem on its base:

> Give me your tired, your poor,
> Your huddled masses yearning to breathe free,
> The wretched refuse of your teeming shore.
> Send these, the homeless, tempest-tost to me.
> I lift my lamp beside the golden door!

5. Which of the following is an example of the United States acting on the ideas expressed in the poem?

(1) At the U.S.–Canadian border, officials stop cars, check their occupants' citizenship, and ask what goods they are bringing into the country.

(2) The 1921 immigration law limited the number of emigrants from other countries.

(3) The amnesty program in the 1980s allowed many people who had entered the United States without proper papers to stay.

Check your answers on page 223.

Lesson 21

Applying Information from Graphic Material

In Unit 1 you learned how to preview and find details in graphic material. In Unit 2 you made inferences from graphic material. In this lesson you will apply information from graphic materials to new situations.

TRY THIS

The following table shows the average high temperatures in Mexico City and in Monterey. Study the table. Then use the information to answer the question.

Average Monthly High Temperatures

	Mexico City	Monterey		Mexico City	Monterey
January	66	68	July	73	90
February	69	72	August	73	92
March	75	76	September	74	86
April	77	84	October	70	80
May	78	87	November	68	71
June	76	91	December	66	65

A company wants to build a plant in Mexico where expenditures for air conditioning will not be high. In which city listed in the table should less air conditioning be needed? _____

Mexico City's high temperatures stay in the 60s and 70s all year. Monterey's temperatures rise into the 80s and 90s during seven months each year. Air conditioning would be needed less in Mexico City than in Monterey.

NOW TRY THIS

The following graph gives more information about Mexico City's climate. It shows how often it rains or snows there each month. Use the information in the graph to answer the question.

Precipitation in Mexico City

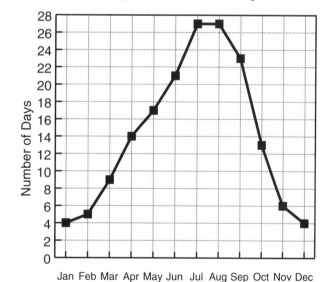

The company wants to build its Mexico City plant in the five months the weather is clearest. During which months should it build?

_____

The company should build during November, December, January, February, and March. During those months it rains or snows fewer than ten days a month. During the rest of the year, precipitation is more frequent.

You can also apply information from a map.

TRY THIS

Study the following map of the time zones in the United States. Notice that as you go west the time grows earlier. Use the information in the map to answer the question.

U.S. Time Zones

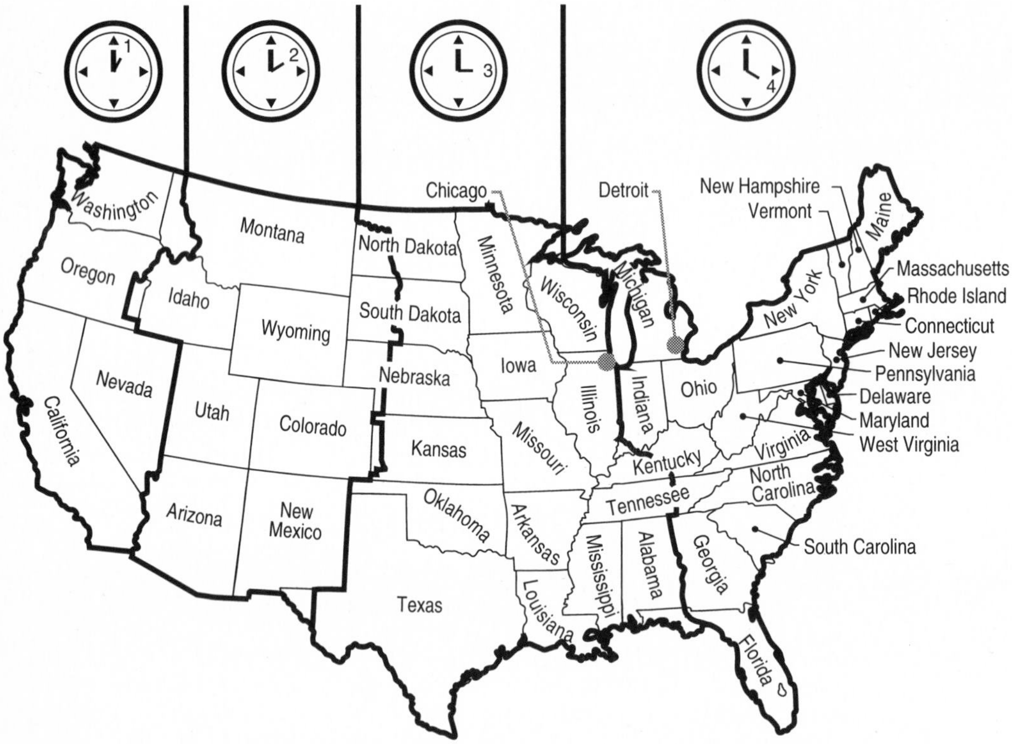

A truck driver must take freight from Detroit to Chicago. The trip takes five hours. Using the time in Detroit, what is the latest time she can begin her trip and arrive in Chicago by noon? _____

The driver must leave Detroit no later than 8 A.M. The map shows that the time in Detroit is one hour later than in Chicago. The driver would be leaving at 7 A.M. Chicago time and would arrive in Chicago at 12 noon, five hours later.

How to Apply Information from Graphic Materials

STEP 1: Preview and study the graphic.

STEP 2: Ask yourself: How can this information be used to answer real-world questions?

Use the information in each graph, map, and table to answer the questions.

Question 1 is based on this bar graph.

1. Which of the following sales histories is most like the early history of car registrations?

   (1) Personal computers were introduced in the 1970s. By 1990, millions had been sold.
   (2) For a while the Beta VCR sold well. Then Beta sales dropped.
   (3) Air conditioners for home use became available in the 1930s. Sales have slowly but steadily risen since then.

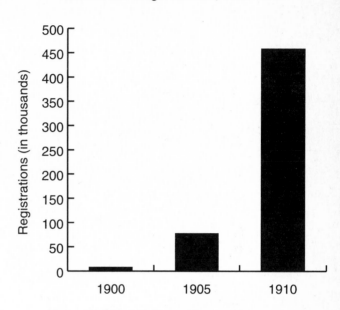

Automobile Registrations, 1900–1910

Note: The first U.S.–made gasoline cars were introduced in 1896.

Question 2 is based on this line graph.

2. Phil has ordered fish for his family's grocery store since Year 1 on the graph. How much fish did he probably order in Year 4?

   (1) more than he ever ordered in one year
   (2) about the same amount he ordered in Year 2
   (3) less than he ever ordered in any earlier year

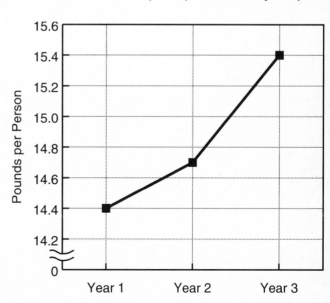

U.S. Fish Consumption (three recent years)

Question 3 is based on this line graph.

3. Information in the graph suggests that ads for coffee have NO effect on
   (1) the brand of coffee people drink
   (2) the type of coffee people drink, instant or brewed
   (3) the amount of coffee people drink

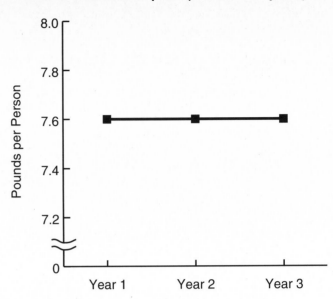

U.S. Coffee Consumption (three recent years)

Questions 4 through 6 are based on the following map.

U.S. Population Density

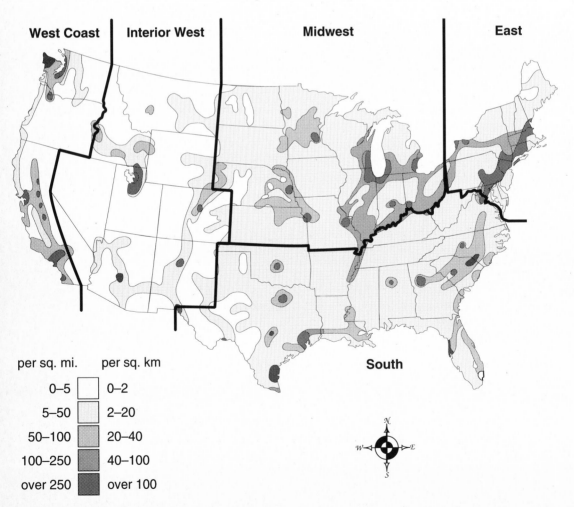

4. A company wants to build a new warehouse near several large population centers. Which of the following regions would be the best choice?

   (1) the middle or southern part of the East
   (2) the western part of the Midwest
   (3) the interior West

5. In the 1950s the military was looking for a place to test atomic bombs. Which region did the government most likely pick?

   (1) the West Coast
   (2) the South
   (3) the Interior West

6. The person most likely to use this map would be

   (1) a retired person who wants to move to a warm, dry climate
   (2) a planner who needs to decide where to place social service agencies
   (3) a farmer who wants to buy livestock

Question 7 is based on the following information.

Presidential Vetoes, 1945–1969

President	Vetoes	Party in Control of Congress
Truman (Democrat)	250	Republican
Eisenhower (Republican)	181	Democratic
Kennedy (Democrat)	21	Democratic
Johnson (Democrat)	30	Democratic

7. The table suggests that

   (1) Democratic presidents use their veto power more often than Republican presidents
   (2) vetoes are more likely when a president does not belong to the party that controls Congress
   (3) Presidents Kennedy and Johnson felt they had more important things to do than veto bills

Check your answers on page 224.

Lesson 22

Classifying Information in Categories

Information can often be classified. For example, there are three levels of government in the United States: federal, state, and local. All laws can be classified as belonging to one of those three levels.

You probably need to classify information in categories occasionally. To do this, you need to know what each category can contain. Using that knowledge, you can classify a piece of information in its proper category.

Political opinions can be classified. In the 1890s, there were three political parties in the United States. Each part had opinions on the issues of the day.

Democrats
- believed governments should leave business alone
- wanted to lower the tax on imported goods so those goods would cost less

Republicans
- believed government should favor big business
- wanted to keep the high tax on imported goods so those goods would cost more

Populists
- believed government should control big business and own certain businesses
- wanted to lower the tax on imported goods so those goods would cost less

In the 1890s a man was heard to say, "The railroads cheat people with their high prices. The government should run the railroads."

What party did the man probably vote for? _____

The man probably voted for the Populists. He agreed with them on a key point: the government should control or own certain businesses. The man thought the government should control or own the railroad business.

NOW TRY THIS

Read the following opinion of a woman in the 1890s and answer the question.

"We have to keep low-cost foreign goods out of this country. Then people will buy American goods."

What party did the woman probably vote for?_____

The key point in the Republicans' stand during the 1890s was that they wanted to keep the high tax on goods from other countries. The woman, hoping that high taxes would keep foreign goods from being imported, probably voted for the Republicans.

Sometimes authors let you know they are classifying. They may write something like, "There are three kinds of . . ." or "Here are two ways to . . ." Other times you may need to classify information without help from the author.

<table>
<tr><td colspan="2" align="center">**How to Classify Information in Categories**</td></tr>
<tr><td>STEP 1:</td><td>Make sure you know what each category you are using can contain.</td></tr>
<tr><td>STEP 2:</td><td>When you read, look for words that signal classification, such as *types of, kinds of, ways to,* and so on.</td></tr>
<tr><td>STEP 3:</td><td>Ask yourself: Which category best contains this new piece of information I have read?</td></tr>
</table>

EXERCISE 22

Read the following passages and answer the questions.

Questions 1 and 2 refer to the following information.

Learning how to behave is part of socialization. Children usually learn how to behave from their parents. Here are three methods parents can use to teach a child how to behave.

(1) *positive reinforcement*—giving or doing something pleasant after good behavior

(2) *punishment*—giving or doing something unpleasant after bad behavior

(3) *negative reinforcement*—removing something unpleasant after good behavior

1. Julia says "You're a good boy!" when her son puts away his toys. She is using

   (1) positive reinforcement
   (2) punishment
   (3) negative reinforcement

2. Manny's daughter hits her friend during an argument. Manny says, "Just for that, you'll stay in your room until dinnertime." Manny is using

   (1) positive reinforcement
   (2) punishment
   (3) negative reinforcement

Questions 3 and 4 refer to the following information.

People usually borrow money from one of these three kinds of lending institutions:

(1) *commercial bank*—Offers many different services to both companies and persons, including loans, savings retirement plans, and checking.

(2) *savings and loan*—Lends money, especially for building, buying, or remodeling houses. Pays out profits to people who place their savings there.

(3) *credit union*—Saves money for the members of a group. Lends them money.

3. Jake and Sue wanted money to buy a car. Jake belonged to an organization that pooled his savings together with his co-workers'. Jake borrowed money from this organization. What kind of lending institution was it?

   (1) commercial bank
   (2) savings and loan
   (3) credit union

4. The Blaines wanted money to buy land. They went to the place where they had their personal checking and savings accounts and their business account. What kind of lending institution was it?

   (1) commercial bank
   (2) savings and loan
   (3) credit union

Questions 5 and 6 refer to the following information.

Before the 1800s each product was handmade by one worker. No two products were exactly alike. Later new ways to make things were invented. Three of those methods of manufacturing are still used today.

Robot Welders at a General Motors Assembly Plant

(1) *division of labor*—Each worker does one particular task in the process of making a product.

(2) *use of standard parts*—Each identical part of a product is made in the same way and to the same measurements so one part can be replaced by another.

(3) *automation*—Machines are used to make things.

5. Kent has a tune-up done on his car. All the old spark plugs are taken out, and new ones are put in. What method of manufacturing does this illustrate?

(1) division of labor
(2) use of standard parts
(3) automation

6. Some of the workers at Larry's company are losing their jobs to robots. What method of manufacturing does this illustrate?

(1) division of labor
(2) use of standard parts
(3) automation

Check your answers on page 224.

2 ANALYZING WHAT YOU READ

When you read, you are constantly thinking about what you're reading—even if you're not aware of it. You are analyzing, or examining, ideas and facts and their relationships. Analyzing what you read helps you understand it better.

In this chapter you will practice analyzing cause and effect, recognizing conclusions, and distinguishing facts from opinions and from hypotheses.

Lesson
23

Analyzing Cause and Effect

When something happens, you usually like to know why. Why did the price of meat go up? Why did the network cancel your favorite TV show? Why did a plane crash? When you ask *why*, you're looking for a **cause**.

You also usually want to know what happens because of something you or others do. What will happen if you pay a bill late? What will a medication do? What were the results of the Persian Gulf War? When you ask a question like that, you're looking for an **effect**.

In Lesson 7 you learned to recognize cause and effect relationships in passages. You learned to look for clue words like *because*, *effect*, and *result*. You also learned that cause-effect relationships are sometimes described without clue words.

TRY THIS

Read the following passage, looking for cause-effect relationships. Then answer the question.

Before 1787 each state had its own courts. These courts settled disputes between people in the state. The power of a state court ended at the state's borders. It had no authority to make a person outside the state obey its rulings. If a person from one state sued a person from another state, no court had the power to hear the case and enforce a ruling.

When the U.S. Constitution was written, Congress was allowed to set up central courts, called federal courts. The federal courts were established to settle disputes between people from different states.

Why were federal courts established?

(1) Federal courts were established because there were not enough state courts.
(2) Federal courts were established to settle disputes between people within a state.
(3) Federal courts were established to settle disputes between people from different states.

In this passage, the writer discusses the cause-effect relationship described in Choice (3). The *cause* was the inability of state courts to deal with disputes involving citizens from different states. The *effect* was the establishment of federal courts to handle such disputes.

In the passage about the establishment of federal courts, the writer discusses both the cause and the effect. Sometimes, however, only the cause or only the effect is discussed. It's up to you to figure out the missing cause or effect.

TRY THIS

Read the following passage, looking for cause-effect relationships. Answer the question.

Along the edges of the Sahara Desert, herders graze their animals on low grasses and shrubs. Because of the growing population's demand for more meat and animal products, the areas along the edge of the desert are being overgrazed. As animals eat away the vegetation, the topsoil blows away and the desert sands blow in.

Because of overgrazing along its edge, the Sahara Desert

(1) is increasing in size
(2) is decreasing in size
(3) is becoming more fertile

You were right if you chose the first answer. When animals overgraze, the vegetation that holds the soil disappears. With nothing to hold it, the soil blows away and sand from the desert blows in. All this is stated in the passage. To answer the question you had to figure out the effect of this process: the desert is spreading into areas that used to support grazing and is getting larger.

How to Analyze Cause-Effect Relationships

STEP 1: As you read, ask yourself why something has happened (the cause).

STEP 2: As you read, ask yourself what might happen as a result of something (the effect).

Read each of the following paragraphs and answer the questions.

Question 1 refers to the following paragraph.

Countries of southern Europe—Portugal, Spain, Italy, and Greece—lack resources for fuel. The lack of fuel resources has made the growth of industry in these countries slow.

1. What has caused the slow growth of industry in the countries of southern Europe?
   (1) language differences among the countries
   (2) greater local interest in agriculture than in industry
   (3) lack of fuel resources

Question 2 refers to the following paragraph.

In 1970 the number of U.S. children in nursery school was just over a million. By the end of the 1980s, that number was over 2.5 million.

2. Which of the following was a likely result of the change in nursery school enrollment?
   (1) The number of children in high school also increased.
   (2) More couples got divorced.
   (3) The demand for nursery school workers increased.

Question 3 refers to the following paragraph.

Because of new laws, students in several states must stay in school or give up their driver's licenses. West Virginia was the first state to pass such a law. There, teenagers aged 16 through 18 lose their licenses if they are absent from school ten days in a row without an excuse. Other states have similar laws or are thinking of passing them.

3. West Virginia probably passed the law about teenagers' licenses because it wanted to

   (1) motivate students to stay in school and graduate
   (2) limit the number of drivers under the age of 18
   (3) force teenagers to walk to school for their health

Question 4 refers to the following paragraph.

Before 1929 most Americans looked up to business leaders. They felt that businessmen could lead the nation. With the Great Depression of the 1930s, many Americans lost faith in business leaders.

4. Which of the following was probably a result of Americans' change in attitude toward business leaders?

   (1) More people began to support labor unions.
   (2) People bought fewer goods during the depression.
   (3) More people voted for businessmen to represent them in government.

Question 5 refers to the following paragraph.

More people than ever before are staying single and living alone. Others are postponing marriage until they are older. Every year about half as many people get divorced as get married. The divorces result in many single-parent households.

5. Which of the following is one likely result of the changes in the family described in the paragraph?

   (1) People remarry more now than in the past.
   (2) There are more households now than in the past.
   (3) Families are larger now than in the past.

Check your answers on page 224.

Lesson 24

Recognizing Conclusions

When social scientists study a subject, they gather information about it. Often they come to a conclusion about the subject they have been studying.

A conclusion is a reasoned, logical judgment or opinion based on facts and ideas. It is usually stated at the end of a passage, but it may be stated at the beginning.

Read the following paragraph. Look for the conclusion the author draws and the facts upon which it is based. Answer the question.

The population explosion is mainly due to our ability to prevent, control, and cure disease. Ridding water, milk, and food of disease-causing agents has stopped the spread of cholera, smallpox, and typhoid. Vaccines give people protection from certain diseases, and antibiotics cure once-fatal diseases. Better sanitation and health care have allowed more children to survive to adulthood. As more adults have healthy children, the population increases.

The author concludes that the main cause of the population explosion is

(1) a growth in the world's water and food supply
(2) our ability to prevent, control, and cure disease
(3) vaccinations that prevent disease

The author states the conclusion in the first sentence of the paragraph. The rest of the paragraph gives reasons that support this conclusion: cleaner water, milk, and food; vaccines and antibiotics; and sanitation. All of these help people survive to become adults who have children. Choice (2) is the correct answer to the question.

Choice (1) is wrong because the paragraph does not say the food and water supply has increased. Choice (3) is wrong because it is too specific. Vaccinations are just one part of improved health care that helps people live longer.

NOW TRY THIS

Read the following paragraph and look for the conclusion. Answer the question.

In a city the feeling of anonymity—of not being known to others—can be great. In New York researchers have studied the crime rate in three types of public housing: high-rises (8 or more floors), mid-rises (6 or 7 floors), and walk-ups (3 floors). In high-rises 68 crimes per 1,000 families were reported. In mid-rise buildings the rate dropped to 41 crimes per 1,000 families. In walk-ups the rate was 30 crimes per 1,000 families.

The researchers found that the anonymity of high-rises is the most likely cause of their high crime rate. In the public spaces of high-rises—lobbies, elevators, and hallways—people are anonymous. No one knows who belongs in the building and who doesn't.

Which of the following is the conclusion stated in the paragraph?

(1) In high-rises 68 crimes per 1,000 families were reported.

(2) The anonymity of high-rises is the most likely cause of their high crime rate.

(3) In the public spaces of high-rises . . . people are anonymous.

The sentence from the paragraph that states the researchers' conclusion is the one in Choice (2). The other sentences give facts from the paragraph that support this conclusion. The researchers used these facts to reach their conclusion.

How to Recognize Conclusions

STEP 1: Look for words that sometimes signal conclusions, such as *found, revealed, showed, concluded, thus, therefore.*

STEP 2: Ask yourself: Which statement is supported by the facts and ideas presented?

EXERCISE 24

Read each of the following passages and answer the questions.

Question 1 refers to the following passage.

The Great Depression of the 1930s followed a decade of prosperity. Many people wonder how such a bad economic downturn could follow a prosperous period. A closer look at the 1920s, however, shows that that decade's prosperity masked weaknesses in the economy.

For example, farmers did not share in the boom of the 1920s. Farm prices dropped about 40 percent. Farm profits fell so far that many farmers could not repay their debts.

Workers did not share in the prosperity either. The prices of goods rose about four times as fast as workers' wages did. The workers could not afford the goods they were producing, so many bought on credit.

Last, the stock market became a popular "game" to play. People were buying stocks for more than they were really worth. Many people bought stocks on credit.

*Charles A. Lindbergh made the first nonstop solo flight
from New York to Paris in 1927.*

1. The conclusion drawn by the passage is that
   (1) the 1930s was a bad economic period in the United States
   (2) the 1920s was a prosperous period in the United States
   (3) the prosperity of the 1920s hid problems in the economy

Question 2 refers to the following passage.

In the United States, powers are divided between the federal government and the state governments. This system of government is called federalism.

In practice, the federal government exerts influence over areas nor-
mally reserved to the states. When Congress gives states grants of tax
money, it often attaches conditions to its use. For example, in the 1970s
any state that did not lower its speed limit to 55 miles an hour lost federal
highway money. Likewise, in the 1980s any state that did not raise its
drinking age to 21 lost highway money. To receive some other federal
funds, states must show that they employ women and minorities in accept-
able volumes. States must often meet clean air and water standards for
some federal grants.

2. The conclusion drawn by the passage is that
   (1) the federal government influences the way states use their powers by
       attaching conditions to grant money
   (2) federal highway money is given to states under certain conditions
   (3) states must meet certain hiring and environmental standards to receive
       some federal grants

Question 3 refers to the following passage.

More mothers are working outside the home than ever before. A recent study revealed that older and college-educated mothers are much more likely to work than younger mothers and mothers without high school diplomas.

In June 1988, 60 percent of college-educated mothers worked outside the home, but only 34 percent of mothers without a high school diploma did. Also, 53 percent of mothers aged 25 to 44 worked, but only 46 percent of mothers aged 18 to 24 did.

3. The conclusion drawn by the study of new mothers was that

(1) more mothers are working today than ever before
(2) older and college-educated mothers are more likely to work than younger mothers and mothers without high school diplomas
(3) 46 percent of mothers aged 18 to 24 worked in 1988

Question 4 refers to the following passage. The sentences in the passage are numbered to help you answer the question.

(1) The world's population is growing. (2) More food is needed to feed the growing number of mouths. (3) Yet world grain production is decreasing after thirty years of increase. (4) Some people believe recent droughts are the cause. (5) But a report done by one group found that loss of farmable land is the main reason.

(6) In the 1960s and 1970s land that was easily eroded was farmed. (7) The topsoil that produced grains there no longer exists. (8) Further, so much water was pumped for irrigation that the water table below the farms became too low. (9) These lands have now been lost to farming. (10) Eroded farmlands and land lost to deserts each year reduce the amount of land available to feed a growing world population.

4. The conclusion in the passage is in

(1) Sentence 1
(2) Sentence 4
(3) Sentence 6
(4) Sentence 9
(5) Sentence 10

Question 5 refers to the following passage.

Head Start was begun in 1965 to help poor children. Head Start centers run preschool programs to give poor children a "head start" on their education. The programs try to develop the children's language skills, get the children ready to read, and teach them counting and numbers.

In the 1980s a study showed Head Start makes a difference. The study compared first and second graders who had been in Head Start to those who had not. As a group, children who had been in Head Start were doing better in school than those who had not. However, they were not doing as well as children from middle-class families.

5. What was the conclusion of the study about Head Start?

(1) Head Start tries to develop children's language and math skills to prepare them for grade school.
(2) Poor children who have been in Head Start do better than those who have not, but not as well as middle-class children.
(3) Head Start would not be a benefit for middle-class children.

Check your answers on page 224.

Recognizing Facts, Opinions, and Hypotheses

Suppose you are planning to buy a car. First you consider the facts: Is the car within your price range? Does it have the features you want? What gas mileage does it get? Next, you may ask your family and friends for their opinions: What do they think of the car? Once you consider the facts and opinions, you may form this hypothesis: If I buy this car, I'll probably like it.

Being able to distinguish facts, opinions, and hypotheses when you read will improve your ability to understand what you read.

- Facts can be proved by measurement, observation, or documentation.
- Opinions are personal beliefs that may or may not be based on facts.
- Hypotheses are good guesses based on facts. With more information, hypotheses can be accurate or inaccurate.

TRY THIS

Read the following passage, looking for the facts, opinions, and hypotheses in it. Then answer the question.

A growth in population means an increase in the amount of garbage people discard. In the United States we throw away about 400,000 tons of garbage a day. Because landfills are getting full, new ways to use or get rid of garbage must be found.

Recycling is one way to reduce the amount of garbage that goes into landfills. Yet many people believe that recycling is a waste of time, so they don't do it.

One recycling group feels that most people would be willing to recycle if it were more convenient to do so. Several towns have agreed to try this group's recycling plan on a trial basis. Each household is given special bins for glass, paper, and aluminum. The materials are picked up from the curb in front of their houses and apartments. In one town 85 percent of the households recycle. In another, the success rate is 95 percent.

Label each of the following ideas from the passage as a fact, as an opinion, or as an hypothesis.

_____ 1. In the United States we throw away about 400,000 tons of garbage a day.
_____ 2. Recycling is one way to reduce the amount of garbage that goes into landfills.
_____ 3. Recycling is a waste of time.
_____ 4. Most people would be willing to recycle if it were more convenient to do so.
_____ 5. In one town 85 percent of the households recycle.

The first statement is a fact. It can be proved by referring to records kept at landfills. The second statement is also a fact. It can be proved by comparing landfill records before and after recycling.

The third statement is an opinion. The passage says that some people believe this, whether or not it is based on facts. The fourth statement is an hypothesis. It is a guess about what most people would do under certain conditions.

The fifth statement is a fact. It can be proved by referring to records about the number of households that recycle. This fact shows that the hypothesis in the fourth statement was accurate: most people do recycle now that recycling is convenient.

NOW TRY THIS

Read the following passage, looking for the facts, opinions, and hypotheses in it. Then answer the question.

Education is the most important activity under the control of state and local governments. States spend far more on education than they do on any other service. More people have jobs in education than in any other field.

In some states, such as Texas, the state government maintains significant control over local school boards. In other states, like New Hampshire, control is in the hands of local governments. Many educators think that local control of education throughout the United States would improve students' performance.

Label each of the following ideas from the passage as a fact, as an opinion, or as an hypothesis.

_____ 1. Education is the most important activity under the control of state and local governments.
_____ 2. States spend far more on education than they do on any other service.
_____ 3. Local control of education throughout the United States would improve students' performance.

The first statement is an opinion. There may be differing opinions about what the most important state and local government activity is. The words *most important* are the clue. When people think something is the *most, best, worst,* or *least,* they are often stating an opinion.

The second statement is a fact. You can prove it by looking at states' spending records.

The third statement is an hypothesis. Educators are making a good guess about the relationship between widespread local control of education and student performance. This hypothesis could be tested with more information and experience. It could be proved accurate.

How to Recognize a Fact, an Opinion, and an Hypothesis

STEP 1: Ask yourself: Can this be proved by measurement or observation? If so, it is a fact.

STEP 2: Ask yourself: Is this someone's personal view that cannot be proved right or wrong? If so, it is an opinion.

STEP 3: Ask yourself: Is this a good guess based on facts, and can it be proved accurate or inaccurate with more information? If so, it is an hypothesis.

EXERCISE 25

Study each passage and graphic. Answer the questions that follow each.

Question 1 refers to the following passage.

Many Americans wanted to stay neutral during World War I. President Woodrow Wilson was among them. In fact, the United States did not enter the war until 1917, three years after it started.

Americans' feelings about foreign affairs became stronger during the 1920s and 1930s. Most wanted nothing to do with the rest of the world—especially the movement toward war in Europe and the Far East. President Franklin Roosevelt sometimes opposed this isolationist feeling. Some people called him a warmonger.

1. Label each of the following ideas from the passage as a fact or as an opinion.

_____ a. President Woodrow Wilson wanted the United States to stay neutral during World War I.

_____ b. The United States did not enter the war until 1917.

_____ c. President Franklin Roosevelt enjoyed the idea of going to war.

Questions 2 is based on the following table.

Marriages and Divorces in the United States (in thousands)

	Marriages	Divorces
1980	2,413	1,182
1981	2,438	1,219
1982	2,495	1,180
1983	2,444	1,179
1984	2,487	1,155
1985	2,425	1,187
1986	2,400	1,159
1987	2,421	1,157
1988	2,389	1,183
1989	2,419	1,099
1990	2,448	1,175

2. Using information in the table, label each of the following ideas as a fact, as an opinion, or as an hypothesis.

_____ a. Each year more people marry than divorce.

_____ b. Getting a divorce is too easy.

_____ c. If couples were aware that nearly half the people who marry divorce, they might give more thought to their plan to marry.

Question 3 is based on the following table.

State Weekly Unemployment Compensation Maximums, 1989 (in dollars)

State	Amount	State	Amount	State	Amount
Alabama	$ 145	Louisiana	$ 181	Oklahoma	$ 197
Alaska	188–260	Maine	171–256	Oregon	229
Arizona	145	Maryland	205	Pennsylvania	266–274
Arkansas	209	Massachusetts	255–382	Puerto Rico	110
California	166	Michigan	263	Rhode Island	240–300
Colorado	214	Minnesota	254	South Carolina	147
Connecticut	234–284	Mississippi	145	South Dakota	140
Delaware	205	Missouri	150	Tennessee	155
D.C.	283	Montana	185	Texas	210
Florida	200	Nebraska	134	Utah	208
Georgia	165	Nevada	184	Vermont	169
Hawaii	239	New Hampshire	156	Virgin Islands	162
Idaho	193	New Jersey	258	Virginia	176
Illinois	187–244	New Mexico	166	Washington	209
Indiana	96–161	New York	245	West Virginia	225
Iowa	174–214	North Carolina	228	Wisconsin	200
Kansas	210	North Dakota	183	Wyoming	200
Kentucky	166	Ohio	169–268		

Note: Maximum amounts. When two amounts are shown, the higher includes dependents' allowances.

3. Using information from the table, label each of the following ideas as a fact, as an opinion, or as an hypothesis.

_____ a. In Connecticut, an unemployed person with dependents could receive as much as $284 per week in unemployment compensation.

_____ b. In Indiana unemployed people without dependents don't receive enough money for unemployment compensation.

_____ c. If unemployment compensation maximums were the same in every state, fewer people, if they are laid off, would travel to states with high maximums in order to receive higher benefits.

Question 4 refers to the following passage.

Some social scientists believed that gun control laws affect the suicide rate. To find out if they were right, they looked at suicide rates in two cities, Seattle and Vancouver. Vancouver has strong gun control laws, but Seattle does not.

The scientists found that the two cities' suicide rates were about the same. Even so, suicide victims in Seattle used guns to kill themselves much more often than victims in Vancouver. That was especially true of 18- to 24-year-olds.

4. Which of the following hypotheses did the social scientists test?

(1) More suicides occur in Vancouver than in Seattle.
(2) The availability of guns affects the suicide rate.
(3) Young people usually use guns to kill themselves.

Question 5 refers to the following passage.

As the world population grows, more and more of the world's forests are cut down. Nowhere is this more true than in the Amazon rainforest. Trees in this vast forest are cut down for fuel and wood. Clearing the trees also makes room for farms and cattle ranches.

The plants in the Amazon rainforest are an important agent in removing carbon dioxide from the earth's air. Some scientists suggest that stripping the Amazon rainforest will increase the amount of carbon dioxide in the air. This could lead to warmer weather around the world.

5. Which of the following is the hypothesis suggested in the passage?

(1) Cutting down the Amazon rainforest may affect the earth's air and weather.
(2) The world's growing population uses more and more timber.
(3) Many trees are being cut down in the Amazon rainforest.
(4) Trees are cut down for fuel and wood and to clear the land for farms and ranches.

Check your answers on page 225.

azChapter

3 EVALUATING WHAT YOU READ

As a consumer, you examine and judge the worth of many products before you buy. You also examine and judge ideas you read. When you think about something and then make a judgment about it, you are evaluating.

In this chapter you will practice evaluating whether there is enough information to support a conclusion, evaluating whether information is relevant and logical, and recognizing values.

Evaluating the Amount of Information

Look at the following pieces of a picture. How many pieces do you need to see before you can conclude what the picture shows?

The picture is of the Statue of Liberty. You probably knew that after seeing the first few pieces of the picture. Those few pieces gave you enough information to support the conclusion that the image was of the Statue of Liberty. But you had to have enough pieces to support that conclusion. With fewer pieces your conclusion would not have been based on enough information. It would have been a wild guess. If you draw a conclusion based on too little evidence, you jump to a conclusion.

TRY THIS

A list of some of the laws made during the 1960s and a conclusion about them follows. Read the list and the conclusion carefully and then answer the questions about them.

- The Civil Rights Act of 1960 imposed federal criminal penalties on people who threatened to use force against African-Americans who tried to register or to vote.

- In 1964 the 24th Amendment banned poll taxes. (Five southern states had used poll taxes to keep African-Americans from voting.)

- The Civil Rights Act of 1964 ordered private and public facilities to serve all people regardless of color. It also banned race discrimination in employment.

- The Voting Rights Act of 1965 outlawed qualifying tests for voters in states and counties where fewer than half the people of voting age were registered.

- The Fair Housing Act of 1968 outlawed race discrimination in selling and renting housing.

Conclusion: In the 1960s several laws that assure protection of people's civil rights were passed.

How much evidence does the list provide to support the conclusion?

_____

Does the list give enough evidence to support the conclusion?

_____

The first question asks you to report a fact. The list describes five laws passed in the 1960s that protect civil rights. Three laws assure the right to vote. One law assures the right to be served in places open to the public and to be considered for a job regardless of skin color. The last law listed gives people the right to buy or rent housing wherever they choose, regardless of their skin color.

The second question asks you to evaluate whether the amount of evidence given in the list is *enough* to support the conclusion, which says that *several laws . . . were passed*. When you evaluate the conclusion, the key word about which you must make a judgment is *several*. Just how many are *several*? It depends on the context of the conclusion. If many civil rights were passed in each ten-year period, five laws would probably not be considered to be *several* laws. But since few civil rights laws are passed in a typical decade, the five laws passed in the 1960s can certainly be described as *several*.

Sometimes when you evaluate whether there is enough evidence to support a certain conclusion, your judgment will be that there is not.

TRY THIS

Read the following conclusion and answer the question about it.

Conclusion: Race discrimination in hiring had not existed before the 1960s.

Does the list of 1960s civil rights laws give enough evidence to support this conclusion? _____

The question asks you to evaluate whether the amount of evidence given in the list is *enough* to support another conclusion. In this case, the list provides *no* information to support the conclusion. It makes no mention of the period before the 1960s. Indeed, the government acted on employment discrimination in 1964, but that doesn't mean that discrimination didn't exist before the 1960s. In fact, it is reasonable to assume that the government acted *because of* discrimination that had existed for a long time.

Just as you can evaluate conclusions based on passages, you can evaluate conclusions based on information in tables.

TRY THIS

Read the following table and conclusion, and then answer the question that follows.

Median Incomes for Men Compared to Their Educational Backgrounds

Educational Background	Median Income
Grade school	$18,939
Some high school	$21,269
High school diploma	$25,394
College degree	$34,380

Note: *Median income* is income in the middle. Half the people make more than the median income, and half make less than the median income.

Conclusion: More education generally leads to higher pay.

Does the information in the table support or fail to support this conclusion? _____

The conclusion is supported by the information in the table. The table shows that the median income for men with more education is higher than for men with less education.

When you evaluate a conclusion drawn from a table, you may find that the information in the table does not support the conclusion.

Review the table in the previous activity. Then read the following conclusion and answer the question about it.

Conclusion: Every college-educated man has a higher income than men with less education.

Does the information in the table support this conclusion? Explain.

_____

The information in the table does not support the conclusion. The table reports median incomes, not individual incomes. Remember that half of college-educated men make less than $34,380. Some college-educated men probably make less than the median income for groups with less than college educations.

You can evaluate conclusions based on graphs and maps just as you can those based on tables or passages.

Study the graph and answer the question.

Which of the following conclusions is supported by the information in the graph?
   (1) Young people prefer to vote for young people.
   (2) People over 35 are more likely to vote than people under 35.
   (3) Older people vote more frequently than younger people.

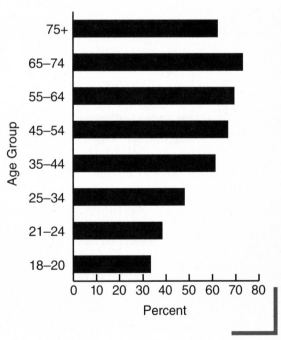

Percent Who Voted in 1988, per Age Group

The second conclusion is supported by the graph's information. As age increases, the percent of voters per age group rises (except for the very oldest group). More than 50 percent of people over 35 vote. Less than 50 percent of all younger voters vote. So people over 35 are more likely to vote than people under 35.

The graph doesn't show anything about the ages of people who run for office, so Conclusion (1) is not supported. Conclusion (3) is also not supported because the graph does not report how frequently people vote. It reports about voting rates in only one year.

How to Evaluate Whether There Is Enough Information to Support a Certain Conclusion

STEP 1:   Examine the information and the conclusion.

STEP 2:   Ask yourself: Does the information give enough evidence to support the conclusion?

EXERCISE 26

Read each passage and study each graphic. Answer the question that follows each.

Question 1 refers to the following paragraph.

People need fresh water. About 97 percent of all earth's water is in the salty oceans and seas. That leaves only 3 percent fresh water. Two-thirds of that is in the Antarctic ice cap around the South Pole. In fact, the fresh water in lakes, in rivers, and in the ground—the sources of most of the water people use—is less than one-third of 1 percent of the water on earth. In other words, for every gallon of salt water on earth there is less than a tablespoon of fresh water that people can use.

1. Which of the following conclusions is supported by the information in the paragraph?
   (1) We must be careful not to pollute lakes, rivers, and groundwater.
   (2) The Antarctic ice cap will probably never be useful to people as a source of fresh water.
   (3) People use too much fresh water for cooking, bathing, and cleaning.

Question 2 is based on the following pictograph.

The Six Fastest-Growing Careers in the 1990s

Computer Programmer	𝕏𝕏𝕏𝕏𝕏𝕏𝕏𝕏𝕏𝕏𝕏𝕏𝕏𝕏𝕏
Computer Systems Analyst	𝕏𝕏𝕏𝕏𝕏𝕏𝕏𝕏𝕏𝕏𝕏
Dental Assistant	𝕏𝕏𝕏𝕏𝕏
Home Health Aide	𝕏𝕏𝕏𝕏𝕏
Medical Assistant	𝕏𝕏𝕏𝕏𝕏
X-Ray Technician	𝕏𝕏𝕏𝕏

𝕏 = 50,000 new job openings

2. Which of the following conclusions is supported by the graph?

   (1) In the 1990s there will be more new jobs related to computers than to health.

   (2) Computer programmers make more money that people in health fields.

   (3) Nearly a million people will enter or switch to the four health-related careers listed in the graph.

Question 3 is based on the following information.

Before 1972 people could register, or sign up, to vote only if they had lived in one place for a long time. In 1972 the Supreme Court ruled that states could not demand long residency requirements. The following table shows the requirements the states have now.

Residency Requirements for Voter Registration

None		30 Days		Other
Alabama	Missouri	Alaska	North Dakota	California
Arkansas	Nebraska	Arizona	Ohio	Colorado
Connecticut	New Hampshire	Idaho	Pennsylvania	Kansas
Delaware	New Mexico	Illinois	Rhode Island	Minnesota
District of	North Carolina	Indiana	Utah	Oregon
Columbia	Oklahoma	Kentucky	Washington	Vermont
Florida	South Carolina	Louisiana		Wisconsin
Georgia	South Dakota	Michigan		
Hawaii	Tennessee	Mississippi		
Iowa	Texas	Montana		
Maine	Virginia	Nevada		
Maryland	West Virginia	New Jersey		
Massachusetts	Wyoming	New York		

3. Which two of the following conclusions are supported by the information about residency requirements?

   (a) More people in states with no residency requirements vote than in other states.

   (b) Some states ignored the Supreme Court's ruling on residency requirements.

   (c) The Supreme Court's 1972 ruling on residency requirements made more people eligible to vote.

   (d) People who move from one state to another may lose the chance to vote in the next election after they move.

Question 4 is based on the following map.

World Oil Reserves and Trade Routes

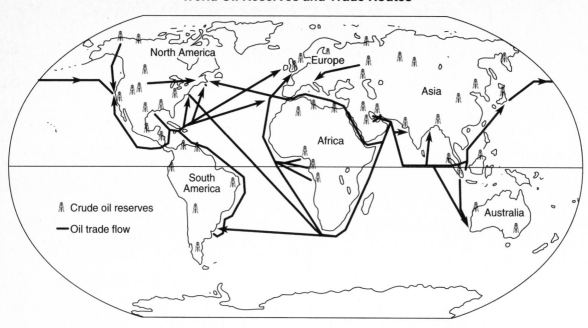

4. Which of the following conclusions is supported by the map?

(1) Oil spills are more likely above the equator than below it.

(2) The cost of oil increases almost every year.

(3) Oil is more commonly used for fuel today than it was in the past.

Check your answers on page 225.

Lesson 27

Evaluating the Relevance of Information

Do you remember the pieces of the Statue of Liberty in Lesson 26? Beginning with the second piece they included buildings. The buildings don't really help you figure out what the picture is. They are irrelevant: they have little or nothing to do with the main picture.

As you learned in Lesson 26, when you evaluate a conclusion you need to be sure there is enough information to support it. You also need to make sure you use only the information that is relevant, the information that relates to the point of the conclusion.

TRY THIS

Read the following paragraph and conclusion. Answer the question.

Every society has rules about marriage. Some societies allow a man to have more than one wife. Some allow a woman to have more than one husband. As in the United States, in some societies people are encouraged to marry for love. In others, such as India's, marriages are often arranged by parents. Arranged marriages have been shown to be just as successful and happy as love marriages.

Conclusion: Love before marriage has little to do with whether a marriage is successful.

Which of the following statements from the paragraph supports the conclusion?

(1) Every society has rules about marriage.
(2) Some allow a woman to have more than one husband.
(3) As in the United States, in some societies people are encouraged to marry for love.
(4) Arranged marriages have been shown to be just as successful and happy as love marriages.

Choice (4) supports the conclusion. It suggests that love before marriage is not necessary, since arranged marriages can be as successful as love marriages. Therefore, Choice (4) is relevant to the conclusion.

The other choices, on the other hand, do not support the conclusion. They tell about marriage, but they don't say anything about the success of marriages. They are irrelevant to the conclusion.

TRY THIS

Read the following passage and conclusion. Answer the question.

Health-care costs are rising every year, so health insurance costs are going up, too. More and more, employers are shifting this cost to their workers instead of paying it themselves.

In 1989 more than three out of four striking workers—78 percent— went out on strike because of health benefits. That 78 percent figure was 60 percent more than in 1986. This trend has continued into the 1990s.

Conclusion: Health-care benefits have become the main reason for strikes.

Which two of the following statements from the paragraph most directly support the conclusion?

(a) Health-care costs are rising every year, so health-insurance costs are going up too.
(b) In 1989 more than three out of four striking workers—78 percent—went out on strike because of health benefits.
(c) That 78 percent figure was 60 percent more than in 1986.
(d) This trend has continued into the 1990s.

The conclusion says that health-care benefits have become the main reason for strikes. Statements (b) and (d) most directly support it. They show that well over half the strikes in 1989 were because of health-care benefits and that in the 1990s even more strikes are about those same benefits. This means that since 1989, the main cause for strikes has been health-care benefits.

Statement (c) indirectly supports the conclusion. It gives background information that helps you understand how significant the number of health-care strikes in 1989 was. Statement (a) also provides useful background information, but does not say anything about the causes for strikes.

How to Evaluate the Relevance of Information

STEP 1: Look at conclusions an author draws, and at the conclusions *you* want to draw.

STEP 2: Ask yourself: Is there relevant supporting information? Does it really relate to the point of the conclusion?

EXERCISE 27

Study each passage and graphic. Then answer the question about each.

Question 1 is based on the following table.

Voters in the 1988 Presidential Election, by Gender

	Persons of Voting Age	Persons Reporting They Voted	Percent of Total
Male	84,531,000	47,704,000	56.4%
Female	93,568,000	54,519,000	58.3%
Total	178,099,000	102,223,000	57.4%

1. A political scientist looked at the table and came to this conclusion: Most adults in the United States voted in the 1988 presidential election. Which number from the table supports this conclusion most directly?

_____

Question 2 is based on this circle graph.

Air Pollution Sources

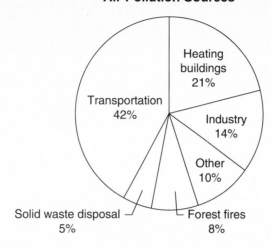

2. An environmentalist drew this conclusion from the graph: If we could take only one step to reduce air pollution, the most effective would be to use auto fuels that pollute less than gasoline. Which section of the circle graph most directly supports this conclusion?

_____

Question 3 is based on the following passage.

President John Kennedy wanted a strong civil rights law, medical help for the elderly, and more aid for education. He was unable to convince Congress to pass these bills during his short presidency.

When Kennedy was assassinated in 1963, Lyndon Johnson became president. He was elected to a full term in 1964. That year Congress passed the Civil Rights Act. In 1965 Congress created Medicare. By 1965 the government was spending three times more on education than it had before Kennedy was elected.

3. One conclusion that can be drawn from this information is that Kennedy's hopes for legislation affecting civil rights, medical assistance for the elderly, and education were realized after his death. Which of the following sentences from the paragraph is IRRELEVANT to (does NOT support) this conclusion?

(1) President John Kennedy wanted a strong civil rights law, medical help for the elderly, and more aid for education.
(2) He was elected to a full term in 1964.
(3) That year Congress passed the Civil Rights Act.
(4) By 1965 the government was spending three times more on education than it had before Kennedy was elected.

Question 4 is based on the following graph.

U.S. Families with Annual Incomes over $50,000 in 1988 Dollars

4. A sociologist drew this conclusion from the graph: The percents of whites and of African-Americans making over $50,000 annually increased the same amount between 1968 and 1988. On which two of the following facts reported by the graph did the sociologist base that opinion?

(a) Twenty percent of all whites and 10 percent of all African-Americans had incomes over $50,000 in 1978.

(b) Between 1968 and 1988 the percent of whites with incomes over $50,000 increased by 7 percent—from 17 percent to 24 percent.

(c) Between 1968 and 1988 the percent of African-Americans with incomes over $50,000 increased by 7 percent—from 6 percent to 13 percent.

(d) Between 1968 and 1988, a greater percent of whites than of African-Americans made over $50,000 annually.

Question 5 is based on the following map.

Western and Soviet Bases During the Cold War

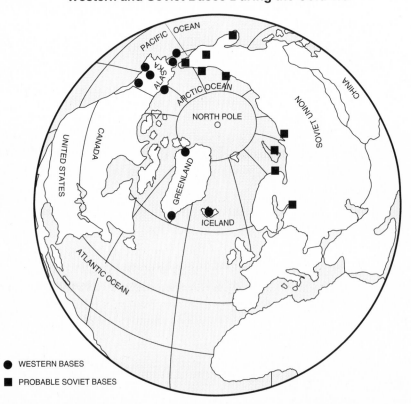

● WESTERN BASES

■ PROBABLE SOVIET BASES

5. Conclusion: The West was made up of the United States and other countries.

The map shows Cold War military bases. On which of the following facts drawn from the map is the above conclusion based?

(1) All the Western bases were located in Canada, Greenland, Iceland, and the United States.

(2) The Soviet Union had one more base than the West.

(3) Alaska had five bases within its borders.

Question 6 is based on the following passage.

Smokestacks from coal-burning factories in the Midwest pollute the air with gases. These gases are blown by high winds into the Northeast. There they mix with water in the air to form acid, and acid rain falls on the forests and lakes below.

Trees are harmed when they soak up the acid through their roots. Lakes collect the acid rain as it falls, causing plants and fish in the lakes to die.

6. Scientists have determined that at least 1,200 lakes in the Northeast have been polluted by acid rain. On which two of the following observations must the scientists have based their conclusion?

(a) Some factories in the Midwest burn coal for energy.

(b) Gases mix with water in the air.

(c) Trees in the Northeast show evidence of having soaked up acid through their roots.

(d) The level of acid in lakes in the Northeast has increased.

(e) The number of plants and fish in lakes in the Northeast has decreased.

Check your answers on page 226.

Lesson 28

Evaluating the Logic of a Conclusion

Look again at the first three pieces of the picture of the Statue of Liberty you first saw on page 155.

Suppose the first two pieces gave you the idea that the full picture would be of a harbor and buildings. Based on the information in the first two pieces and your own knowledge, that would be a logical conclusion.

Suppose you looked at the fourth frame and continued to conclude that the picture would be of a harbor. Based on the new information and your own knowledge, that would not be a logical conclusion. Harbors do not have statues holding torches and wear crowns like the one worn by the Statue of Liberty. You would have jumped to the wrong conclusion because you did not logically consider all the available information.

Concentrating on irrelevant information can lead you to a wrong conclusion, too. If you paid too much attention to the harbor and buildings, you might have concluded that the complete picture would show an island or shorelines. Your conclusion would not be logical because you made too much of information in the picture that was not relevant.

In real life, mistakes in logic can cause serious problems. Unworthy candidates can be elected; someone can take too much of a prescription medicine; or the cost of a home-improvement project can run way over the estimate.

TRY THIS

Read the following paragraph and answer the question.

A voter read this ad in his local newspaper: "Elect Florence Hartwig as your next senator. She's from Camden and wants you to send her to Washington on election day." The voter was from Camden, too. The voter was sure that Hartwig would look out for the town's interest in receiving certain federal funds, so he voted for her.

Explain why the voter's conclusion—that he should vote for Hartwig—was or was not logical.

_____

_____

The voter's conclusion was not logical partly because it was based on too little information. The ad didn't say anything about Hartwig's position on the federal funds in question. The voter's conclusion was also illogical because it was based on irrelevant information. That Hartwig is from Camden doesn't mean she would value Camden's interests if they conflicted with those of her state or of the country. Her conscience might force her to vote against Camden's interests.

NOW TRY THIS

Read the following paragraph and answer the question.

A foreign company opened a factory in the United States. The manager, who was a foreigner, began interviewing people for jobs. The first two applicants were young, and each had worked for several companies already. The manager concluded that Americans have little loyalty toward their employers.

Explain why the manager's conclusion was or was not logical.

_____

_____

The manager's conclusion was not logical partly because it was based on too little information. It may have been unavoidable necessity that caused the applicants to change jobs frequently. Further, the manager drew a conclusion about millions of American workers based on interviews with only two of them. Basing a conclusion about many on evidence from only a few is called over-generalizing.

How to Evaluate the Logic of a Conclusion

STEP 1: Look at the conclusions an author draws and at those you want to draw.

STEP 2: Ask yourself: Is the conclusion logical, or is it based on too little and/or irrelevant information?

EXERCISE 28

Study the following passages and graphics and answer the question(s) about each.

Question 1 is based on the following table.

**U. S. Exports and Imports by Principal Commodity Groupings, 1990
(in millions of dollars)**

Item	Exports	Imports
Agricultural commodities	38,715.7	22,378.2
Beverages and tobacco	5,411.3	2,068.4
Crude materials	15,468.6	11,118.6
Fish and preparations	2,800.0	5,202.4
Manufactured goods	298,686.6	388,806.2
Petroleum and products	6,712.3	61,356.5
Other mineral fuels	4,971.5	2,742.5
Other	2,178.9	1,214.3
Total	374,944.9	494,887.1

1. A farmer looked at the *Agricultural commodities* row in the table and said, "The United States doesn't have a trade deficit. We Americans sell a lot more agricultural products than we buy." Explain why the farmers's conclusion was or was not logical._____

_____

_____

Question 2 is based on the following passage.

In 1948 public opinion polls were a new business. That year's polls showed that more people planned to vote for Thomas Dewey than for Harry Truman for president. They also showed that many voters were undecided.

Pollsters predicted that Dewey would be the winner. The *Chicago Tribune* printed its front-page headline even before the votes were counted: *DEWEY DEFEATS TRUMAN*. Yet in one of the biggest upsets ever, Truman got 24 million votes to Dewey's 22 million.

2. Explain why the pollsters' prediction was not logical._____

_____

_____

Question 3 is based on the following paragraph.

Early people were hunter-gatherers. They traveled in bands, hunting animals and gathering plants for food. Today small groups of people in scattered parts of the world still follow this way of life. Social scientists have noted that such groups maintain peace among their members very effectively. Survival depends on cooperation among group members, so peace and harmony are necessary. If one member gets angry or otherwise disturbs the group's peace, the group uses nonviolent means to bring about a change in that person's behavior.

3. Some groups of hunter-gathers in southwestern Africa carry bows and poison arrows. A tourist concluded that one such group was warlike and violent. Explain why the tourist's prediction was or was not logical.

_____

_____

Questions 4 and 5 are based on the following table.

**State and Local Taxes Paid by Home-Owning Families of Four
with Incomes of $20,000**

Albuquerque, N. Mex.	$1,504
Atlanta. Ga.	$1,897
Baltimore, Md.	$2,148
Chicago, Ill.	$1,707
Detroit, Mich.	$2,400
New York, N.Y.	$1,913
Omaha, Nebr.	$1,642
Philadelphia, Pa.	$2,527
Portland, Oreg.	$2,281
Salt Lake City, Utah	$1,866

Note: Based on one wage earner per family with two school-age
children. Figures are for the late 1980s.

4. A couple looked at the table and concluded that people in Philadelphia
pay higher state and local taxes than those in Albuquerque. The couple's
conclusion was

   (1) logical because the Philadelphia taxes reported are over $1,000 higher
   than Albuquerque's
   (2) logical because the couple probably considered all the information
   shown in the table
   (3) illogical because not everyone makes $20,000 a year

5. A young, single man looked at the map and figured he would pay less
than $1,900 in state and local taxes if he bought a house in Atlanta. The
man was

   (1) right because the table shows $1,897 in state and local taxes paid in
   Atlanta
   (2) right because the table reports taxes for home-owing people
   (3) wrong because the figures are for a family of four

Question 6 is based on the following information.

Radiation from accidents in nuclear power plants can be dangerous. The
following list gives information about four such accidents.

   1952   Chalk River, near Ottawa, Canada

   Partial meltdown; dangerous radioactive water collected inside
   plant; no injuries.

   1957   Windscale Pile, near Liverpool, England

   Fire; radiation spread over 200 square miles.

   1979   Three Mile Island, near Harrisburg, Pennsylvania

   Overheating; partial meltdown; some radiation spread over surrounding area.

   1986   Chernobyl, near Kiev, U.S.S.R.

   Explosion and fire; radiation spread over part of what was then
   the Soviet Union and over parts of eastern, northern, and southern Europe.

6. A man concluded that the nuclear accident at Chernobyl was the worst of those listed. Explain why the man's conclusion was or was not logical.

_____

_____

Check your answers on page 226.

Lesson 29

Recognizing Values

What do you value? What do you think is important? Your family and friends? Money and status? Honesty? Law and order? Freedom? Different people value different things. People's values and beliefs are often revealed in the things they do, and in the decisions they make.

When you read, you can often find or figure out the values and beliefs a writer holds.

TRY THIS

Read the following passage and answer the question.

The U.S. space program was spurred by a Soviet satellite named Sputnik. After Sputnik I was launched in October 1957, Americans were stirred to send their own rocket ships into space. In the 1960s and 1970s people visited the moon. In the 1980s space probes explored Mars, Jupiter, Saturn, and beyond.

Three products of the space program have been (1) information about the planets and the universe, (2) improved communication and weather data, and (3) everyday items for use in the home, such as Teflon-coated pans and powdered fruit drinks.

The Surface of the Earth from Apollo Nine

Suppose a manufacturer says, "To me the most important products of the space program are those that can be used to improve everyday life on earth." Which of the following does the manufacturer probably value most?

_____ scientific information about the universe for its own sake

_____ practical information that affects his life and work directly

The manufacturer thinks the most important outcome of the space program is information that can lead to products that improve everyday life. Therefore the manufacturer probably values information that can be used or applied—information that affects his life and work directly. He probably finds such information more important than information for its own sake—information that does not necessarily have a practical use or application.

NOW TRY THIS

Answer the following question based on the information in the passage about the space program.

Which of the three products of the space program would a foreign news reporter probably value the most?

_____ information about the planets and the universe

_____ improved communication and weather data

_____ everyday items for use in the home

A reporter's job is to communicate information. A foreign news reporter would probably value anything that improves such communication.

How to Recognize Values

STEP 1: Think about the information in a passage you read.

STEP 2: Ask yourself: What part of this information does the writer seem to value most? What part of this information would be most important to a person based on that person's interests?

Read each of the following passages and answer the question(s) about each.

Questions 1 are 2 refer to the following passage.

A group of Sioux in South Dakota turned a community hall into a factory. There they made electronic components. Forty people held jobs in the factory. They were known for meeting deadlines and turning out good products.

Soon the Sioux decided to expand their operation. They wanted to provide fifty jobs for another group of Sioux who lived across the Missouri River from them. They asked the Bureau of Indian Affairs in Washington, D.C., for $8,000 for more tools.

An official visited their plant and was impressed. He decided to give them $115,000 to build a whole new factory, to landscape the grounds, and to pave a road. The Sioux refused the money. All they wanted was $8,000 so they could provide jobs for their fellow Sioux.

1. Which of these values was most important to the Sioux?
   (1) getting as much government money as possible
   (2) filling large orders for products even if quality suffered
   (3) providing for the welfare of their people

2. Which of these values was most important to the official from Washington?
   (1) improving the physical condition of the Sioux's factory
   (2) providing jobs for unemployed Sioux
   (3) helping a successful business expand

Question 3 refers to the following paragraph.

The First Amendment to the U.S. Constitution forbids Congress to interfere with Americans' freedoms of religion, of speech, and of the press. It grants that Americans can assemble freely in order to ask the government to right wrongs.

3. By adopting this amendment, the states showed that they valued
   (1) individual liberty
   (2) strong government
   (3) newspapers

Questions 4 and 5 refer to the following paragraph.

In 1990 a Med fly was found in southern California. Med flies eat fruits and vegetables, crops that earn billions of dollars for California farmers each year. The state had helicopters spray an insect killer called malathion. People were told to cover their cars, to move outdoor furniture inside, and to stay inside whenever the helicopters flew over. Many people were concerned that malathion would hurt them and their children.

Crop Dusting (Spraying) an Orange Grove by Helicopter

4. The state put the highest value on

    (1) its economy and the welfare of farmers
    (2) the comfort and peace of mind of its residents
    (3) the safety of the helicopter pilots

5. Environmental groups probably thought the most important issue was

    (1) the amount of money farmers could lose if Med flies ate their crops
    (2) the effects malathion might have on other animals, plants, and humans
    (3) the right of the state government to spray malathion

Question 6 refers to the following passage.

Stealing is almost unknown in hunting-gathering groups. Whenever a large animal is killed, the meat is shared, so there is no need to steal food.

Most hunting-gathering people own very little: a few items of clothing, pots for cooking, weapons for hunting, some ornaments, and a few musical instruments. If someone asks for something, he or she is given it. People who often give to others are respected.

Aborigines in Western Australia

6. Hunting-gathering people put a high value on

   (1) creating laws against stealing
   (2) owning property
   (3) sharing with the group

Questions 7 and 8 refer to the following information.

A woman received the following letter in the mail.

Dear Grayford Resident:

   When you receive your census form, please fill it out and return it promptly to the U.S. Census Bureau.

   As you know, every ten years the federal government conducts a census to count our nation's population. The census also gathers information on the age, gender, race, income, and standard of living of our citizens. It is essential that all Grayford residents participate in this national effort.

   When residents take the time to fill out their census forms, they help to hold the line on their property taxes. They make sure Grayford gets its share of the funds available from the state income tax and the state motor fuel tax. These funds are given to communities on a per-person basis. The money contributes significantly to the well-being of our village.

   If you do not fill out your form and return it, the amount of state funds for the village will be reduced. If funds are reduced, the village will be forced to increase property taxes to fill the gap.

   The census is your direct way to help hold down your property taxes. Don't miss your chance to help.

Sincerely,

The Mayor of Grayford

7. For the mayor of Grayford, the most important information the census provides is about

   (1) the incomes of the people of Grayford
   (2) the number of people in Grayford
   (3) the amount of fuel Grayford uses

8. From his letter, you can tell the mayor of Grayford places a high value on

   (1) harmony between people
   (2) keeping property taxes as low as possible
   (3) providing as many services as possible

Check your answers on page 227.

On the next 16 pages you will find twenty short readings in the five areas of social studies: history, geography, economics, political science, and behavioral science. They will help you prepare for the Social Studies Test of the GED in three ways. You can use them to

- refresh what you already know about social studies
- expand your general knowledge of social studies
- practice the reading skills you have studied in Units 1, 2, and 3

HISTORY READINGS

BIG BUSINESS

Big business was born in the late 1800s. Industrialization meant that more goods could be produced and sold. More goods meant more profits for factory owners. With no laws to stop them, many businessmen fought to wipe out competing companies and win complete control over their industries. Each one wanted to have a monopoly in his industry.

One businessman, Andrew Carnegie, started a steel company and made it grow by paying low wages and charging lower prices than other steel companies. He bought competing steel companies and expanded his company during business slumps.

Another businessman, John D. Rockefeller, created a huge oil monopoly. He bribed government officials, took money from railroad companies, bought competing oil companies, and forced others out of business.

Such wealthy businessmen made enormous personal fortunes, yet they also gave millions of dollars to libraries, schools, hospitals, and churches.

1. The main idea of the second paragraph is that Andrew Carnegie
   (1) paid low wages
   (2) created a large steel industry
   (3) expanded his company during business slumps

2. In the final paragraph, the information is organized by
   (1) cause and effect
   (2) contrast
   (3) time sequence

3. As it is used in the first paragraph, the word *monopoly* means
   (1) a company that controls a particular industry
   (2) a large, fully automated factory
   (3) a law that allows some companies to operate without competition

4. Which of the following illustrates a monopoly?
   (1) A utility company controls the production and sale of gas and electricity in a region.
   (2) AT&T broke into several small companies that sell long-distance telephone service. Those companies compete with other long-distance companies.
   (3) McDonald's has thousands of restaurants all over the world.

A factory fire that killed 143 women is tragic. But a factory fire that killed 143 women because the doors had been locked to keep union leaders out is truly terrible. That is what happened in the Triangle Shirtwaist Factory in 1911.

The struggle to unionize was hard. In the industrial era, men, women, and children worked up to seven 12-hour days a week. They worked in unsafe factories, mills, and mines for low pay. Some businesses fired workers who joined unions. Others hired police or private guards to spy and make trouble for unions. Strikes (when workers walked off the job) and lock-outs (when company owners refused to let workers in) sometimes ended in violence and prison terms for the workers. The government often sided with business.

Today workers take for granted the eight-hour day, the five-day week, overtime pay, and vacation time. All these benefits and conditions were fought for and won by workers who joined together to form labor unions to represent their interests.

5. Of the following, who is most likely to have said, "These people should be thankful they have jobs. If they don't want to work 60 hours a week, I'll find people who will."

   (1) a factory owner
   (2) a factory worker
   (3) a union leader

6. During a recent labor dispute, a large company told its workers that they had to return to work by a certain day or be replaced by new workers. The company was threatening a

   (1) strike
   (2) lock-out
   (3) benefit

During the worst of the Great Depression of the 1930s, Franklin Roosevelt became president. He promised "a new deal for the American people." His program tried to stimulate the economy in three ways:

- The New Deal offered relief to the poor and the unemployed through cash payments. It also created jobs for them on public works, such as bridges and roads.
- The New Deal laid the basis for recovery from the depression. It encouraged fair business practices and fair pricing of goods. It paid farmers not to plant some crops so farm prices would go up.
- The New Deal tried to reform the economy so that such a horrible depression could not occur again. Social Security and insured bank deposits were parts of this attempt.

Although the New Deal helped people in many ways, it couldn't completely free the country from the depression. War in Europe did.

In Germany Adolf Hitler had strong-armed his way into power in 1933. His Nazi Party, with its racist beliefs, turned Germany into a military giant. Germany took control of parts of Czechoslovakia and Austria. Then in 1939 Hitler attacked Poland. Great Britain and France declared war on Germany. Hitler's troops continued to invade other countries. They won control of France. Britain—and later the Soviet Union—were left to fight Nazi Germany and its ally, Italy (see map on next page).

Roosevelt began to build war machines—planes, ships, and tanks—for the Allies. The production of war goods created jobs and lifted the United States out of the depression. It also helped the Allies fight off Germany until the United States could strengthen its own troops. Meanwhile, Japan had been ruthlessly building an empire in Asia and the Pacific. When Japan attacked the U.S. Navy at Pearl Harbor in Hawaii in 1941, the United States officially entered the war.

The World at War: 1939–1945

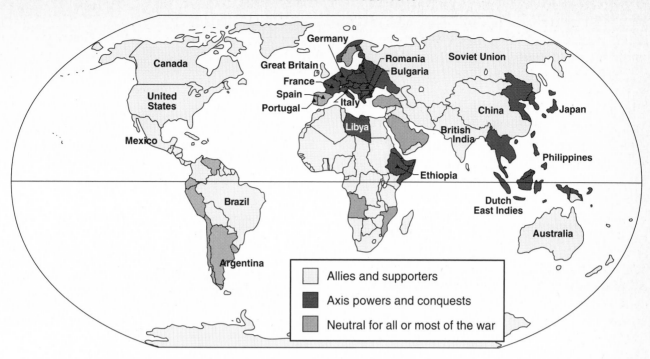

The United States entered the war in December 1941.

The Soviet Union entered the war against Germany in June 1941. It was neutral against Japan until August 1945.

World War II stretched on for four more years. The war in Europe took millions of lives and left the continent in rubble. Hitler killed himself in April 1945, when he realized Germany would lose.

The war in the Pacific lasted another four months—until the United States dropped two atomic bombs on Japan in August 1945. World War II ended, and the atomic age began.

7. President Roosevelt established the New Deal program in the 1930s to
   (1) prepare the United States for war
   (2) sell planes, ships, and tanks to the Allies
   (3) fight the Great Depression

8. Which of the following is a conclusion drawn by the writer of the passage?
   (1) The Great Depression ended because of the New Deal.
   (2) Although the New Deal helped the economy, the war actually ended the Great Depression.
   (3) The Great Depression ended when Japan bombed Pearl Harbor.

9. When Germany invaded the Soviet Union (see map), the United States supplied the Soviet Union with equipment to fight the Nazis. The Soviet Union probably benefited most from
   (1) ships
   (2) submarines
   (3) tanks

After World War II the countries of the world became divided into three groups. The United States and the democratic nations of Western Europe came to be called the Western bloc, or the Free World. The Soviet Union set up communist governments in Eastern Europe. They formed an alliance called the Warsaw Pact. These and other communist countries—like China and Cuba—were called the Eastern bloc, or the Communist World. The developing countries in Africa, Asia, and Latin America came to be known as the Third World.

A cold war arose between the Free World and the Communist World. (The Third World wanted nothing to do with the cold war.) Both sides built up their supplies of nuclear weapons. The two superpowers, the United States and the Soviet Union, never fought each other directly. In one major confrontation, however, the cold war became hot: U.S. troops, as part of a United Nations force, fought the communist invasion of Korea in the early 1950s.

10. What group of countries

(a) became allies with the United States as the Free World? _____

_____

(b) became allies of the Soviet Union as the Communist World? _____

_____

(c) came to be known as the Third World? _____

_____

11. Why was the relationship between the Free World and the Communist World known as "the cold war"?

_____

_____

12. Which of the following sentences from the passage supports the conclusion that the United States and the Soviet Union were in an arms race?

(1) After World War II the countries of the world became divided into three groups.

(2) A cold war arose between the Free World and the Communist World.

(3) Both sides built up their supplies of nuclear weapons.

THE CIVIL RIGHTS MOVEMENT

In the United States the civil rights movement began in 1954 when the Supreme Court ruled, in *Brown vs. Board of Education of Topeka* (Kansas), that schools could not be segregated. The court reasoned that separate educational facilities are always unequal and violate the Fourteenth Amendment, which guarantees "equal protection of the laws." Presidents Eisenhower and Kennedy used federal troops to force formerly all-white schools in the South to enroll African-American students.

In the 1960s Dr. Martin Luther King, Jr., and others led marches to call for voting rights and other civil rights for African-Americans. Many marchers were victims of violence. Some civil rights workers were

Dr. Martin Luther King Leading a Civil Rights March in Washington, D.C., on August 28, 1963

murdered. Dr. King himself was shot to death in 1968—but not before he had seen key civil rights laws passed under the Johnson administration.

13. Why did the Supreme Court find that segregated schools go against the Constitution? _____

_____

14. The passage implies that the civil rights laws of the 1960s were due

    (1) largely to the efforts of Dr. Martin Luther King
    (2) only to the efforts of President Lyndon Johnson
    (3) strictly to the efforts of the Supreme Court

THE LAST THIRTY YEARS

Lyndon Johnson became president in 1963. His Great Society program tried to ease poverty in the United States. It focused its spending on welfare and education.

Johnson also spent money on Vietnam, a small country in southeast Asia that was fighting a civil war between its communist north and capitalist south. The United States tried to help South Vietnam drive the communists back into the North. As the war dragged on, U.S. students and others began to protest U.S. involvement. Sometimes the protests became violent. Coupled with riots in inner cities, the protests turned the end of the '60s and the early '70s into a violent period.

U.S. involvement in Vietnam ended in 1973, when the last troops left under President Nixon. But the country still couldn't settle down. Nixon was suspected of covering up a burglary and of other abuses of power. "Watergate"—as the scandal was called—led to his resignation in 1974.

Under Presidents Ford and Carter, the late 1970s was a quieter period for the United States. Nevertheless, when President Carter found no way to gain release for more than a hundred Americans taken hostage by Iran in 1979, people became discontented with his administration.

In 1980 the people elected Ronald Reagan to the presidency. Inflation that had been mounting under the two previous presidents was gradually curbed. The 1980s became a time of great prosperity for some. Consumers bought billions of dollars of goods on credit. Businessmen bought whole companies the same way—with "junk" bonds. But farmers suffered, and many had to sell their land.

By the beginning of the 1990s, the stock market had fallen hundreds of points. Experts said it was "correcting" itself because stock in companies had been overvalued.

Despite their domestic problems in the early 1990s, Americans were happy to see freedom spring up in the Eastern bloc as Eastern European countries and the Soviet Union began to reject communism for capitalism and to hold democratic elections.

15. According to the passage, what was the United States trying to do by its involvement in the Vietnam War?

    _____

    _____

16. What caused the late '60s and the early '70s to be a violent time?

    _____

    _____

17. According to the passage, the main domestic problem facing the United States in the early '90s was

    (1) international
    (2) economic
    (3) communist

18. Which two of the following events in the early '90s brought about an end of the cold war?

    (a) The stock market fell.
    (b) Eastern bloc countries began to adopt capitalism.
    (c) Eastern bloc countries held democratic elections.

GEOGRAPHY READINGS

THE ENVIRONMENT AND AGRICULTURE

As you read this passage, find the places it mentions on the map below.

One important way we use the environment is for agriculture. Agriculture gives us food, materials for making clothing, and materials for building homes. How people practice agriculture depends on the kind of environment they live in.

When North Americans think of agriculture, they usually think of large farms with tractors and harvesters. That's an accurate picture of farming in most of North America, where there are plains areas, rich soil, and moderate temperatures and rainfall.

In other parts of the world land is often too steep to farm the way it is in North America. In some mountain regions in South America and Asia, farmers move earth to make terraces on mountain slopes. The terraces are like steps going up the slopes. Because the terraces are flat, farmers can grow crops on them.

In some places soil is not very fertile; it isn't rich enough to grow food crops. Soil in the hot, wet rainforests of South America and central Africa is like that. There people burn down trees both to clear land and to fertilize the soil. They plant food crops for one or two years and then move on to a new spot.

Some places are too cold to grow food. In the northernmost parts of North America, Inuit people eat a lot of meat and fish to make up for the lack of plants in their diet. The meat and fish help the people keep warm in their cold climate.

In some dry lands people irrigate the land with water for agriculture. For thousands of years people in northeast Africa have used water from the Nile River for irrigation. In the western United States, people have dammed rivers to store water to irrigate farmlands.

In dry lands where too little water is available for growing crops, people often graze animals to use for food and clothing. For ex-

World Climates

NORTH AMERICA

EUROPE

ASIA

Atlantic Ocean

Pacific Ocean

AFRICA

Equator

SOUTH AMERICA

Indian Ocean

AUSTRALIA

Mountains; cold and wet

Hot and wet

Warm summers and cool winters; medium rain

Cold; little rain or snow

Desert or grassland; hot and cold; little rain

Cool summers and cold winters; medium rain

ample, the nomads of northern Africa and of southwest and central Asia travel with their animals. In other dry lands, people run huge cattle and sheep ranches, such as those in the North American West and in Australia.

In places with heavy rainfall, people grow crops that need a lot of water. In rainy southeast Asia, rice, which grows standing in water, is a popular crop.

19. Which of the following sentences from the first paragraph expresses the main idea of the passage?

    (1) One important way we use the environment is for agriculture.
    (2) Agriculture gives us food, materials for making clothing, and materials for building homes.
    (3) How people practice agriculture depends on the kind of environment they live in.

20. Based on the information in the passage, why would it not be logical to conclude that there is too little farmland to support the world's growing population?

    _____

    _____

21. The map suggests that the agriculture practiced in northeast Asia is probably most similar to that practiced in the northern part of

    (1) Africa
    (2) North America
    (3) South America

INDUSTRIALIZATION AND POPULATION GROWTH

The world has more than 5 billion people now. Two decades ago it had only 4 billion. At this rate of growth, the world's population will be more than 6 billion ten years from now. The population is growing so quickly because many more people are born worldwide each year than die.

Before the Industrial Revolution, death rates in countries affected by the revolution were higher than they are today. Their populations grew slowly even though their birth rates were high. Because of better medicine,

food supplies, and health practices, death rates in industrializing countries began to drop. Their populations grew more rapidly because their birth rates stayed high. Both birth and death rates later fell in those countries once they were fully industrialized. With low birth and death rates, today's industrialized countries grow slowly.

The developing nations in the world are just beginning to industrialize. Because they are not yet fully industrialized nations, their populations are still growing at a tremendous rate.

22. The article discusses three stages in population growth. Complete the following paragraph by writing *high* or *low* in the blanks to describe each stage of population change.

    Before a country becomes industrialized, its birth rate is (a) _____ and its death rate is (b) _____. When a country is in the process of industrializing, its birth rate is (c) _____ and it its death rate is (d) _____. When a country is fully industrialized, its birth rate is (e) _____ and its death rate is (f) _____.

23. Why do death rates fall when a country is developing?

    _____

    _____

24. Which of the following could explain why birth rates fall in developed countries?

    (1) There is more food for the people in developed countries.
    (2) There is better medicine in developed countries.
    (3) People in developed countries don't need a lot of children to work and support the family.

25. The passage supports the conclusion that the next ten years' billion-person world population increase will be spread

    (1) evenly across all the countries in the world
    (2) mostly through developed nations
    (3) mostly through developing nations

People have created borders between cities, states, and countries. Wind, rivers, lakes, and seas don't recognize man-made borders, though. Neither do air and water pollution.

Air pollution in the United States comes from three main sources. Most comes from cars and other vehicles. This is especially true in southern California, where car exhausts contribute to smog. Air pollution also results from home and office heating. This source is largely responsible for the pollution in New York City. Industrial emissions, such as from factories' smokestacks, also pollute the air. Such pollution is common around Chicago.

Winds spread air pollution. Pollution from smokestacks in the U.S. Midwest travels on winds to the Northeast and to Canada. There it mixes with moisture in the air and falls as acid rain. Not only North America is affected by acid rain. Heavy industry causes acid rain in northern Europe, too.

Most water pollution is caused by industrial dumping. In Europe the Rhine River is badly polluted by the many industries along its banks. In the United States, factories dump nearly four times as much waste into water as sewage plants do. The Cuyahoga River in Cleveland was once so polluted with chemicals, fuels, and trash that it occasionally caught fire.

Water is also polluted by sources other than industrial dumping. Sewage—human waste and garbage—pollutes water in some places. Fertilizers and insecticides used in agriculture often run off into surface and groundwater and pollute it. Animal waste pollutes some streams and lakes. When oil spills occur, they pollute the oceans.

Air and water pollution have unhealthy effects on plants, animals, and people. Recent efforts by governments, businesses, and individuals have helped to reduce or control pollution. It will take a lot more effort on the part of many to rid the environment of the hazards of pollution.

26. What are the three main causes of air pollution in the United States?

    (a) _____

    (b) _____

    (c) _____

27. Explain whether or not examples in the passage allow you to conclude that acid rain is caused by pollution from industries. _____

    _____

28. Acid rain destroys forests and lakes. Which of the following industries is probably hurt the most by acid rain?

    (1) banking
    (2) recreation
    (3) transportation

29. In the morning a homeowner sprays chemicals on his sloping lawn to get rid of destructive insects. In the afternoon a heavy rain washes the chemicals into a stream and pollutes it. This water pollution is most like that caused by

    (1) industry
    (2) agriculture
    (3) animals

30. An environmentalist said, "If businesses were not able to pass pollution-control costs on to consumers, they would find ways to control or prevent pollution." Is this statement a fact or an opinion?

    _____

CONSUMER CREDIT

The "buy now, pay later" method of purchasing goods began in the United States. When consumers buy on credit, they take possession of something but pay for it later. Payment can often be made in installments. If an article is not paid in full by the due date (usually after 25–30 days), interest is charged on the unpaid balance—the amount still owed. The interest rate charged often depends on the size of the outstanding balance. Over months and years, the monthly interest due on an unpaid balance can add up to a lot of money.

Consumers can get credit from a variety of businesses: banks, credit unions, finance companies, stores, and gasoline companies. Consumer credit fuels an economy: people buy more on credit than they would if they had to pay right away. For example, a person can buy a house and appliances on credit long before he or she could save enough money to pay cash.

Some consumers misuse credit. They charge more and more purchases without paying off their credit balance. They end up going deeply into debt.

The following graph shows the debt Americans owed in installment payments in 1980 and in each year from 1985 through 1990.

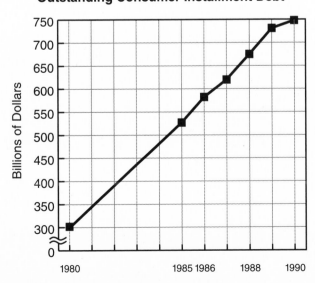

Outstanding Consumer Installment Debt

31. What is an "unpaid balance"? _____

_____

32. A woman buys a $12,000 car on credit and pays for it in installments. Altogether she will pay
    (1) less than $12,000
    (2) $12,000
    (3) more than $12,000

33. A finance company plans to run television ads to encourage people to borrow money. Which of the following ideas from the passage might the finance company use in its ad?
    (1) When consumers buy on credit, they take possession of something but pay for it later.
    (2) Over months and years, the monthly interest due on an unpaid balance can add up to quite a lot of money.
    (3) [Some consumers] end up going deeply into debt.

34. According to the graph, about how much more did Americans owe in consumer installment debt in 1990 than in 1980?
    (1) $300 billion
    (2) $450 billion
    (3) $750 billion

THE FEDERAL BUDGET DEFICIT

Many people make budgets. They figure how much money they make—their income. Then they figure how much they need to spend—their expenses. Most people try to make sure their incomes are higher than their expenses so that they don't sink into debt. In fact, most people like to save some of their income. Like some people, the U.S. government makes a budget every year.

The graphs on page 186 show where the federal government's income comes from and how the government spends its money.

Sources of the Federal Government's Income, 1988–1989

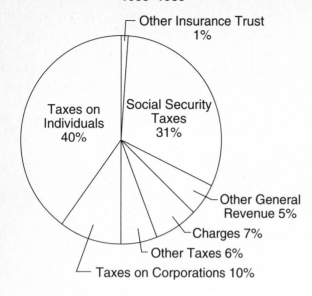

Other Insurance Trust 1%

Taxes on Individuals 40%

Social Security Taxes 31%

Other General Revenue 5%

Charges 7%

Other Taxes 6%

Taxes on Corporations 10%

The Federal Government's Expenses 1988–1989

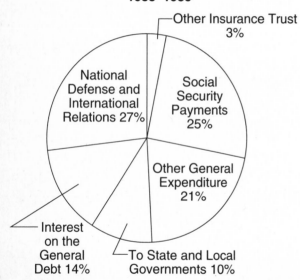

Other Insurance Trust 3%

National Defense and International Relations 27%

Social Security Payments 25%

Other General Expenditure 21%

Interest on the General Debt 14%

To State and Local Governments 10%

When the government spends more than it takes in, it goes into debt just as people do. To make up the difference, the government borrows money. This creates a budget deficit. Like people, the government must pay interest on its loans. As the graph titled *The Federal Government's Expenses* shows, 14 percent of the federal expenditures in 1988–1989 went to pay interest on debt.

In almost every year since the Great Depression, there has been a deficit in the government's budget. In the 1980s the deficit had risen to more than $200 billion—

higher than it had ever been before. That meant that the government had spent $200 billion more than it had.

Such a huge deficit is dangerous for the country, according to most people. They want a balanced budget. Others say a government is not like a family so its debt must be thought of differently. For one thing, because the government borrows from people by selling them interest-bearing bonds, those people benefit from the deficit. If they spend their earnings, the government benefits as well.

35. Which of the following best explains the main idea of the passage?
    (1) Many people make budgets that keep them out of debt and help them save money.
    (2) In 1988–1989, 14 percent of the federal government's income went toward paying the interest on its loans.
    (3) The federal government has a growing budget deficit, but people have different opinions about how dangerous that is.

36. What is the largest source of the federal government's income? _____

37. Which of the following statements from the passage expresses an opinion?
    (1) When the government spends more than it takes in, it goes into debt just as people do.
    (2) In almost every year since the Great Depression, there has been a deficit in the government's budget.
    (3) Such a huge deficit is dangerous for the country.

The government plays a positive role in the economy: it regulates business. It makes laws to ensure that businesses operate fairly and safely. Among other things, regulations cover dealings among businesses and businesses' treatment of workers and consumers.

One example of the way the government protects businesses from each other is the antitrust laws that prevent monopolies.

Many laws assure that workplaces are safe for workers. Others set minimum wages. Still others ban discrimination in hiring and promotion: a person can't be refused a job because of his or her race, sex, or age.

Laws prevent false advertising and protect consumers from dangerous products and pollution. The Federal Drug Administration (the FDA) tries to protect people from unsafe drugs. The U.S. Department of Agriculture (USDA) sets standards and inspects food for safety. The government also tries to control pollution by fining companies that pollute and giving tax breaks to those who enact pollution controls.

Without government regulation, some businesses would undoubtedly adopt practices injurious to other businesses, workers, or consumers.

38. What three groups does the government's regulation of business protect?

_____, _____,

_____

39. Which of the following statements from the passage expresses a fact?

(1) The government plays a positive role in the economy.
(2) Many laws assure that workplaces are safe for workers.
(3) Without government regulation, some businesses would undoubtedly adopt practices injurious to other businesses, workers, or consumers.

The United States competes with other countries by trying to export its goods and services. Recently, however, the United States has been importing more than it has been exporting. This has created a trade deficit for the United States.

One way the United States can improve its balance of trade is to import less. U.S. consumers could help in such an effort by buying fewer goods from other countries. Yet many U.S. consumers buy foreign goods, such as cars and electronic equipment, because they think such goods are better than U.S. goods.

Another way the United States can improve its balance of trade is to export more goods to other countries. That can happen only if U.S. goods are in demand because of their quality. To create goods that will be in demand, the United States needs a well-educated workforce, especially in technological fields. Creating such a workforce will require the dedicated effort of business managers, workers, unions, schools, and others.

40. How is a trade deficit created?_____

_____

41. An educator who read this passage drew this conclusion: The 25 percent high school dropout rate in the United States is bad for the country's balance of trade.

Is there enough information in the passage for the educator to draw this conclusion? If so, what information supports

the conclusion?_____

_____

_____

POLITICAL SCIENCE READINGS

CHECKS AND BALANCES

To make sure that no part of government becomes too powerful, the drafters of the U.S. Constitution divided power among three branches of government: the executive branch, the legislative branch, and the judicial branch.

The Constitution further limits power by providing for a system of checks on each branch, as shown in the table below. The top part of the table shows the powers of each of the three branches of government. The bottom part shows how those powers are checked by the powers of another branch.

Like the federal government, every state has a constitution. These constitutions set up the states' governments with separate powers. Each state's executive branch is headed by a governor.

42. When President Ronald Reagan vetoed a civil rights bill in 1988, he checked the power of _____.

43. When Congress voted in 1988 to override Reagan's veto of the civil rights bill, it checked the power of _____.

44. When the Supreme Court ruled in 1935 that the National Industrial Recovery Act was not allowed by the Constitution, it checked the power of _____ and of _____.

45. When Congress refused to approve the appointment of Robert Bork as Supreme Court justice in 1987, it checked the power of _____.

46. Tell two ways state governments are like the federal government.

    (a) _____

    (b) _____

U.S. Government: Division of Powers

Executive Powers (President)	Legislative Powers (Congress)	Judicial Powers (Courts)
Enforces laws.	Makes laws.	Interprets laws.
Can veto bills.	By 2/3 vote in each house, can pass a law over a veto.	Can declare laws unconstitutional.
Appoints judges and other officials.	Approves a president's appointments of judges and other officials.	
Signs treaties with other nations.	Approves treaties.	
	Can impeach a president.	

Checks on Executive Powers	Checks on Legislative Powers	Checks on Judicial Powers
Congress can override a president's veto.	President can veto a bill Congress approves.	
Supreme Court can declare a law signed by the president unconstitutional.	Supreme Court can declare a law made by Congress unconstitutional.	
Congress must approve a president's appointments.		A president appoints judges.
Congress must approve treaties signed by the president.		Congress can remove a judge from office.
Congress can remove a president from office.		

FEDERALISM

The U.S. Constitution set up a special relationship between the states and the federal government. To prevent powers of the states from being swallowed up by the federal government, this paragraph was included in the Constitution:

The powers not delegated to the United States by the Constitution, nor prohibited by it to the states, are reserved to the states respectively, or to the people.

That means that the states have any powers that the Constitution (a) does not give to the federal government and (b) does not deny to the states. This division of power is called federalism. Under federalism, states can't print money or go to war because those are powers only the federal government has. On the other hand, the Constitution leaves it to the states to create and run school systems, to protect their citizens from crime, to provide social services, to oversee health services, and to do many other things that benefit their residents.

Under federalism some powers are given to both the federal government and state governments. Both federal and state governments can impose taxes, for example.

To protect federalism as the form of government in the United States, the Constitution declares itself the supreme law of the land. It says that no state can have a law that disagrees with the Constitution. To enforce this, the Supreme Court must sometimes overturn a state law. For example, in 1973 the Court ruled that no state could outlaw abortions.

47. According to what you have read, which of the following best describes the division of power in a federalist form of government?
    (1) Most power belongs to the central government.
    (2) Most power belongs to the states.
    (3) Power is divided between the central government and state governments.

48. Which of the following illustrates a power shared by the central and state governments under federalism?
    (1) Fifty states make up the United States of America.
    (2) States have national guard units, and the federal government has an army.
    (3) People in all fifty states elect the president of the United States.

49. From where does the Supreme Court get the power to overturn a state law?

_____

50. Tell whether each of the following illustrates a power of the federal government, state governments, or both federal and state governments.

    _____ (a) A high school curriculum is planned.
    _____ (b) Troops were sent to war in the Persian Gulf.
    _____ (c) A worker's earnings are taxed.

51. How do states raise the money they need to provide services to their citizens?

_____

THE RIGHTS OF CITIZENS

Rights is a word you hear often these days. People demand civil rights, equal rights, women's rights, gay rights, and other rights.

From the beginning the United States has recognized that people have certain rights. Three main rights are listed in the Declaration of Independence: the rights to life, liberty, and the pursuit of happiness.

Although the original Constitution did not mention citizens' rights, amendments made citizens' rights part of the Constitution. Some of the rights granted by constitutional amendments are described in the table on page 190.

Amendment	Rights Granted
1st	freedom of speech
	freedom of religion
	freedom of the press
	the freedom to assemble (to meet in groups)
	the freedom to petition the government (to ask it to change things)
4th	protects citizens from unreasonable searches of their persons (bodies) or houses
5th	protects people from being tried twice for the same crime
	protects people from having to testify against themselves in court
	protects people from having their lives, liberty, or property taken away without due process of law
6th	grants a person
	• the right to a speedy and public trial
	• the right to a trial by jury
	• the right to know what he or she is accused of
	• the right to face his or her accusers
	• the right to a lawyer

Amendment	Rights Granted
14th	freed slaves and granted them all the rights of citizenship
	guaranteed equal protection under the law for all citizens
15th	granted African-American men the right to vote
19th	granted women the right to vote
26th	granted 18-year-olds the right to vote

52. The Supreme Court ruled that arrested people have the right to remain silent. On which of the constitutional amendments described in the table was this ruling based? _____

_____

53. An editor who defends an unpopular opinion in a newspaper is protected by which constitutional amendment?

_____

BEHAVIORAL SCIENCE READINGS

CHILDREN AND SOCIALIZATION

Parents are usually the first socializers of a child. The larger family—sisters and brothers and sometimes grandparents—is an important early socializer too. As a child grows older, more socializers enter his or her world.

When children begin to have contacts outside their families, they are socialized by their peers. The peers for young children are their playmates. A child learns how to cooperate, how to play games by the rules, and how not to be bullied.

Many people have studied the role of television in a child's socialization. On TV children see ways men and women act, but some people think that some adult role models shown on TV are not good for children to see. Some people also think TV ads for toys and junk food teach children to value material things too highly and to learn unhealthy eating habits. Most important, many people believe that violence on TV makes children act violently. Some studies suggest that this is correct.

54. A peer is a person who
   (1) has equal standing with another person
   (2) is trained to socialize others
   (3) is socialized mainly by TV

55. A parent can NOT influence his or her child's early socialization by
   (1) knowing the child's playmates
   (2) monitoring the child's TV watching
   (3) putting in long hours at work

56. Which of the following conclusions can be drawn from information in the passage?

   (1) Children should be kept at home to protect them from bad influences.

   (2) It might be better for children if they didn't see violence on TV.

   (3) If a child chooses the wrong playmates, he should not be allowed to watch television.

57. People who criticize TV ads seen by children probably think that adults should NOT

   (1) have any more material things than they absolutely need

   (2) place too much value on material things

   (3) keep any potato chips around the house

TEENAGERS AND SOCIALIZATION

Teenagers are especially concerned with what other teens think, what they wear, and how they act. During adolescence the effect of the peer group is very strong. It can be so strong that a teenager will take on roles and values that conflict with those taught by his or her parents.

For example, a teenager's peers may pressure him or her to take drugs or drink to show his or her independence from parental control. A teenager who takes his peers' suggestions shows that he or she has become less dependent on parental approval and more dependent on peer approval.

For some teenagers a gang takes the place of the family. The older members of the gang are role models for the younger ones. The gang teaches its own values and beliefs, which often conflict with those of the larger society. Gangs are strong influences when families are weak. They appeal mostly to teenagers who feel they have no family and don't belong to the rest of society.

58. As part of the socialization process, most teenagers adopt the values of

   (1) their parents

   (2) their peers

   (3) gang leaders

59. Which of the following best expresses the main idea of the last paragraph?

   (1) Some teenagers who need a sense of belonging join gangs and take on the gang's values.

   (2) For some teenagers gang leaders take the place of parents as role models.

   (3) Gangs' values are usually in conflict with teenagers' families' values.

SOCIAL CLASSES

Strata means layers or levels. *Stratification* in a society refers to levels or classes. The United States has three main classes: lower, middle, and upper. Usually a person's income, education, and lifestyle determine which class he or she belongs to. A person's race and ethnic background are often factors, too. More African-Americans and Hispanic people are in the lower class than are white people.

Percent of Persons Below the Poverty Level

Age	White	African-American	Hispanic
Under 16	16.2	46.7	40.6
16 to 21	12.1	36.0	27.5
22 to 44	8.5	25.1	21.2
45 to 64	7.4	23.5	20.4
65 and over	10.1	33.9	27.4
All ages	10.5	33.1	28.2

Unlike in many countries, in the United States a person is able to move from one class to another. For example, many African-Americans who were born into the lower class move into the middle class because their educations give them access to higher incomes.

60. List five factors that help to determine a person's class.

   (a)_____

   (b)_____

   (c)_____

   (d)_____

   (e)_____

61. According to the chart, the percent of persons living below the poverty level decreases until what age? _____

62. A woman who becomes an alcoholic, loses her job, and has her children taken from her is likely to

    (1) move into a class lower than the one she has been in

    (2) stay in the class she has been in

    (3) move into a class higher than the one she has been in

SOCIAL STATUS

Everyone has a certain status or position in society. A person's status depends on three main factors: his or her class, job, and lifestyle. Material possessions—in this context they are called *status symbols*—are signs of a person's status. In the United States, the more expensive possessions you have, the higher your status in society is likely to be.

A person's status at birth is largely based on his or her family's status. In the United States there is also achieved status. When poor people work their way through school into good jobs and middle-class lifestyles, they trade in their ascribed status for achieved status. It's similar to the way an actor who becomes a star achieves a new status.

63. Ascribed status is the status you

    (1) earn by hard work

    (2) are born with

    (3) gain by owning status symbols

64. Tell whether each of the following illustrates ascribed status or achieved status.

    _____ (a) A woman trains and becomes a professional athlete.

    _____ (b) A baby is born to the president.

    _____ (c) A man whose father is a miner becomes a surgeon.

    _____ (d) The son of a corporation president is convicted of a violent crime and is disowned by his family.

65. The leader of a church, a synagogue, a mosque, or another religious group may earn less money than the people he or she serves. Within that group, though, the leader probably has the highest status. Which of the factors that determine status makes this so?_____

Check your answers on page 227.

SOCIAL STUDIES READINGS 3 SKILLS CHART

To review the readings skills covered by the items in Social Studies Readings 3, study the following parts of Units 1, 2, and 3.

Unit 1	Comprehending What You Read	Item Number
Chapter 2	Recognizing Stated Main Ideas	
Lesson 5	Finding the Sentence That States the Main Idea	19
Chapter 3	Understanding the Details	
Lesson 6	Reading for Details	7, 10, 15, 22, 31, 38, 58, 60
Lesson 7	Seeing How Details Are Organized	2, 26, 46
Lesson 8	Finding Details in Tables	61
Lesson 9	Finding Details in Graphs	34, 36

This section will give you practice answering questions like those on the GED. The ten questions in this Practice are all multiple choice, like the ones on the GED.

As you do this Practice, use the reading skills you've studied in Units 1, 2, and 3:

- Preview each passage or graph before you read it. Preview the questions, too.
- Read each passage, looking for its main idea and noting the details it contains.
- If you don't understand a word, try to infer its meaning from its context.
- Make inferences about things not stated directly in passages.
- Apply the ideas and facts in the passages and graphic materials to new situations.
- Look for cause-effect relationships, conclusions, facts, opinions, and hypotheses.
- Evaluate whether conclusions are supported by enough relevant, logical evidence.
- Recognize how people's values affect their beliefs and actions.

Directions: Choose the one best answer to each item.

Items 1 through 3 refer to the following passage.

During the Great Depression, one of the key programs of President Franklin Roosevelt's New Deal was Social Security. The Social Security Act of 1935 set up payments to aid people who were unemployed or too old to work. The program worked like insurance. Workers and their employers paid into a fund. Workers then received an income when they retired or were unemployed.

Supporters of Social Security argued that it was a kind, humane program. They also pointed out that it was, in effect, paid for by the workers themselves. Opponents of Social Security called it "socialistic." They claimed people would no longer want to work if they could get money from the government.

1. Social Security is like insurance in that
   (1) people are given money by the government
   (2) people pay money into a fund and get it back later
   (3) employers pay money into a fund
   (4) it is socialistic
   (5) it is kind and humane

2. What was probably the main reason the Social Security Act was needed?
   (1) It helped Roosevelt get elected.
   (2) Many unemployed and retired people had no way to support themselves.
   (3) Some people had few economic difficulties during the Great Depression.
   (4) People wanted to retire before they were 65.
   (5) People were tired of working and wanted something for nothing.

3. Which of the following is an opinion about Social Security?

   (1) It was started in 1935.
   (2) It was part of Roosevelt's New Deal.
   (3) It was a kind, humane program.
   (4) Workers paid into the program.
   (5) It paid jobless and retired workers.

Items 4 and 5 refer to the following passage.

The government used to regulate the airlines. It controlled fares and routes.

In the late 1970s the government began to deregulate the airline industry. By the early 1980s many small, new airlines had formed. They could charge lower fares than large airlines because it cost them less to operate. Large airlines suffered huge losses. They thought deregulation was a terrible influence on their industry.

To reduce operating costs, large airlines started using a "hub" system. Planes flew from different cities into an airline's hub airport. There passengers changed to planes that headed for their final destinations. The hub system reduced the number of empty seats on planes, so the larger airlines began to make money again.

4. In the early 1980s airplane passengers benefited from deregulation because

   (1) fares were reduced
   (2) flights were safer
   (3) more seats were empty
   (4) the hub system made travel faster
   (5) planes were more comfortable

5. Which of the following statements from the passage expresses an opinion?

   (1) The government used to regulate the airlines.
   (2) In the late 1970s the government began to deregulate the airline industry.
   (3) [Small airlines] could charge lower fares than large airlines.
   (4) Deregulation was a terrible influence on [the airline] industry.
   (5) To reduce operating costs, large airlines started using a "hub" system.

Items 6 and 7 refer to the following passage.

Child abuse is physical, emotional, or sexual mistreatment of a child. Because most child abuse occurs in the home, the actual occurrence of child abuse is hard to determine. Reports of child abuse in the United States have risen steadily from 700,000 cases in the middle of the 1970s to 2 million cases ten years later.

News reports and TV shows have brought the nature and frequency of child abuse to everyone's attention. Therefore, the increase in the number of reports of child abuse may be due more to people's greater awareness than to actual increases in abuse.

The causes of child abuse have been the focus of research. One fact has become clear: more than 90 percent of child abusers were abused when they were children.

6. Which of the following statements from the passage expresses an hypothesis?

   (1) Child abuse is physical, emotional, or sexual mistreatment of a child.
   (2) Most child abuse occurs in the home.
   (3) News reports and TV shows have brought the nature and frequency of child abuse to everyone's attention.
   (4) The increase in the number of reports of child abuse may be due more to people's greater awareness than to actual increases in abuse.
   (5) More than 90 percent of child abusers were abused when they were children.

7. From the information in the passage it is reasonable to conclude that

   (1) most child abuse is emotional
   (2) only parents abuse children
   (3) the number of reports of child abuse will continue to rise
   (4) the rate of child abuse is falling
   (5) anyone abused as a child will abuse children

Items 8 through 10 refer to the following passage and graph.

The United States gives foreign countries money and credit on goods. Most of this aid is for military, agricultural, and industrial purposes.

The graph that follows shows the cost of U.S. foreign aid from 1945 through 1985.

U.S. Aid to Foreign Countries
(in billions of dollars)

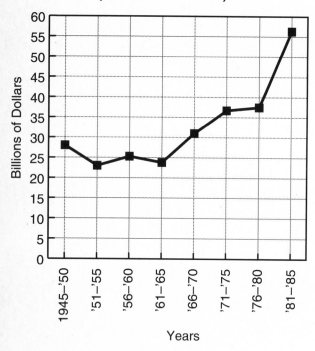

8. Which of these is an example of U.S. foreign aid?

(1) The United States played in all the Olympic Games except the 1980 games.
(2) The United States met with the former Soviet Union to discuss limiting weapons.
(3) The United States sold wheat to the former Soviet Union.
(4) Americans buy Japanese cars.
(5) The U.S. Peace Corps helps other countries make improvements in farming and health care.

9. Which of the following conclusions is supported by information in the graph?

(1) The amount of U.S. foreign aid has increased every year since 1945.
(2) The United States has consistently given billions of dollars to other countries during each five-year period since World War II.
(3) Most of the aid that the United States gives other countries is for military purposes.
(4) Most of the aid that the United States gives other countries is for agriculture and industry.
(5) Voter support for U.S. foreign aid is decreasing.

10. Which piece of information from the graph supports this conclusion?

The United States increased foreign aid greatly after 1980.

(1) The cost of foreign aid between 1981 and 1985 increased almost $20 billion over the previous five years.
(2) The cost of foreign aid between 1981 and 1985 was higher than its cost between 1945 and 1950.
(3) About $24 billion was spent in foreign aid from 1961 through 1965.
(4) The graph reports foreign aid costs in five-year periods.
(5) In each period shown on the graph, the cost of foreign aid exceeds $20 billion.

Check your answers on page 231.

GED PRACTICE 3 SKILLS CHART

To review the reading skills covered by the items in GED Practice 3, study the following parts of Units 1, 2, and 3.

GED PRACTICE 3 CONTENT CHART

The following chart shows which area of social studies each item in GED Practice 3 refers to.

Area of Social Studies	Item Number
Geography	1, 2, 3, 8
Economics	4, 5, 9, 10
Political Science	6, 7

Posttest

The following Posttest is similar to the Social Studies Test of the GED. Taking it will help you find out how your skills have improved by using this book. It can also help you find out what you need to review or learn more about.

The Posttest has 32 multiple-choice items—half as many as there are on the GED. The items are based on readings in history, geography, economics, political science, and behavioral science. The questions test your understanding of the readings and your ability to apply information and think critically.

RCA Radiola Super VIII, circa 1925

SOCIAL STUDIES POSTTEST

Directions: Choose the <u>one best answer</u> to each item.

<u>Item 1</u> is based on the following paragraph.

In Japan, cheerfully slapping someone on the back is considered rude. In Thailand, pointing your toes at someone is an insult. Such body language and gestures carry different meanings in different cultures. In the United States both men and women shake hands, but in India women do not shake hands. And in Arabia, men stroll down the street holding hands with each other as a sign of friendship.

1. Which of the following ideas from the paragraph is its main idea?

   (1) In Japan, slapping people on the back is rude.
   (2) Holding hands is a sign of friendship.
   (3) Body language and gestures have different meanings in different cultures.
   (4) Pointing your toes at someone is rude in Thailand.
   (5) Both men and women in the United States shake hands.

<u>Item 2</u> is based on the following paragraph.

In the 1800s slavery was an emotionally charged issue. It divided the United States. Many believed it was morally allowable; others believed it was immoral.

2. Which of the following recent issues has a similar effect on the country?

   (1) freedom of speech
   (2) new taxes
   (3) defense spending
   (4) abortion
   (5) space exploration

<u>Items 3 and 4</u> are based on the following graph.

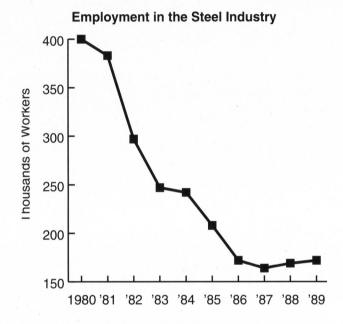

Employment in the Steel Industry

3. Which of the following conclusions can be drawn from the graph?

   (1) There was a sharp decline in the number of jobs in the steel industry during the 1980s.
   (2) Fewer people wanted to work in the steel industry in the 1980s than before.
   (3) Steel was replaced by other metals as the material of choice in the 1980s.
   (4) The number of people working in the steel industry will drop sharply again in the 1990s.
   (5) During the 1980s new methods of steel production requiring few people were introduced.

4. Which of the following pieces of information from the graph supports the conclusion that employment levels in the steel industry became stable during the second half of the 1980s?

   (1) Employment in steel didn't return to its 1980 level during the 1980s.
   (2) During the 1980s there were fewer jobs in steel each year (with two exceptions) than the year before.
   (3) In 1989 about 175,000 people worked in the steel industry.
   (4) 1986 was the first year the number of jobs in steel dropped below 200,000.
   (5) From 1986 through 1989 the number of jobs in steel did not vary much.

Items 5 through 8 are based on the following passage.

Marshes and swamps often border seacoasts. These wetlands are sources of food. Many food fishes are hatched in these wetlands. A major part of fishermen's catches of shrimp, scallops, clams, and other seafood comes from marshes. Marshes and swamps also help clean seawater by trapping pollutants in their muddy bottoms.

Wetlands are especially common where rivers meet oceans. People have often settled in such areas. They have learned to drain the wetlands and fill them in. They live, farm, and build industries on the newly created land. Wetlands are disappearing. People in Holland, Asia, and the eastern United States have been converting them to their use.

5. How do people change wetlands to make them useful?

   (1) They drain and fill them in to create dry land.
   (2) They settle near wetlands.
   (3) They allow food fishes to breed in them.
   (4) They create wetlands along seacoasts.
   (5) They let the ocean flood them.

6. Which of the following explains why wetlands are disappearing all over the world?

   (1) need for more fish
   (2) changes in climates
   (3) growth in populations
   (4) competition among countries
   (5) decline in the number of cities

7. Which of the following is most likely to result if wetlands keep disappearing?

   (1) The sea level will rise.
   (2) People will lose farmland.
   (3) The weather along seacoasts will change.
   (4) Seawater will be more polluted.
   (5) People will settle in other places.

8. An economist would probably be most interested in

   (1) the amount of pollution wetlands prevent
   (2) the plants that grow in wetlands
   (3) human settlement around wetlands in the past
   (4) the value of seafood caught in wetlands
   (5) the natural beauty of wetlands

Item 9 is based on the following passage.

A Polish immigrant who worked in a clothing factory in the early 1900s described her work this way:

"At seven o'clock we all sit down to our machines and the boss brings to each one the pile of work that he or she is to finish during the day. . . . Sometimes the work is not all finished by six o'clock. . . .

"The machines go like mad all day, because the faster you work the more money you get. Sometimes in my haste I get my finger caught and the needle goes right through it. . . . I bind the finger up with a piece of cotton and go on working. We all have accidents like that."

9. The woman's description is about
   (1) the freedom immigrants felt in America
   (2) opportunities immigrants had in America
   (3) the working conditions many immigrants suffered in America
   (4) the way industry makes clothing
   (5) the benefits that come with having a job

Items 10 and 11 are based on the following graph.

Homeless People in the United States

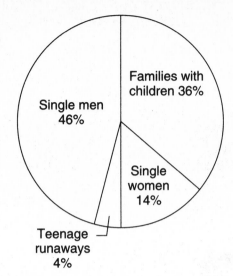

10. Teenage runaways account for what percent of the homeless?
    (1) 100%
    (2) 46%
    (3) 36%
    (4) 14%
    (5) 4%

11. Which of the following statements is supported by information in the graph?
    (1) The number of homeless people is growing.
    (2) More than half of the homeless are single adults.
    (3) Homelessness is more common today than in earlier years.
    (4) Single women are the largest group of homeless people.
    (5) Drugs and alcohol cause a good deal of homelessness.

Items 12 through 14 are based on the following information.

Descriptions of the responsibilities of five of the departments that make up the executive branch of the federal government follow.

Department of Agriculture—Keeps prices fair for farmers and consumers. Maintains quality standards for food.

Department of Defense—Directs the army, navy, air force, and marine corps. Buys weapons.

Department of the Interior—Preserves and develops the nation's resources. Manages federal land, including parks.

Department of State—Handles U.S. relations with other governments. Speaks for the U.S. at the United Nations.

Department of the Treasury—Receives all money paid to the government. Pays government's expenses.

12. Morton is a government worker who inspects meat products. He makes sure they are processed correctly. Morton works for the Department of

(1) Agriculture
(2) Defense
(3) the Interior
(4) State
(5) the Treasury

13. Charmaine works for the Internal Revenue Service. She checks people's tax returns. Charmaine works for the Department of

(1) Agriculture
(2) Defense
(3) the Interior
(4) State
(5) the Treasury

14. Deena is a ranger in a national forest in Colorado. Deena works for the Department of

(1) Agriculture
(2) Defense
(3) the Interior
(4) State
(5) the Treasury

Items 15 and 16 refer to the following map, which shows where the British were defeated by the Americans and French in the battle that ended the American Revolution. The black areas indicate areas filled with French troops.

The Battle of Yorktown

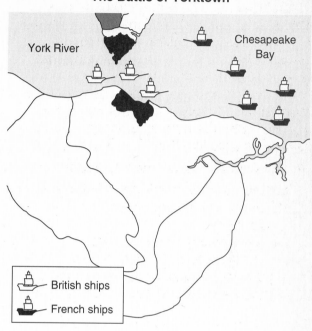

15. Which of the following conclusions is supported by the map?

(1) The Battle of Yorktown was a long, hard fight.
(2) The British had more troops than the Americans and French.
(3) The Americans were better trained than the British.
(4) The French played an important role in the defeat of the British.
(5) The Battle of Yorktown was fought entirely on water.

16. A man looked at the map and thought, "The British ships could have escaped via the Chesapeake Bay." The man's conclusion was wrong because

(1) the York River empties into Chesapeake Bay
(2) the York River is too shallow for ships
(3) the York River flows through Virginia
(4) the British had few ships left
(5) the British ships were blocked and outnumbered by French ships

Items <u>17 through 19</u> are based on the following passage.

For years U.S. factories used one way of manufacturing: the assembly line. The assembly process was broken down into the smallest steps, and each worker did just one step. The worker was seen as just another machine.

The assembly line was created by Henry Ford for use in his car factories. It was quickly adopted by other automakers and other industries as well.

When Japan began selling cars successfully to American consumers, the three largest U.S. automakers believed the reason for the Japanese success was their workforce. Japanese workers were thought to be loyal, obedient, and willing to work long hours for the company. But when Japan began making cars in the United States with American workers, the cars sold equally as well. The automakers had to look for another explanation for the Japanese success.

The answer wasn't the workers. The answer was in the manufacturing system itself. In the Japanese system, workers are parts of teams, and each worker learns not just one job but as many jobs as possible. Workers are allowed and encouraged to make decisions, such as to stop the assembly process if they spot a defect.

17. At first U.S. automakers explained Japanese automakers' success by

(1) the way Japan markets cars
(2) the way Japan builds cars
(3) the price of Japanese cars
(4) the style of Japanese cars
(5) the attitude of Japanese workers

18. Unlike Japanese workers, Ford's workers

(1) made little money
(2) enjoyed their work
(3) worked with robots
(4) made no decisions
(5) learned several jobs

19. Which of the following industries could use the assembly-line method of production?

(1) insurance
(2) law enforcement
(3) TV manufacturing
(4) farming
(5) air transportation

<u>Item 20</u> refers to the following globe.

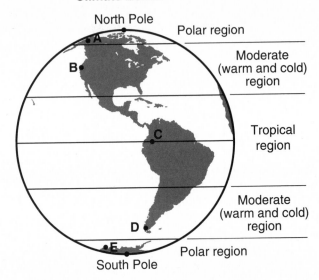

Climate Zones

20. If you wanted to live in a mild climate, the best place would probably be

(1) A
(2) B
(3) C
(4) D
(5) E

refers to the following paragraph.

A reporter studied senators' campaign spending and found that the amount spent on television ads depends on two factors. In a close race a senate candidate might spend as much as 90 percent of his or her campaign dollars on TV ads. In heavily populated states, like California, a candidate pays more for air time than a candidate in a more sparsely populated state such as South Carolina.

21. The main idea of the passage is that

    (1) the amount a senate candidate spends on TV ads depends on the closeness and location of the race

    (2) senators spend too much money on television ads

    (3) senators are forced to spend a great deal of time raising funds for TV ads

    (4) air time in populous states is more expensive than in other states

    (5) money spent on TV ads affects who wins a senate race

Item 22 refers to the following paragraph.

About 178,000 African-American soldiers fought in the Civil War. Yet only 110 African-Americans became officers. Seven thousand white officers were in charge of the "colored troops." Many of the African-American soldiers were former slaves, and all were paid lower wages and received fewer supplies than white soldiers. According to one historian, they performed superbly.

22. Which of the following statements about African-American Civil War soldiers is supported by the passage?

    (1) They were promoted just as white soldiers.

    (2) They were given equal pay for equal work.

    (3) They had little knowledge of slavery.

    (4) They were assigned to troops that were not integrated.

    (5) They did not fight well.

Items 23 through 25 are based on the following passage.

What effect does television have on children? According to one researcher, plenty.

An Illinois child psychiatrist says parents should pay attention to the shows their children watch. Young children think the characters on TV are real people. They identify with the characters and often emulate their behavior. Because of that identification, violent cartoon characters can influence a child just as a violent person in real life can.

The psychiatrist also says that too much TV, even "good" TV, can keep a child from active play, and play is essential for a child's social and mental development.

Another researcher suggests that parents can become too involved in children's viewing habits. A study in California found that small children left on their own are more likely to tune into educational shows like "Sesame Street." But when they watch TV with their parents, children choose cartoon and clown shows.

23. When a child emulates behavior, the child

    (1) fears the behavior he or she sees

    (2) dislikes the behavior he or she sees

    (3) ignores the behavior he or she sees

    (4) laughs at the behavior he or she sees

    (5) imitates the behavior he or she sees

24. How can a parent best use the information provided by the researcher in Illinois?

    (1) Do not allow children to watch TV.

    (2) Allow a limited amount of TV watching.

    (3) Punish children for watching violence on TV.

    (4) Use the TV as a baby-sitter.

    (5) Don't let children play alone.

25. Which of the following conclusions is supported by the research done in California?

    (1) Parents should control which TV shows children watch.

    (2) Television has no effect on children.

    (3) Children are more likely to watch educational shows when alone.

    (4) Children like the violence they see on cartoon shows.

    (5) Cartoon and clown shows are the best shows for children.

Item 26 is based on the following quotation.

"The responsibility of great states is to serve and not to dominate the world."

                    —President Harry Truman

26. Each of the following illustrates the United States following Truman's belief EXCEPT

    (1) giving foreign aid to countries

    (2) trading with other countries

    (3) doing research in Antarctica

    (4) hosting the United Nations

    (5) damming rivers in the West

Item 27 is based on the following information.

    In the 1800s the United States pushed its border to the Pacific Ocean.

27. Which of the following statements is an opinion about this growth?

    (1) The United States bought land west of the Mississippi from France.

    (2) It was right for the American people to settle from coast to coast.

    (3) Mexico gave the United States land in the Southwest after it lost a war.

    (4) Pioneers created trails that led to the West.

    (5) The move west led to fights with the Indians who were living on the land.

Items 28 through 30 refer to the following information and map.

    Once the Nineteenth Amendment to the Constitution was passed in 1920, no state could deny people the right to vote because of their sex.

Women's Voting Rights Before 1920

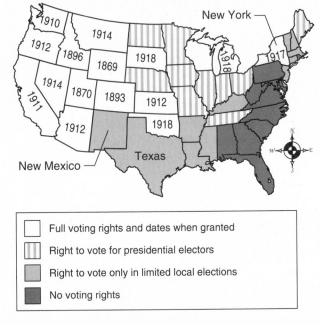

☐ Full voting rights and dates when granted

▥ Right to vote for presidential electors

▧ Right to vote only in limited local elections

■ No voting rights

28. Before 1920, in which region did women have the least say about government?

    (1) the Southeast

    (2) the Northeast

    (3) the Midwest

    (4) the Southwest

    (5) the Northwest

29. Which of the following is a fact shown by the map?

    (1) Women make intelligent voters.

    (2) Women should not have been given the right to vote.

    (3) Women had to fight harder to vote than other groups.

    (4) Women in New York voted for many good candidates.

    (5) Women in Texas could not vote for president before 1920.

30. Which of the following pieces of information from the map helps support the conclusion that people in the West were more willing to grant voting rights to women?

(1) Some states did not allow women to vote at all before 1920.

(2) Women in all the western states could vote before 1920.

(3) Women in New Mexico could vote only in local elections before 1920.

(4) Most states allowed women to vote in some elections before 1920.

(5) After 1920 women in the West could vote in all elections.

Item 31 is based on the following information.

Good weather has led to a very large crop of oranges.

31. Which of the following is most likely to happen as a result?

(1) People will stop buying oranges.

(2) Farmers will sell their land.

(3) The price of oranges will go down.

(4) More orange trees will be planted.

(5) Fewer oranges will be shipped to stores.

Item 32 is based on the following paragraph.

The generation of people who were children during the Great Depression (in the 1930s) tended to watch their spending and save a lot of money after they grew up.

32. Which of the following statements offer an hypothesis for this?

(1) This same generation had to fight World War II during the 1940s.

(2) The parents of this generation had fought in World War I.

(3) The hard years of the depression made this generation fear being without money.

(4) This generation is now in their sixties and seventies.

(5) Franklin Roosevelt was president during the Great Depression.

Check your answers on page 231.

SOCIAL STUDIES POSTTEST SKILLS CHART

To study the reading skills covered by the items in the Social Studies Posttest, review the following parts of this book.

		Item Number
Unit 1	Comprehending What You Read	
Chapter 1	Preparing to Read	9
Chapter 2	Recognizing Stated Main Ideas	1
Chapter 3	Understanding the Details	5, 10, 28
Unit 2	Inferring as You Read	
Chapter 1	Inferring Word Meanings	23
Chapter 2	Inferring Details	18, 22
Chapter 3	Inferring the Unstated Main Idea	21
Unit 3	Thinking Critically as You Read	
Chapter 1	Applying What You Read	2, 12, 13, 14, 19, 24, 26
Chapter 2	Analyzing What You Read	6, 7, 17, 20, 27, 29, 31, 32
Chapter 3	Evaluating What You Read	3, 4, 8, 11, 15, 16, 25, 30

SOCIAL STUDIES POSTTEST CONTENT CHART

The following chart shows the type of content each item in the Social Studies Pretest is based on.

Content	Item Number
History	2, 9, 15, 16, 22, 26, 27, 32
Geography	5, 6, 7, 8, 20
Economics	3, 4, 17, 18, 19, 31
Political Science	12, 13, 14, 21, 28, 29, 30
Behavioral Science	1, 10, 11, 23, 24, 25

Answers and Explanations

In this section are the answers—with explanations—for the questions asked in the Pretest, the Exercises, the Social Studies Readings, the GED Practices, and the Posttest. The reading skill and the social studies content area are indicated for all questions except those in the exercises.

PRETEST (page 1)

1. **(4)** Since raising taxes is unpopular, states looked for other sources of revenue. Many found that lotteries were a good way to raise extra money. (Thinking Critically as You Read/Analyzing What You Read/Political Science)

2. **(3)** The paragraph says that states get money from taxes, from charges for services, and from Washington. It then says that states wanted to broaden their revenue bases. From this, you can figure out that *revenue base* means "all sources of income." (Inferring as You Read/Inferring Word Meanings/Political Science)

3. **(1)** Since she likes working with her hands, and since jobs in the computer field will keep increasing, Gloria could take courses to prepare herself to work as a computer technician. (Thinking Critically as You Read/Applying What You Read/Economics)

4. **(3)** The third sentence of the paragraph is general enough to state the main idea of the paragraph. All the other sentences contain details that support that idea. (Comprehending What You Read/ Recognizing Stated Main Ideas/History)

5. **(2)** Two crops that feed people—wheat and rice—are grown in the eastern part of China. So it's likely that people live there, where

food can be easily grown. (Inferring as You Read/Making Inferences/Geography)

6. **(1)** All the sentences give information about the space we like to keep between ourselves and others. This is the topic of the paragraph. (Comprehending What You Read/ Preparing to Read/Behavioral Science)

7. **(5)** A store clerk is not a close family member or a friend, so you would tend to keep a clerk at a social distance. A girlfriend, a doctor, your grandfather, and your child would all come closer. (Thinking Critically as You Read/Applying What You Read/ Behavioral Science)

8. **(2)** According to the graph, bank cards are used more often than all the other cards combined. People must find them the most convenient to use. (Thinking Critically as You Read/Evaluating What You Read/ Economics)

9. **(5)** This is an example of the Supreme Court overturning state laws. It shows that the Court ensures that state laws follow the Constitution. (Thinking Critically as You Read/Applying What You Read/Political Science)

10. **(3)** The areas on the map with the darkest shading show the free states. (Comprehending What You Read/ Understanding the Details/History)

11. **(1)** If all the territories now marked for voters' choice had become slave-owning areas, more than half the country would have allowed slavery. (Thinking Critically as You Read/Analyzing What You Read/History)

12. **(4)** The map shows that large sections of the country were free and large sections were not. The issue of slavery divided the country. There is not enough information in the map to support any of the other conclusions. (Thinking Critically as You Read/Evaluating What You Read/History)

13. **(2)** The words *should not* signal an opinion. You may agree with it, but you cannot prove it with details from the map. (Thinking Critically as You Read/Analyzing What You Read/History)

14. **(3)** The sharp decrease in the value of farmland must have caused economic difficulties for farmers in the 1980s. (Thinking Critically as You Read/Evaluating What You Read/Economics)

15. **(1)** A senator from a wheat-producing state would probably be more concerned than the other people listed about the value of farmland. He or she would think about the effect of land values in his or her state. (Thinking Critically as You Read/Evaluating What You Read)

16. **(5)** Barrow has cold winters and cool summers. It gets very little rain and has only short ground plants. These details all fit the description of a tundra climate. (Thinking Critically as You Read/Applying What You Read/Geography)

17. **(4)** San Diego has warm summers (near 80°F) and mild winters (about 55°F). Most of its rain falls during the winter. These details match the description of a Mediterranean climate. (Thinking Critically as You Read/Applying What You Read/Geography)

18. **(3)** New York City has hot summers (about 82°F) and cold winters (freezing). Rain or snow falls throughout the year. These details match the description of a continental climate. (Thinking Critically as You Read/Applying What You Read/Geography)

19. **(2)** The only detail that doesn't help describe a climate is the number of people who live in an area. (Thinking Critically as You Read/Evaluating What You Read/Geography)

20. **(1)** The paragraph is about colonists' opposition to British rule. The other sentences give details that illustrate their opposition. (Comprehending What You Read/Recognizing Stated Main Ideas/History)

21. **(1)** Discontent with British rule must have led many colonists to seek independence. (Inferring as You Read/Making Inferences/History)

22. **(4)** The divorce rate is stated in the second sentence of the passage. (Comprehending What You Read/Understanding the Details/Behavioral Science)

23. **(5)** The second and third paragraphs explain that attitudes about marriage and divorce have changed. The last paragraph says that laws changed. You can infer that people let their lawmakers know they wanted divorce made easier. (Inferring as You Read/Making Inferences/Behavioral Science)

24. **(5)** This question asks you for a hypothesis—a possible explanation. At the end of the fourth paragraph, a researcher suggests this explanation for the greater number of divorces today. (Thinking Critically as You Read/Analyzing What You Read/Behavioral Science)

25. **(2)** You can infer that when families are split by divorce, the children live with just one parent. (Thinking Critically as You Read/Analyzing What You Read/Behavioral Science)

26. **(3)** This statement explains why the graphs are shown side by side. (Inferring as You Read/Inferring the Unstated Main Idea/Economics)

27. **(4)** The man was wrong. If you add the sales of all American cars and the sales of all Japanese cars, you'll see that more American cars were bought in 1989. (Thinking Critically as You Read/Evaluating What You Read/Economics)

28. **(2)** Roosevelt wanted to help needy people. Social Security payments help disabled people who cannot work. (Thinking Critically as You Read/Applying What You Read/History)

29. **(5)** The questions asks for a conclusion. The fifth choice is supported by the observation that voters return the same people to office. (Thinking Critically as You Read/Evaluating What You Read/Political Science)

30. **(3)** Whether the IRS will collect less money cannot be determined until tax collection in the years following the Taxpayer Bill of Rights is studied. (Thinking Critically as You Read/Analyzing What You Read/Political Science)

31. **(1)** This statement is the only fact; it can be proved true. The other statements are all opinions that cannot be proved right or wrong. (Thinking Critically as You Read/Analyzing What You Read/Political Science)

32. **(4)** This conclusion was stated in the first sentence of the paragraph. The rest of the paragraph explains how the scientist reached the conclusion. (Thinking Critically as You Read/Analyzing What You Read/Behavioral Science)

UNIT 1   COMPREHENDING WHAT YOU READ

EXERCISE 1 (PAGE 17)

1. The words **rules** and **children** are repeated often.

2. **(3)** The first sentence and the repeated words are strong clues about the topic.

3. These words stand out: **leader, thinker, writer**, and **scientist**.

4. The paragraph is about **Benjamin Franklin**. The first sentence and the repeated name, *Franklin*, are the strongest clues about the topic.

5. The words **computers** and **jobs** are repeated.

6. The topic of this paragraph is the effect of **computers** on **jobs**. The first sentence and the repeated words are strong clues about the topic.

7. The word **founded** is repeated in every sentence.

8. **(2)** The last sentence tells the topic. The other sentences give examples of colonies founded for religious reasons.

EXERCISE 2 (PAGE 21)

1. As the title says, the topic of the table is **female workers in the United States**.

2. As the subtitle tells, the table covers the time from **1940** to **1990**.

3. The **title** and the **subtitle** give the information for answering questions 1 and 2.

4. **(a) and (c)** The column headings tell what information the table gives.

5. The title shows that the topic is **average height for boys**.

6. The graph covers ages from **birth to 18 years**.

7. **(3)** The label on the side of the graph shows that the heights are reported in inches.

EXERCISE 3 (PAGE 23)

1. The topic is **job satisfaction**. The first sentence and the repeated words, *job, satisfaction*, and *satisfied*, are the clues.

2. Answers will vary. You may have thought of things that could or do make you satisfied with a job.

3. Answers will vary. By scanning the paragraph, you might have predicted that you could find out what gives most people job satisfaction.

EXERCISE 4 (PAGE 29)

1. The topic is **laws**, or laws England made.

2. **Main idea: (a). Supporting sentences: (b), (c), and (d).** The supporting sentences give examples of laws colonists didn't like.

3. The topic is **teenage unemployment**, or teenage unemployment rates.

4. **Main idea: (a). Supporting sentences: (b), (c), and (d).** The supporting sentences give details about teenage unemployment rates.

5. The topic is **teenage years**, or problems and challenges of teenage years.

6. **Main idea: (a). Supporting sentences: (b), (c), and (d).** Choice (b) gives an example of a teenage problem. Choices (c) and (d) give details about what teenage problems and challenges are.

EXERCISE 5 (PAGE 32)

1. The topic is **Antarctica**.

2. **(3)** The main idea is that Antarctica is an icy desert. To support the main idea, the first sentence explains that Antarctica is cold and dry; the second sentence explains that it has ice but lacks vegetation.

3. The topic is **the beginning of the American Revolution**.

4. **Main idea: (a). Supporting sentences: (b), (c), and (d).** Beginning with the second sentence in the paragraph, every sentence tells details about the events in Massachusetts that began the American Revolution.

5. The topic is **jobs**, or job categories.

6. **The first sentence** states the main idea. It says there are three categories of jobs. The other sentences in the paragraph tell about those categories in more detail and give examples of jobs in each category.

7. The topic is **teenage suicide**, or the rate of teenage suicide.

8. **(3)** The main idea is that the rate of teenage suicide is rising. The first two sentences in the paragraph give details about recent suicide rates.

9. The topic is **warning signs of teenage suicide**.

10. **(1)** The main idea is that there are warning signs of suicide. The other sentences in the paragraph give three examples.

11. The topic is **African-American men's roles in the American Revolution**.

12. **(3)** The main idea is that thousands of African-American men had important roles in the Revolution. All the other sentences in the paragraph give examples of those men's roles.

13. **(1)** The main idea is that the vote was extended by amendments. The other two sentences give examples of those amendments.

14. **(1)** The main idea is that the economy has something to do with how many jobs there are. The other two sentences give details that explain how the economy affects job availability.

15. **(3)** The main idea is that the Constitution still works, even though it is old. The first two sentences give details about how old the Constitution is. The last sentence gives the detail that explains why it still works.

EXERCISE 6 (PAGE 39)

1. **(1)** The first sentence says that early in the Revolutionary War an English victory looked probable. The rest of the sentences explain why that was so.

2. England sent **30,000** men. Scanning the paragraph for a number may have helped you answer the question.

3. **(a) and (c)** To answer this question, scanning the paragraph for these words may have helped: *George Washington*, *large and well-trained*, *defeated*, and *destroyed*. You may also have remembered which parts of the paragraph had the details you needed.

4. **(a) and (c)** The second and fourth sentences mention these details. Scanning for the capitalized word, *Hessians*, may have helped you. You also may have remembered that the Hessians' defeat was mentioned near the end of the paragraph.

5. **(3)** The question asks you to identify a detail that gives an example of the main idea. Choice (1) is the main idea, so it is not an example. Choice (2) does not mention French support or give an example of it.

6. **(2)** This detail is mentioned in the middle of the paragraph in the sentence that begins with *Up to then*. You may have had to reread part of the paragraph to find it.

7. **(b) and (c)** The question asks you to identify details that give examples of the main idea. Choices (a) and (d) do not mention unsatisfactory aspects of retirement.

EXERCISE 7 (PAGE 45)

1. This sentence introduces the part of the paragraph about the bad side of middle age: **Middle age has its down side**.

2. The paragraph mentions these three bad points about middle age: (a) **it's harder to keep in physical shape**, (b) **you realize you're getting older**, and (c) **you may feel less positive about life**.

3. This sentence introduces the part of the paragraph about the good side of middle age: **In other ways, middle age has its benefits**.

4. The paragraph mentions these three good points about middle age: (a) **it can bring a feeling of "having arrived,"** (b) **you can feel settled and satisfied with what you've accomplished**, and (c) **you may feel good that your children are grown and managing on their own**.

5. **(3)** The first part of the paragraph is about the down side of middle age. The second part is about the benefits of middle age. The first part contrasts with the second.

6. A child begins to speak sometime around his or her first birthday.

7. A child can say as many as 20 words by about **eighteen months**.

8. At age two, a child expresses each thought in **one or two words**.

9. A child can say about 900 words at **three years of age**.

10. **(1)** The paragraph uses time order to explain how a child's vocabulary grows from 1 word at age one to 900 words at age three.

11. These phrases are clues that the paragraph is organized by classification: **two main reasons**, **one reason**, and **The other reason**.

12. People lose their jobs by **being laid off**. People lose their jobs by **being fired**.

13. **(2)** The details in the paragraph are in two groups. The first group is about job loss due to the economy. The second group is about job loss due to poor performance.

EXERCISE 8 (PAGE 48)

1. The footnote explains that **the figures are for 1986**.

2. **$413**. In the *Job* column, find *Clerk*. Find the figure for that row in the *Earnings for Males* column.

3. **$291**. In the *Job* column, find *Clerk*. Find the figure for that row in the *Earnings for Females* column.

4. **$409**. In the *Job* column, find *Mechanic*. Find the figure for that row in the *Earnings for Females* column.

5. **Male drivers**. They earned $375, which is more than the $296 that female drivers earned.

6. According to the table, iron is used in **machines**, **cars**, **pipes**, and **ships**. You could have answered with any two of those uses.

7. **Nuclear energy**. In the *Metals* column, find *Uranium*. Find what the *Uses* column says for that row.

8. **Five**. Find *Silver* in the *Metals* column. In that row, count the number of places listed in the *Major Mining Locations* column.

9. **No**. Find *Aluminum* in the *Metals* column. In that row under *Major Mining Locations*, see if the United States is listed.

EXERCISE 9 (PAGE 54)

1. **About 7.5 million**. (You would be correct if you answered 7.6 million.) You need to estimate the answer because the point for 1980 is almost even with the *7.5* on the side of the graph.

2. **About 4 million**. (You would be correct if you answered 3.9 million.) You need to estimate the answer because the point for 1960 is almost even with the *4.0* on the side of the graph.

3. **(1)** The line of the graph goes down between 1940 and 1950. Between each other pair of years, it goes up.

4. The number of unemployed workers was lowest in **1950** and highest in **1940**. They have the lowest and highest points on the line of the graph.

5. **About 30 million**. (You would be correct if you answered 29 million.) You need to estimate the answer because the bar for 1900 reaches almost to the *30* on the side of the graph. The numbers on the side represent millions.

6. **About 105 million**. (You would be correct if you answered 106 or 107 million.) You need to estimate the answer because the bar for 1980 stops about halfway between the *100* and the *110* on the side of the graph. The numbers on the side represent millions.

7. **1950**. The bar for 1950 reaches a point just above the *60* on the side of the graph. The numbers on the side represent millions.

8. **(2)** The bar for 1940 is about half as long as the bar for 1980. Compared to the halfway mark on the 1980 bar, the bar for 1970 is longer and the one for 1910 is shorter.

9. **(3)** The largest section of the graph represents the continent with the most people.

10. **10%.** The section that represents North America has *10%* in it.

11. **Antarctica** is not included, as the footnote to the graph explains.

12. **(1)** Africa and North America each have 10% of the world's population.

EXERCISE 10 (PAGE 60)

1. The Battle of **Lexington** (1775) is the earliest date shown.

2. The Battle of Savannah is shown with a black circle, which means that it was won by the **British**.

3. The two forts in New York were **Ft. Ticonderoga** and **West Point**.

4. The last battle shown, with the latest date, is the Battle of **Yorktown** (1781).

5. Ft. Sunbury was located in **Georgia**.

6. **(3)** Of the three choices, only California is covered with the pattern that means $21,000 to $24,000.

7. **Texas** has a higher average yearly wage than Tennessee. The pattern that covers Texas is darker than the one that covers Tennessee.

8. The pattern shows that the average yearly wage in Pennsylvania was in the category **$19,000 to $21,000**.

9. The three states covered with the darkest pattern are **Alaska**, **Connecticut**, and **New York**.

SOCIAL STUDIES READINGS 1

History Readings (page 62)

1. **(2)** The words *British settlement* appear twice at the beginning of the paragraph. All the details in the paragraph are about the the British settlement of America. (Previewing Paragraphs)

2. There were **thirteen** colonies in 1750. (Reading for Details)

3. There were **more than 1.5 million** people in the colonies by 1750. (Reading for Details)

4. The paragraph mentions three reasons that people came to the colonies: **for freedom to follow their own religions**, **to escape poverty**, and **because they were forced to come**. You could have answered with any two of those reasons. (Seeing How Details Are Organized)

5. **(1)** The main idea sentence tells which differences among the colonies the paragraph discusses. The supporting sentences give examples of those differences.(Finding the Main Idea and Supporting Sentences)

6. **(2)** The details in the paragraph are in three categories, one for each of the groups of colonies. (Seeing How Details Are Organized)

7. The **New England colonies**, the **middle colonies**, and the **southern colonies**. (Reading for Details)

8. The four middle colonies were **New York**, **Pennsylvania**, **New Jersey**, and **Delaware**. (Reading for Details)

9. The **middle colonies** had many small farms. (Reading for Details)

10. The **southern colonies** had large plantations. (Reading for Details)

11. **Main idea: (a) Supporting sentences: (b) and (c).** Choices (b) and (c) give examples of reasons the colonists were unhappy with British rule. (Finding the Main Idea and Supporting Sentences)

12. **(2)** This detail is stated in the third sentence of the paragraph. (Reading for Details)

13. Besides taxes, the paragraph mentions three reasons the colonists were unhappy with British rule: they didn't like **(a) laws that forced them to sell certain goods only to Britain; (b) laws that forced them to buy certain goods from Britain; (c) being ruled by a faraway country**. You could have answered with any one of those reasons. (Reading for Details)

14. **(1)** This is the main idea. All the other sentences in the paragraph explain the two struggles in more detail. (Finding the Sentence That States the Main Idea)

15. Fighting in the American Revolution began in **1775**. (Reading for Details)

16. The Constitution was written in **1787**. (Reading for Details)

17. As the first two sentences say, geography studies (a) **the earth** and (b) **the relationship between the earth and human beings**. (Reading for Details)

18. The paragraph says the earth affects people's choice of work, clothes, and houses. Your answer could be one of those examples or one that was not in the paragraph. (Reading for Details)

19. The paragraph says people affect the earth by digging mines, building dams, and discarding waste. Your answer could be one of those examples or one that was not in the paragraph. (Reading for Details)

20. **(3)** The answer is stated, in slightly different words, in the first sentence of the paragraph. (Reading for Details)

21. **Parts of the ocean**, or **the oceans**, separate the continents from each other. This detail is in the sentence that begins *Since then*. (Reading for Details)

22. The **Pacific Ocean** is larger than all the continents. (Reading for Details)

23. **(1)** The other sentences in the paragraph explain how the earth changes or, like Choices (2) and (3), give examples of change. (Finding the Main Idea and Supporting Sentences)

24. **Weathering** causes rocks to break down. (Reading for Details)

25. **(a) and (b)** Of the choices, only these two can move weathered rock. (Seeing How Details Are Organized)

26. **(1)** Other sentences in the paragraph, like Choice (2), explain why there are different climate regions. Some, like Choice (3), give examples of climate regions. (Finding the Sentence That States the Main Idea)

27. The tropical region is located **near the equator**; the warm and cold regions, **between the tropical and polar regions**; the polar regions, **near the North and South Poles**. (Finding Details in Maps)

28. The warmest climate region is (a) **the tropical region**. It is warm there (b) **because the sun hits that area almost directly**. (Reading for Details)

29. As the first sentence says, most people contribute **in three ways**. (Reading for Details)

30. **(2)** When consumers spend money on goods and services, they are buying things. (Reading for Details)

31. **(3)** The last three sentences explain that taxpayers support the community through taxes paid to the government. (Reading for Details)

32. Workers sell **their labor** on the labor market. (Reading for Details)

33. **(a) and (c)** When workers' skills are rare (a), they are in small supply. When an employer needs workers' skills a lot (c), those skills are in great demand. Both situations make wages higher. Situations (b) and (d) would make wages lower. (Seeing How Details Are Organized)

34. **(4)** If many people have certain skills, those skills are in greater supply. The price (wages) paid for those skills is lower. (Reading for Details)

35. **(1)** This is explained in Example 1. (Reading for Details)

36. **(3)** This is explained in Example 2. (Reading for Details)

37. **(1)** This is explained in Example 3. (Reading for Details)

38. As the first prediction says, there will be more **women** and **young people** in the labor market. (Reading for Details)

39. **(1)** As the second prediction says, there will be about 20 million more jobs in the year 2000. (Reading for Details)

40. As the last prediction says, the demand for workers with **post high school education** and **job training** will increase most. (Reading for Details)

Political Science Readings (page 68)

41. **(1)** The other sentences in the paragraph explain or give examples of how the Americans' first two governments did not have the right amount of power. (Finding the Main Idea and Supporting Sentences)

42. **(1)** As the second sentence says, the colonists thought the British government was too powerful. (Reading for Details)

43. **(3)** The passage says there was no president under the Articles. There were states: *each state did pretty much what it wanted to do.* There was **a weak Congress.** (Reading for Details)

44. **(3)** The last sentence of the paragraph above the table says that the Constitution brought a stronger central government. (Reading for Details)

45. (a) **Articles of Confederation**, because courts were only in the states; (b) **Constitution**; (c) **Articles of Confederation**; (d) **Constitution**. (Finding Details in Tables)

46. **(3)** The first and second sentences explain that a federal system divides powers. (Reading for Details)

47. **The Constitution** made federalism the form of government in the United States. (Reading for Details)

48. **(2)** The last sentence of the paragraph gives the answer. Other sentences show that Choices (1) and (3) are not shared powers. (Reading for Details)

49. **(2)** The second sentence of the paragraph explains this. (Reading for Details)

50. The president is part of the **executive branch**; Congress is part of the **legislative branch**; the Supreme Court is part of the **judicial branch**. (Reading for Details)

51. The **legislative branch** of government makes laws. (Reading for Details)

Behavioral Science Readings (page 70)

52. **(2)** The first sentence says that all people develop in much the same way. (Reading for Details)

53. People experience **physical**, **cognitive**, and **psychological and social** changes. (Reading for Details)

54. Learning to talk is a **cognitive** change. (Reading for Details)

55. A young child has the greatest need for **security**, a feeling of safety. (Reading for Details)

56. As children get older, they need to feel **confident** and **independent**. (Reading for Details)

57. **(3)** The last part of the paragraph explains this. The other two choices have to do with

younger children's need for security. (Reading for Details)

58. **(3)** The other choices tell who adolescents are (Choice 1), explain part of the reason they need to develop a sense of identity (Choice 2), and tell what having a sense of identity means (Choice 4). (Finding the Main Idea and Supporting Sentences)

59. Adolescents are **teenagers**, or are in the teenage years. (Reading for Details)

60. **(3)** This is stated in the next to last sentence in the paragraph. (Reading for Details)

61. **(3)** The categories are the three stages of adulthood. (Seeing How Details Are Organized)

62. **(1)** The second sentence in the paragraph gives the answer. (Reading for Details)

63. Many people in middle adulthood get a sense of accomplishment from **their jobs**. (You might also have answered **community work**.) (Reading for Details)

64. After age 65 people's needs are related to **the fact that their lives are closing**. (Reading for Details)

GED PRACTICE 1 (page 73)

1. **(2)** This question asks about the main idea, which is stated in the first sentence of the paragraph. The problems in the other choices are not mentioned in the paragraph. (Finding the Main Idea and Supporting Sentences/Economics)

2. **(4)** This detail is mentioned just below the middle of the paragraph. Choices (1) to (3) have to do with job-related education, not day care. Choice (5) is not mentioned in the paragraph. (Reading for Details/Economics)

3. **(3)** This detail is mentioned in the last sentence of the paragraph. The paragraph doesn't mention Choices (2), (4), or (5) as related to job-related education. It doesn't mention Choice (1) at all. (Reading for Details/Economics)

4. **(4)** This detail is mentioned in the second sentence of the paragraph. The percent that goes with Choice (1) is 20 percent. No percents are given for the groups in Choices (2), (3), and (5). (Reading for Details/Geography)

5. **(3)** All of the other sentences give examples or explanations that support this idea. (Finding the Main Idea and Supporting Sentences/Geography)

6. **(4)** With slightly different wording, each of the other choices is mentioned in the paragraph. For example, the words *cannot afford* are used twice to mention Choice (5). (Reading for Details/Geography)

7. **(4)** The bar is longest for this group. (Finding Details in Graphs/Political Science)

8. **(1)** The bar is shortest for this group. (Finding Details in Graphs/Political Science)

9. **(4)** The bar stretches to a point about halfway between 60 percent and 70 percent. (Finding Details in Graphs/Political Science)

10. **(4)** The bar for the age group 65–74 is the first one that is shorter than the one for the younger group next to it. The bar for the next older group, 75 and over (75+), is even shorter. (Finding Details in Graphs/Political Science)

UNIT 2 INFERRING AS YOU READ

EXERCISE 11 (PAGE 79)

1. **(1)** *Extinction* is the state of having gone out of existence. The context that follows *extinction* in the passage says that the northern states prohibited slavery and that slaves could no longer be brought to the United States.

2. **(2)** The context that follows *prohibited* in the passage says that by 1808 slaves could no longer be brought to the United States. Since it was action by the northern states that led to the temporary end of slavery, the northern states must have refused to permit slavery. The northern states did not allow— and certainly did not encourage—slavery.

3. **(2)** Slavery had been going out of existence, but the cotton gin gave it new life. That is clear from the fact that the South became dependent on slavery after the invention of the cotton gin and after slavery had been prohibited throughout the United States.

EXERCISE 12 (PAGE 81)

1. **(2)** *Partnership* is defined in the third sentence.

2. A share is **a part into which a corporation is divided**.

3. A **shareholder** is a part owner of a corporation.

4. *Business revenue* means **money earned by businesses**.

EXERCISE 13 (PAGE 85)

1. **(2)** The meaning of *socially dominant* is suggested by two examples. Socially dominant people are more likely (1) to express opinions in groups, and (2) to be leaders. The examples are signaled by the phrase *For example*.

2. **(1)** The last sentence in the paragraph contrasts innate differences with learned behaviors. If a difference is not learned, it must be inborn. The contrast is signaled by the word *or*.

3. **(2)** *Populous* means "full of people." *Populous states* contrasts with *States with few people* in the previous sentence. The contrast is signaled by the phrase *In contrast*.

4. **(2)** *Protracted struggle* in the last sentence contrasts with *short war* in the first sentence. The contrast is signaled by the word *Instead*.

5. *Casualties* here means **deaths**. It contrasts with the idea in the second sentence that the war would cost *few lives*. The contrast is signaled by the word *Instead*.

EXERCISE 14 (PAGE 88)

1. **(1)** The last part of the paragraph indicates that discussions of slavery came up *Time after time*. Choice (2) is contradicted by the passage; Choice (3) isn't suggested by the passage.

2. **(3)** The passage says that the North and South had different viewpoints on slavery. It indicates that *Congress came up with compromises* to try to resolve their differences.

3. **(2)** The passage says that the basic objective of a business is to make a profit. Your experience tells you that businesses have the goal of making money. You can guess, therefore, that *objective* means "goal."

4. **(1)** The passage says that a profit is made if money taken in exceeds money spent. Your experience tells you that a profit is money left over after costs. Therefore, for there to be a profit the amount of money taken in must be greater than money spent.

5. The passage is about two different ways of making sweaters. Therefore, *production* is "the process of **making**, or **manufacturing**."

6. **(2)** After the passage says that *the production of sweaters . . . has been mechanized*, it says sweaters are now made by machine. Mechanized production must be production using machines.

7. **(2)** The second sentence indicates that a bill *becomes* a law, *not* that it *is* a law. Therefore, a bill must be a suggested law.

8. **(2)** The relevant committee for a farm bill is the Committee on Agriculture. That committee's interests are related to farms. They are relevant to farms.

9. The last paragraph indicates that bills are changed on their way to becoming laws. Therefore, *modified* must mean "**changed**."

EXERCISE 15 (PAGE 93)

1. **(2)** The passage says that large countries tend to have many natural resources. It then says that it's not surprising that the United States produces more minerals than most other countries. You can infer that the United States is a large country with more land area than other countries. There is not enough information in the paragraph to allow the inferences in Choices (1) and (3).

2. **(2)** The passage says that the soil is good for farming. Therefore, Choices (1) and (3) can't be correct. Since large farms are possible only in the flat valleys of this mountain area, you can infer that the land is too steep to be usable.

3. General Sherman took Atlanta, an important southern city. Its capture was an important victory for the North. Therefore, you can infer that Sherman fought for the North.

4. **(2)** Lincoln's opponents, the Democrats, wanted immediate peace. You can infer that Lincoln had the opposite opinion and preferred continuing the war in order to obtain a victory.

5. **The Republican party** won the election of 1864. The Democrats wanted to end the war. The Republicans wanted to continue the war. The victory in Atlanta affected the result of the election. Since the war continued until there was a northern victory, you can infer that Atlanta's surrender encouraged people to vote for the Republicans.

6. **(2)** You can infer that if the Democrats had been elected in 1864, the North might have given up on the war and made peace with the South.

7. Only **(a) and (b)** can be inferred—both from the first two sentences of the passage. These sentences taken together suggest that today, as in the past, women earn less than men, Choice (a), even though, in contrast to the past, many women work outside the home, Choice (b).

8. **(1)** You can infer this opinion from the writer's saying that women, many of whom now work outside the home, have made progress and that their situation is better than in the past.

9. **No**. **The writer says that despite progress, women still have a distance to go**.

10. **(1)** The passage says that the rivers of the Rio de la Plata system are useful. It also says that rivers that are short are not useful. You can infer that the Rio de la Plata rivers are not short.

11. **(3)** In its discussion about the Amazon, the passage indicates that useful rivers must pass through populated areas. You can infer that many people live in the area through which the Rio de la Plata system passes, since it is useful. Choice (2) must be wrong. Nothing suggests Choices (1) and (4).

12. **(2)** The passage begins by saying that modern means of transportation have largely replaced river transportation. It says the Rio de la Plata system was more important for transportation until recently. You can infer that more modern means of transportation are now used in the area around the Rio de la Plata system.

13. **(2)** The examples tell how parents and TV give children ideas about how girls and boys should each behave. These examples do not fit with Choice (1). The passage suggests that behaviors are learned from both parents and the television—Choice (2). Choice (3) concerns TV only.

EXERCISE 16 (PAGE 100)

1. **(4)** The cartoon shows a contest between a handgun and a pop gun. The pop gun is labeled "U.S. Handgun Laws." It will lose the contest. From this you can infer that the cartoon's point is that U.S. handgun laws are too weak to control handguns.

2. **(3)** The bars on the graph show that each major car maker's earnings were lower in 1992 than in 1990. You can infer that to earn less money in 1992 than in 1990, the car makers must have sold fewer cars in 1992 than in 1990. You cannot make the inference in Choice (1) because the graph shows earnings, not profits. There is nothing in the graph about U.S. car makers' earnings or about the prices of Japanese cars, so you cannot make the inference in Choices (2) and (4).

EXERCISE 17 (PAGE 104)

1. **(2)** The paragraph discusses the improved muskets used in the Civil War, the lack of change in battle strategies, and the high number of deaths that resulted. Choices (1) and (3) simply restate supporting ideas from the paragraph.

2. **(3)** The women in the experiment expressed more emotion than men but apparently didn't experience more emotion. If the experiment was well run, you can infer that its findings apply to most people. Choices (1) and (4) are stated or implied by the paragraph but relate only to small parts of the paragraph. Choice (2) may be true but is not even implied by the paragraph.

3. **(1)** The paragraph indicates that political affiliation plays a major role in determining how well the president and Congress work together. Its examples show that cooperation is greater when many congresspeople are from the same party as the president.

Choice (2) summarizes the paragraph's examples. Choice (3) makes a statement broader than the ideas expressed in the paragraph. Choice (4) states a truth that is not even implied by the paragraph.

EXERCISE 18 (PAGE 107)

1. **(1)** All the sentences in the paragraph support the main idea offered by Choice (1).

2. **(2)** With the addition of the second paragraph, the topic of the passage becomes broader. It is about how a group's use of natural resources determines their way of life. In this context, the main point of the first paragraph is to give an example of this idea.

EXERCISE 19 (PAGE 110)

1. **(4)** The first paragraph is about competition and how it helps the consumer. The second paragraph is about monopolies and how they hurt the consumer. Choices (1), (2), and (3) offer supporting statements or inferences that can be drawn from the passage.

2. **(3)** The first paragraph describes how a bill moves through Congress. The second tells how bills introduced in Congress change before they reach the president. Choice (1) states a truth that is not mentioned in the passage. Choice (2) restates the first sentence of the passage, which contains only a supporting idea, not the main idea of the passage.

SOCIAL STUDIES READINGS 2

History Readings (page 112)

1. **(2)** In the passage *sectionalism* is described as people placing *more importance on their region than on the United States as a whole.* (Recognizing Definitions and Synonyms)

2. **(1)** The other sentences in the paragraph give examples that support the main idea. (Finding the Sentence That States the Main Idea.)

3. **(3)** The four paragraphs in the passage discuss, in this order, territorial expansion, sectionalism, diversity, and the disagreement over slavery. The last sentence implies that these factors combined led to the Civil War. The statement in Choice (1) is too general to be the main idea of the passage. The statement in Choice (2) does not include any of the ideas in the first three paragraphs of the passage. (Inferring the Main Idea of a Passage)

4. **(1)** The events described in the first paragraph led to war. Because of them war was unavoidable. (Using the General Context)

5. The volunteers the North and South sought were **soldiers**. You can infer this because the paragraph is about events leading up to war. (Understanding Meanings from Context)

6. **(2)** The first sentence says that on the surface the North had all the advantages. The paragraph goes on to list these advantages. Then it adds that these advantages were *crucial to the war effort*. Choice (1) restates only part of the thought from only the last sentence in the paragraph. Choice (3) gives only two examples of the North's advantages. (Inferring the Main Idea of a Paragraph in a Passage)

7. **The North** won the battle of Gettysburg. You can infer this because Gettysburg ended Lee's invasion of the North and became a turning point in the war that had begun with Southern military successes. (Making Inferences from Written Material)

8. **(1)** The third sentence says *Lincoln* **finally** *found capable generals*. He must not have had capable generals at first. (Making Inferences from Written Material)

9. **(1)** The paragraph shows that the North had gained the advantage because of Gettysburg and the appointment of capable generals. The paragraph goes on to say *Even so, the Confederate army persevered*. Choice (2) is not implied by information in the paragraph. Choice (3) ignores the words *Even so*, which introduce a contrast. (Using Examples and Contrasts)

10. The Civil War **(a) ended slavery** (see the beginning of the third paragraph), **(b) strengthened the national government** (see the sentence beginning with *First* in the fourth paragraph), and **(c) encouraged the development of industry** (see the sentence be-

ginning with *Second* in the fourth paragraph). (Reading for Details)

Geography Readings (page115)

11. **(3)** Land formations (terrain) are part of the physical environment, not part of culture. (Seeing How Details Are Organized)

12. **(2)** The first paragraph is about how their environment influences the way people live. The second paragraph is about how their culture influences the way people live. The third paragraph shows how both their environment and their culture influence the way people live. The main idea covers the information in all three paragraphs. The statement in Choice (1) is not even implied in the passage. The statement in Choice (3) is the main idea of the third paragraph but not the main idea of the passage. (Inferring the Main Idea of a Passage)

13. **(3)** The last sentence says *we will always depend on our physical environment*. (Reading for Details)

14. **(2)** The second example in the second paragraph says that the problems of dry and flooded land have been overcome by *modern methods of irrigation and flood control*. Since flood control overcomes flooding, irrigation must overcome dryness. Since dryness is overcome by supplying water, you can infer the meaning of *irrigation*. (Using the General Context)

15. The passage gives four examples to show how the Industrial Revolution has helped people overcome their environment. Although your wording may be different, you should have given one of these examples: (1) **Cities can now be located anywhere because water is no longer the main means of transportation**, (2) **Because of modern irrigation and flood control, land that was once useless can now grow crops**, (3) **Cars allow us to move around freely**, and (4) **Factories make goods that allow us to live better**. (Seeing How Details Are Organized)

16. The passage gives two examples to show how the Industrial Revolution has caused harm to the environment. Although your wording may be different, you should have given one of these examples: (1) **Cars pollute our air** or (2) **Factories pollute the air and water on which we depend**. (Seeing How Details Are Organized)

17. The fourth paragraph explains that a nonrenewable resource is a **resource that cannot be replaced**. (Recognizing Definitions and Synonyms)

18. **(3)** The passage explains how the Industrial Revolution has increased people's effect on and dependence on their environment. The first paragraph introduces the Industrial Revolution. The second and third paragraphs explain how we now affect the environment more than before the Industrial Revolution. The fourth paragraph explains how we are more dependent on the environment now than before the Industrial Revolution. The last paragraph summarizes the points made in the second, third, and fourth paragraphs. (Inferring the Main Idea of a Passage)

Economics Readings (page 116)

19. **(2)** The definition of a capitalist economic system is given in the second sentence of the passage. (Recognizing Definitions and Synonyms)

20. **(2)** The last paragraph says that businesses can charge whatever they wish for products and services. It also implies that to attract customers, businesses keep prices reasonable. This is a benefit to the customer. Even though the passage says that competition under a free enterprise system often results in high-quality products and services, it does not say that *all* products and services are of high quality, so Choice (1) is not correct. The statement in Choice (3) is not implied in the passage and, as your experience tells you, is incorrect. (Making Inferences from Written Material)

21. **(1)** The second paragraph says that if the income of a business is *lower than or equal to its costs, the business will not make a profit.* From that you can infer that making a profit requires an income higher than costs. (Making Inferences from Written Material)

22. The first paragraph implies that low prices attract customers. You can infer that if a business charges high prices, **it will lose customers and won't sell enough to make a profit**. (Making Inferences from Written Material)

23. **(2)** The last paragraph explains why the profit motive benefits customers only when there is competition. (Reading for Details)

24. **(3)** The paragraph says that the government makes laws to protect consumers and gives, as an example, ensuring product safety. Since a guarantee of product safety would protect consumers, you can infer that *ensure* means "guarantee." The definitions offered in Choices (1) and (2) do not fit the context. (Using the General Context)

25. **(4)** The last sentence of the passage implies that businesses decide for themselves what goods and services to provide consumers. (This idea was also stated in the economics reading titled "The U.S. Economic System.") The passage mentions the activities in Choices (1), (2), and (3) as parts of the government's role. (Making Inferences from Written Material)

26. **(3)** The examples in the first paragraph of the passage show that the government controls certain business practices. The second paragraph says that the government provides some products and services. The third paragraph explains that the United States' economic system is basically capitalistic. By summarizing these three ideas, you can infer the main idea of the passage. (Inferring the Main Idea of a Passage)

Political Science Readings (page 118)

27. **(3)** The passage says that the Constitution established three branches of government so that power would not be concentrated in one person or group. Having three branches of government is supposed to prevent tyranny, which you can infer would be government by one person or group with too much power. Choices (1) and (2) do not fit the context. (Using the General Context)

28. Your statement of the second paragraph's main idea should say something like the following: **Each branch of the government has a role to play with regard to the country's laws**. (Inferring the Main Idea of a Paragraph)

29. **(4)** The first paragraph says that the number of representatives from each state depends on the state's population. You can infer that less-populous states have fewer representatives. (Making Inferences from Written Material)

30. **(2)** You can infer from the note to the diagram that money bills must start in the House of Representatives. Choice (1) is wrong because bills are referred to committees, not introduced to committees. Choice (3) is not supported by the diagram, which doesn't show the president introducing a bill to Congress. (Making Inferences from Graphic Material)

31. As the end of the first paragraph says, the cabinet is made up of **the president's advisers, the heads of government agencies appointed by the president**. (Reading for Details)

32. Besides carrying out laws, the president is **(a) the leader of the country, (b) commander-in-chief of the military**, and **(c) leader of his or her political party**. These functions are described in the last paragraph. (Seeing How Details Are Organized)

33. **(1)** The third paragraph says that when *a district court's decision is appealed, the case is heard in an appeals court.* You can infer that an appealed case is taken to a higher court for further consideration. Therefore, a case that is appealed has not been settled to everyone's satisfaction, as in Choice (2), or dropped, as in Choice (3). (Making Inferences from Written Material)

34. *Unconstitutional* means **not supported by the Constitution**. You can infer this from the context provided in the last paragraph. It says that the Supreme Court decides *whether laws can be supported by the Constitution.* It also says that laws found unconstitutional *cannot stand.* (Using the General Context)

35. **(3)** The Supreme Court is the most powerful federal court because when a case is appealed and referred to the Supreme Court, its decision is final, as the last paragraph says. (Reading for Details)

Behavioral Science Readings (page 120)

36. **(1)** The definition of *innate* is given in the sentence that follows its use in the passage. (Recognizing Definitions and Synonyms)

37. The first sentence of the paragraph states the main idea: **One question behavioral scientists ask is why there are gender differences in behavior**. All the other sentences in the paragraph ask related ques-

tions. (Finding the Sentence That States the Main Idea.)

38. As the beginning of the second paragraph says, behavioral scientists study gender differences **by studying behavior differences between men and women in different cultures**. (Reading for Details)

39. **(1)** If a behavior differs from culture to culture, it cannot be innate. It must be something that people learn from their culture. Nothing in the paragraph implies that any behavior difference is unimportant. (Making Inferences from Written Material)

40. **(3)** The first paragraph of the passage discusses the results of lab experiments on gender differences in behavior. The second paragraph discusses the results of cross-cultural studies on the same differences. The results of both types of research are summed up in this statement of the main idea. The statement in Choice (1) mentions only an example from the second paragraph. The statement in Choice (2) contradicts the information in the passage. (Inferring the Main Idea of a Passage)

41. **(3)** The first paragraph says that differences in expressing emotion are cultural, but that differences in aggressiveness are at least partly biological. Therefore Choice (3) is correct and Choice (1) is incorrect. Choice (2) is incorrect because cross-cultural studies have shown that men are typically more socially dominant than women, as the last paragraph says. (Making Inferences from Written Material)

42. **(2)** The first paragraph says that new evidence may force scientists to draw new conclusions about behavioral differences between men and women. You can infer, therefore, that the conclusions scientists have drawn so far are not final. (Understanding Meanings from Context)

43. **(1)** The second paragraph says that scientists have found a relationship between testosterone levels and levels of aggression. Since testosterone is a biological agent, not a social one, the root of gender differences in aggressive behavior seems to be biological. (Making Inferences from Written Material)

44. *Diminish* means **decrease**. The last sentence in the paragraph gives an example that illustrates how gender differences decrease with age. (Using Examples and Contrasts)

1. **(2)** Minimum-wage workers earned at the same hourly rate in 1989 as in 1981. Because prices had gone up, their unchanged income bought them less in 1989. Choice (4) is contradicted by the passage, which illustrates that increasing the minimum wage requires legislation. Choice (5) directly contradicts information in the second sentence of the passage. Nothing in the passage allows you to make the inferences in Choices (1) and (3). (Making Inferences from Written Material/Political Science)

2. **(3)** Congress tried to override the president's veto so that the bill would become law, but didn't have enough votes. You can infer that a bill can become law if enough congresspeople vote for it again after it has been vetoed. Since Choice (3) is correct, Choice (1) is wrong. Nothing in the passage allows you to make the inferences in Choices (2), (4), and (5). (Making Inferences from Written Material/Political Science)

3. **(3)** The last paragraph of the passage states that *the final bill contained a training wage, but only for teenagers who were new workers.* An increase to $5.25 per hour—as in Choice (1)—was originally favored by some members of the House, and a training wage for all new workers—as in Choice (2)—was originally favored by the president. Neither was part of the compromise. The ideas in Choices (4) and (5) are not mentioned in the passage. (Reading for Details/Political Science)

4. **(5)** The passage illustrates how the legislative and executive branches worked together to reach a compromise that solved a problem. None of the ideas in Choices (1), (2), (3), or (4) can be inferred from the passage. (Inferring the Main Idea of a Passage/Political Science)

5. **(2)** Since owners have lost money in recent years, their income must have been lower than their costs. Since players' salaries have risen, you can infer that owners' income from TV networks has not risen as much. Therefore Choice (1) is wrong. No information in the passage allows you to make the inferences in Choices (3), (4), and (5). (Making Inferences from Written Material/Economics)

6. **(5)** The circle represents 100 percent—all—of the sources of energy the United States relies on for energy. The largest section of the graph stands for "oil," so oil is the source of energy the United States relies on most. (Finding Details in Graphs/Geography)

7. **(1)** The sections of the graph that stand for the nonrenewable resources (coal, natural gas, and oil) make up 85 percent of the graph. Therefore, the United States is dependent on nonrenewable natural resources for 85 percent of its energy needs and on other resources for only 15 percent. Since Choice (1) is correct, Choices (2), (3), and (4) cannot be. There is nothing in the graph that allows you to make the inference in Choice (5). (Making Inferences from Graphic Material/Geography)

8. **(2)** The passage indicates that negative campaigning involves candidates *calling one another liars and crooks.* You can infer that a negative campaign is one in which candidates attack each other verbally. (Using the General Context/Political Science)

9. **(3)** The passage ends with a quote from a voter who had been exposed to a negative campaign. This voter said, "*Its not worth voting for anyone.*" You can infer that a negative campaign may make voters form bad opinions of the candidates involved and discourage them from voting at all. (Inferring the Main Idea of a Passage/Political Science)

10. **(1)** The cartoon shows Uncle Sam putting all his money and talent into the arms race. He wonders why the Japanese build better cars. He doesn't seem to realize that the money and talent that the United States could use to develop better cars—and other things—are all spent on the arms race. The cartoon's point is that the United States should spend less on the arms race. (Making Inferences from Graphic Material/Economics)

UNIT 3   THINKING CRITICALLY AS YOU READ

EXERCISE 20 (PAGE 130)

1. **(2)** By rejecting the president's signing of a treaty, Congress checks the president's power to make agreements with foreign countries.

2. **(1)** By appointing some judges, the president can choose people who might rule on legal issues as the president would like. In this way, the president checks the powers of the courts.

3. **(2)** By overriding the president's veto, Congress checks the president's power to veto a bill.

4. **(2)** Inuit people live in the Arctic regions of Canada and Alaska, where snow and ice are plentiful.

5. **(3)** Through the amnesty program, immigrants were welcomed to the United States. Choices (1) and (2) describe ways the U.S. government controls travel and limits immigration to the United States.

EXERCISE 21 (PAGE 135)

1. **(1)** The graph shows that the number of car registrations increased sharply in the first ten years of the twentieth century. Similarly, the sales of personal computers increased sharply in the first years they were on the market. Beta VCR sales rose and then fell. Air conditioner sales rose slowly.

2. **(1)** Because U.S. fish consumption increased sharply during the three years shown on the graph, it probably increased more in Year 4. Phil probably ordered more fish than ever in Year 4.

3. **(3)** Coffee consumption has remained steady at 7.6 pounds per person for the three years shown on the graph. That suggests that with or without advertising, people will not change the amount of coffee they drink. There's no way to tell from the graph whether people switch brands or the type of coffee they drink.

4. **(1)** The map shows that in middle and southern parts of the East there are several large population centers close together. The other regions' population centers are far from each other.

5. **(3)** The military probably looked for an area with few people. The Interior West is the least densely populated area of the United States.

6. **(2)** The planner would use a population map to place social service agencies near people. The retired person would use a climate map; the farmer would use an agricultural products map.

7. **(2)** Since Republicans and Democrats often disagree on issues, a president uses the veto power more often when Congress is controlled by the opposition party.

EXERCISE 22 (PAGE 139)

1. **(1)** Giving praise is a form of reward for good behavior.

2. **(2)** Being sent to her room is a form of punishment because it's unpleasant for the child to be separated from her playmate and made to stay alone.

3. **(3)** A credit union is often operated for a group of employees, as Jake's is.

4. **(1)** A commercial bank is the only lending institution that offers the kinds of services the Blaines used.

5. **(2)** Spark plugs are standard parts that can replace each other.

6. **(3)** Robots are a type of machine used to automate labor.

EXERCISE 23 (PAGE 144)

1. **(3)** Since industry needs fuel for energy, the lack of such resources has caused industry to develop slowly in southern Europe.

2. **(3)** The number of nursery school children more than doubled in twenty years. Certainly more nursery school workers were needed to teach and care for all those children.

3. **(1)** To encourage students to graduate, West Virginia punished them for truancy. For teenagers, who often see driving as a mark of adulthood and independence, having their licenses taken away for cutting school is a severe punishment.

4. **(1)** Labor unions typically oppose business leaders. It is reasonable that the depression encouraged people to look to unions for leadership.

5. **(2)** Single people living away from their parents and families breaking into two households both contribute to an increase in the number of households in the United States.

EXERCISE 24 (PAGE 147)

1. **(3)** Although many people prospered during the 1920s, farmers, workers, and people who bought on credit did not. This leads to the conclusion in Choice (3). Choices (1) and (2) state generalizations from the passage, but not its conclusion.

2. **(1)** The statements in Choices (2) and (3) lead to the passage's conclusion, which is stated in Choice (1).

3. **(2)** The percents given in the passage support the conclusion in Choice (2). Choice (1) states a generalization that is not supported in the paragraph. Choice (3) restates one of the conclusion-supporting facts from the paragraph.

4. **(5)** The passage argues that droughts have not caused decreases in grain production, but that erosion of topsoil, loss of groundwater, and growth of desert areas all are the cause.

5. **(2)** Most of the passage describes the goals of Head Start and a study of Head Start's success. The last two sentences present the study's conclusion.

EXERCISE 25 (PAGE 152)

1. a. **Fact**. This can be proved by referring to President Wilson's writings and speeches.

   b. **Fact**. This can be proved by referring to historical records.

   c. **Opinion**. The last sentence says *Some people called [President Roosevelt] a warmonger*. It was those people's opinion, not a fact that could be proved, that the president enjoyed the idea of going to war.

2. a. **Fact**. The number of marriages each year is about double the number of divorces.

   b. **Opinion**. This is an opinion that cannot be proved by information in the table or by any other statistics. Some people may hold the opposite opinion.

   c. **Hypothesis**. This may or may not be accurate. More information would be needed to test whether it is or not.

3. a. **Fact**. The note below the table says that the higher figure in states with two figures includes dependents' allowances. Therefore, in Connecticut an unemployed person with dependents could receive as much as $284 per week.

   b. **Opinion**. It is a fact that Indiana gives people without dependents the lowest weekly unemployment compensation in the country. It is an opinion, however, that the amount given is not enough.

   c. **Hypothesis**. This may be true. It would have to be tested. The first thing to find out would be whether people, if and when they are laid off, actually do travel to states with high unemployment compensation maximums in order to receive higher benefits.

4. **(2)** Social scientists thought that where gun control laws were strong, the suicide rate would be lower than it would be where gun control laws were not strong. Their investigation proved that they were wrong. They found similar rates of suicide in both cases. But they did find that more suicides were committed using guns than by other methods in places were gun control laws were not strong. The statement in Choice (1) is not made in the passage; the one in Choice (3) is a hypothesis that can be drawn from information in the last two sentences of the passage, but it is not the hypothesis tested by the social scientists.

5. **(1)** The hypothesis is suggested in the last two sentences of the passage. The statements in Choices (2), (3), and (4) are facts from the passage.

EXERCISE 26 (PAGE 160)

1. **(1)** Since lakes, rivers, and groundwater are the source of most of the water people use, we should avoid polluting them. There is so little fresh water on earth that if it is polluted, people will have no water they can use. Conclusion (2) is not supported because the paragraph does not discuss future uses of the Antarctic ice cap. Nothing in the paragraph suggests that Conclusion (3) is valid.

2. **(3)** The graph shows that in the 1990s there will be more than 900,000 new jobs in the four health careers listed. That is nearly a million new health-related jobs. To fill those jobs, nearly a million people will have to enter or switch to one of those four careers in health. Because the graph shows only six—not all—computer and health-related careers, Conclusion (1) is not supported by the graph. The graph shows nothing about salaries, so it does not support Conclusion (3).

3. **(c) and (d)** Conclusion (c) is supported by the information in the paragraph above the table. Before 1972 many people who moved to states with long residency requirements were not able to register and vote for a long time. After 1972, when those states shortened or abolished their residency requirements, people who had not been able to register before could register and vote. Conclusion (d) is supported by information in the table. Some states have a 30-day residency requirement for voter registration. If a person moves to one of those states less than 30 days before an election, he or she will be unable to vote in that election. The graph has no information about voting rates, so Conclusion (a) is not supported. Conclusion (b) is not supported because the graph does not show that any state failed to change its residency requirement.

4. **(1)** The map shows that most oil is transported by water routes north of the equator. It is more likely, therefore, that an oil spill will occur above the equator than below it. The map shows nothing about changes in the cost of oil or the rate of using oil from year to year, so Conclusions (2) and (3) are not supported.

EXERCISE 27 (PAGE 164)

1. The number **57.4%** provides the best support for the conclusion. It shows that more than half of all adults (therefore, most adults) voted in 1988.

2. The graph shows that **Transportation** is the single largest source of air pollution. Using cleaner auto fuels would significantly reduce air pollution—probably more than any other single measure.

3. **(2)** The conclusion doesn't mention President Johnson, so the information about his election in 1964 is irrelevant.

4. **(b) and (c)** These two facts are the ones needed to support the conclusion. The percents of whites and of African-Americans making more than $50,000 both increased by 7 percent between 1968 and 1988. Facts (a) and (d) are irrelevant to the conclusion.

5. **(1)** The map shows Western bases both in the United States and in countries other than the United States. This fact supports the conclusion.

6. **(d) and (e)** If the acid levels in the lakes has increased to the point that plants and fish are dying, it's reasonable to conclude that the lakes are polluted—probably by acid rain. Observations (a), (b), and (c) do not directly support the scientists' conclusions, but they do provide necessary background information.

EXERCISE 28 (PAGE 169)

1. **The farmer's conclusion was not logical**: the United States did have a trade deficit in 1990. **The farmer based his conclusion on only one line—agricultural commodities—in the table.** The United States does export more agricultural products than it buys, but overall, as the *Total* line shows, it imports more products than it exports.

2. **The pollsters did not consider all the information available to them.** It is true that in polls more people said they would vote for Dewey than for Truman. However, since there were many undecided voters, it was not logical to conclude that Dewey would win the election.

3. **The tourist jumped to a conclusion based on too little information.** He or she assumed that the hunting tools carried by the group were weapons. If the tourist had looked further, he or she would have found that the tools were not weapons. The tourist would then have needed much more evidence to be able to conclude that the group was warlike and violent.

4. **(3)** The table says nothing about the amount of state and local taxes paid by people who make less or more than $20,000. Therefore, **it is not possible to draw a logical conclusion about the amount of taxes all people in Philadelphia and Albuquerque pay**.

5. **(3)** The table says nothing about the amount of state and local taxes paid by single people. Therefore, **it is not possible to draw a logical conclusion about the amount of taxes a single person in Atlanta would pay, home-owning or not.**

6. **The man's conclusion was logical. Radiation from the accident at Chernobyl spread over a far wider area than radiation from any of the other accidents listed.**

EXERCISE 29 (PAGE 174)

1. **(3)** By refusing the larger grant, the Sioux showed they valued the people's good more than taking in a lot of money or filling large orders with products of questionable quality.

2. **(1)** The official showed by his offer of more money that he valued what the Sioux had done and wanted to improve their facilities.

3. **(1)** The First Amendment is designed to protect individuals from a too-powerful government. The states valued individual liberty over strong government. They probably valued newspapers, too, but their interests were broader in adopting the amendment.

4. **(1)** By spraying malathion the state tried to protect its economy and the welfare of its farmers.

5. **(2)** A typical environmental group would care about malathion's effects on the environment.

6. **(3)** In hunting-gathering groups, food and other items are shared. Sharing is more important than owning. Because sharing is valued, laws against stealing are not very important.

7. **(2)** The mayor argues for keeping property taxes down by responding to the census. He cares that everyone returns his form so that the state will send as much money to Grayford as it deserves.

8. **(2)** The mayor's argument for returning census forms promptly is based on keeping property taxes from rising.

SOCIAL STUDIES READINGS 3

History Readings (page 177)

1. **(2)** The second paragraph describes how Andrew Carnegie made a steel company grew by forcing other companies out of business. (Inferring the Main Idea of a Paragraph in a Passage)

2. **(2)** The last paragraph contrasts the idea of making a lot of money with the idea of giving money to good causes. (Seeing How Details Are Organized)

3. **(1)** You can infer the meaning of *monopoly* from the fourth sentence in the paragraph. That sentence describes how businessmen drove competing companies out of business to create a company with complete control of its industry. (Understanding Meanings from Context)

4. **(1)** A monopoly operates without competition. It controls the production and sale of a product. The utility company is similar to a monopoly because it provides gas and electricity without competition in its region. McDonald's and the long-distance companies have competitors. (Applying Information from Written Material)

5. **(1)** The statement is critical of workers who are not satisfied with the working conditions an employer sets. The statement was most likely a factory owner's. (Applying Information from Written Material)

6. **(2)** Since the workers were told they would lose their jobs unless they returned to work, the company was threatening a lock-out. (Applying Information from Written Material)

7. **(3)** As the first paragraph says, the New Deal was designed to stimulate the economy. The program began during the Great Depression. (Analyzing Cause and Effect)

8. **(2)** The author concludes that the New Deal did not bring about complete economic recovery. It was increased production of war machines, which created many new jobs, that ended the depression. (Recognizing Conclusions)

9. **(3)** The map shows that Germany's invasion of the Soviet Union probably took place on the ground rather than by sea. Tanks would have been more useful than sea-going vessels. (Applying Information from Graphic Material)

10. (a) **The democratic nations of Western Europe** became allies of the United States in the Free World; (b) **the communist nations of Eastern Europe, together with other communist countries like China and Cuba**, became allies of the Soviet Union in the Communist World; (c) **the developing nations in Africa, Asia, and Latin America** came to be known as the Third World. (Reading for Details)

11. The nuclear weapons buildup mentioned in the second paragraph created the threat of war between the two superpowers. **The two superpowers never fought each other, so there was no "hot" war between them. The "war" remained "cold."** (Using the General Context)

12. **(3)** In an arms race each side tries to stockpile more weapons than the other. It is a race to stay ahead—an arms race. (Evaluating the Relevance of Information)

13. The Supreme Court found that **separate educational facilities violate the Fourteenth Amendment because they are unequal**. (Analyzing Cause and Effect)

14. **(1)** The second paragraph says that Dr. Martin Luther King led marches for civil rights and saw civil rights laws passed before his death. This implies that Dr. King's marches helped to bring about the laws. President Johnson could not have brought about the laws himself. The Supreme Court does not make laws. (Inferring the Main Idea of a Paragraph)

15. The second paragraph says that by its involvement in Vietnam the United States tried to **help South Vietnam drive out communists**. (Reading for Details)

16. According to the second paragraph, the late '60s and early '70s were violent because of **the protests against U. S. involvement in Vietnam and riots in inner cities**. (Analyzing Cause and Effect)

17. **(2)** The fifth and sixth paragraphs imply that credit spending in the '80s led to a stock-market crash in the '90s. (Making Inferences from Written Material)

18. **(b) and (c)** Because Eastern bloc countries began to adopt economic and political freedom like those freedoms in the Free World, the cold war began to end. The basic causes for the dispute between the East and the West ceased to exist. (Analyzing Cause and Effect)

Geography Readings (page 182)

19. **(3)** Beginning with the second paragraph, each paragraph in the passage is about agriculture in different environments. Choices (1) and (2) are too broad to be the main idea of the passage. (Finding the Sentence That States the Main Idea)

20. **The passage does not contain all the information necessary to draw the conclusion**. It doesn't tell how much farmland there is or how much farmland is necessary to support a certain number of people. (Evaluating the Logic of a Conclusion)

21. **(2)** The pattern that covers northeast Asia is like the pattern that covers the north part of North America. (Making Inferences from Graphic Material)

22. (a) **high** (b) **high** (c) **high** (d) **low** (e) **low** (f) **low** The second paragraph provides the information you need to answer this question. (Reading for Details)

23. When a country is developing, death rates fall **because of better medicine, food supplies, and health practices**. (Analyzing Cause and Effect)

24. **(3)** People in most countries that are not industrialized—not developed—depend on agriculture to feed themselves and make a living. Even small farms require many hands to produce a sufficient yield. (Making Inferences from Written Material)

25. **(3)** Of the choices, only developing nations have high birth rates and low death rates. Their populations will grow more in the next ten years than those of other countries. (Evaluating the Logic of a Conclusion)

26. The three main causes of air pollution in the United States are (a) **cars and other vehicles**, (b) **home and office heating**, and (c) **industrial emissions**. These causes are spelled out in the second paragraph. (Seeing How Details Are Organized)

27. **The two examples from two different parts of the world—northeastern North America and northern Europe—provide enough evidence to show that air pollution from industries causes acid rain**. (Evaluating the Amount of Information)

28. **(2)** People who like outdoor recreation might stay away from areas polluted by acid rain. This would hurt businesses that cater to those people. Banking is an indoor industry; the transportation industry does not depend on the lakes and trees polluted by acid rain. Neither industry would be as severely hurt as the recreation industry. (Applying Information from Written Material)

29. **(2)** The fifth paragraph says that *insecticides used in agriculture often run off into surface and groundwater and pollute it*. In the example, insecticides used in lawn care run off into a stream. (Classifying Information in Categories)

30. The statement is **an opinion**. There is no way to know what businesses would do if they had to operate under new conditions, so the statement cannot be a fact. (Recognizing Facts, Opinions, and Hypotheses)

Economics Readings (page 185)

31. An unpaid balance is the **amount still owed on a debt after its due date**. (Reading for Details)

32. **(3)** Because the woman pays for her car in installments, she must pay interest on the unpaid balance. The interest payments add to the base cost of the car. (Applying Information from Written Material)

33. **(1)** Consumers might be encouraged to borrow money by an ad that reminds them that they can "buy now, pay later." They would probably not be encouraged to borrow money by an ad that reminds them that the interest on a loan can be very expensive (Choice 2) or that taking out a loan could drive them into debt (Choice 3). (Recognizing Values)

34. **(2)** In 1980 Americans owed about $300 billion in consumer installment debt. In 1990 they owed about $750 billion, or roughly $450 billion more than in 1980. (Finding Details in Graphs)

35. **(3)** The purpose of the statement in Choice (1) is to introduce the contrast between the way people and the federal government budget. The statement in Choice (2) points to an example drawn from one of the graphs. The main thrust of the passage, as shown in the last three paragraphs, is that the federal government's deficit is growing but that people have differing opinions about the danger of that growth. (Inferring the Main Idea of a Passage)

36. The largest source of the federal government's income is **taxes on individuals**, which the graph entitled *Sources of the Federal Government's Income* shows accounts for 40 percent of the total income, more than any other source. (Finding Details in Graphs)

37. **(3)** Both Choices (1) and (2) can be proved by reference to records. Choice (3) expresses an opinion with which some people disagree, according to the last paragraph. (Recognizing Facts, Opinions, and Hypotheses)

38. As the first paragraph says, the government's regulation of business protects **businesses**, **workers**, and **consumers**. (Reading for Details)

39. **(2)** Choice (1) expresses an opinion with which some people disagree. Choice (3) expresses an hypothesis that might or might not be valid if it were tested. Choice (2) can be proved a fact by referring to laws. (Recognizing Facts, Opinions, and Hypotheses)

40. A trade deficit is created **when a country imports more than it exports**, as implied in the first paragraph. (Making Inferences from Written Material)

41. **Yes**, there is enough information in the passage to support the educator's conclusion. The passage says that to improve its balance of trade **the United States needs a well-educated workforce, especially in technological fields, to create a demand for U.S. products in foreign markets**. If 25 percent of all high school students drop out, the workforce will not be educated enough to help the United States compete in foreign markets and improve the country's balance of trade. (Evaluating the Amount of Information)

Political Science Readings (page 188)

42. Ronald Reagan's veto checked the power of **Congress**. When Congress uses its lawmaking power to pass a bill, the president can override that power by vetoing the bill. (Applying Information from Graphic Material)

43. The vote in Congress checked the power of **the president**. When a president uses the power to veto a bill, Congress can override that veto by a two-thirds majority vote in both houses. (Applying Information from Graphic Material)

44. The Supreme Court's decision checked the power of both **Congress** and **the president**. Even after both Congress and the president use their powers to create a law, the Supreme Court can override those powers by declaring that law unconstitutional. (Applying Information from Graphic Material)

45. The refusal of Congress to approve the appointment checked the power of **the president**. When a president uses his power to appoint a judge, Congress can override that power by refusing to approve the appointment. (Applying Information from Graphic Material)

46. State governments are like the federal government in that (a) **both have constitutions** and (b) **the constitutions of both set up governments with separate powers**. (Seeing How Details Are Organized)

47. **(3)** The passage does not suggest that either the federal government or state governments have more power than the other. It merely says each has some power. (Evaluating the Relevance of Information)

48. **(2)** Because both states and the federal government can have military forces, they share the power to provide for defense. (Applying Information from Written Material)

49. The Supreme Courts gets the power to overturn a state law from **the U.S. Constitution**. This is implied in the last paragraph. (Making Inferences from Written Material)

50. (a) Planning a high school curriculum is **a power of state governments** because the Constitution leaves to states the power to control education in their states. (b) Going to war in the Persian Gulf was **a power of the federal government** because the Constitution allows only the federal government to go to war with a foreign government. (c) The Constitution allows both the federal and state governments to tax a person's income, so taxing earnings is **a shared power**. (Applying Information from Written Material)

51. States raise the money they need **by imposing taxes**. As the third paragraph says, the power to impose taxes is a power shared by the federal and state governments. This implies that state governments raise money for themselves through taxes. (Making Inferences from Written Material)

52. The Supreme Court based its ruling on **the Fifth Amendment**, which protects people from having to testify against themselves in court. (Applying Information from Graphic Material)

53. The editor is protected by **the First Amendment**, which grants freedom of speech. (Applying Information from Graphic Material)

Behavioral Science Readings (page 190)

54. **(1)** The second paragraph says that a child's peers are his or her playmates. Playmates share an equal status with each other. (Using Examples and Contrasts)

55. **(3)** If a parent is away from a child for long hours, he or she has limited influence on a child's early socialization. A parent can influence a child's early socialization, though, by being sure that the child chooses playmates and television shows that reflect the parent's values. (Applying Information from Written Material)

56. **(2)** Choice (2) is supported by the last paragraph—and especially the last sentence—of the passage. The passage implies that persons outside the family are important to a child's socialization, so Choice (1) is wrong. In the passage, no link is drawn between a child's choice of peers and television watching, so Choice (3) is wrong. (Evaluating the Logic of a Conclusion)

57. **(2)** Some people criticize TV ads because they think ads teach children to value material things *too highly*. That does not imply that they think they should own only necessary material things, as Choice (1) says. Rather, it implies that they think they should not put too much value on material things. (Applying Information from Written Material)

58. **(2)** The support for this answer is in the first paragraph of the passage. (Reading for Details)

59. **(1)** The last two sentences in the paragraph are about teenagers who need a sense of belonging. Those teenagers are the topic of the paragraph. The rest of the paragraph explains how such teenagers join gangs and adopt their values. (Inferring the Main Idea of a Paragraph in a Passage)

60. The passage mentions the following five factors that help to determine a person's class: (a) **income**, (b) **education**, (c) **lifestyle**, (d) **race**, and (e) **ethnic background**. (Reading for Details)

61. The percent of people living below the poverty level decreases until age **65 and over**. At those ages, it rises. (Finding Details in Tables)

62. **(1)** The woman has lost the income and lifestyle that have defined her class. She has probably moved into a class lower than the one she had been in. (Applying Information from Written Material)

63. **(2)** The first sentence of the second paragraph gives the information you need to find the meaning of *ascribed status*. (Using the General Context)

64. (a) This illustrates **achieved status** because the woman had to train to gain her status. (b) This illustrates **ascribed status** because the child's status is dependent on the father's status. (c) This illustrates **achieved status** because the man had to study to become a doctor. (d) This illustrates **achieved status** because the man's own actions brought about a decline in his status. (Applying Information from Written Material)

65. Status is determined by a person's class, job, and lifestyle. In this case, the religious leader's **job** determines his or her status in the group. (Applying Information from Written Material)

GED PRACTICE 3 (page 194)

1. **(2)** Workers contribute to the Social Security fund and receive money from it later. This is similar to paying premiums to an insurance company and collecting money when an insured event occurs. (Reading for Details/History)

2. **(2)** During the Great Depression, there were no government "safety nets" to help the large number of people who were unemployed or disabled. Because of the extent of the problem, government action was needed. (Analyzing Cause and Effect/History)

3. **(3)** The words *kind* and *humane* signal an opinion. The other choices state facts that can be proved. (Recognizing Facts, Opinions, and Hypotheses/History)

4. **(1)** Flying for less money on small airlines was a benefit of airline deregulation for the passengers. (Making Inferences from Written Material/Economics)

5. **(4)** The word *terrible* indicates an opinion. The other choices state facts that can be proved. (Recognizing Facts, Opinions, and Hypotheses/Economics)

6. **(4)** This is an educated guess that could be proved or disproved with more information. (Recognizing Facts, Opinions, and Hypotheses/Behavioral Science)

7. **(3)** The passage indicates that reports of child abuse have increased. It is reasonable to conclude that they will continue to increase. (Recognizing Conclusions/Behavioral Science)

8. **(5)** The Peace Corps is a form of foreign aid. At no cost to the host countries, American volunteers help those countries. (Applying Information from Written Material/History)

9. **(2)** The graph shows that each year between 1945 and 1985, the United States has given billions of dollars in foreign aid. None of the other conclusions is supported by the graph. (Evaluating the Amount of Information/Economics)

10. **(1)** The graph shows a sharp rise of almost $20 billion in foreign aid for the period from 1981 through 1985. (Evaluating the Relevance of Information/Economics)

POSTTEST (Page 199)

1. **(3)** All the other sentences give examples that support this main idea. (Comprehending What You Read/Recognizing Stated Main Ideas/Behavioral Science)

2. **(4)** Slavery was an emotionally charged issue; so is abortion. People were divided about whether slavery was moral or immoral. People are divided about the morality of abortion too. (Thinking Critically as You Read/Applying What You Read/History)

3. **(1)** Only the first conclusion can be supported by the graph. The other conclusions are speculations not based on information in the graph. (Thinking Critically as You Read/Evaluating What You Read/Economics)

4. **(5)** Since the number of jobs in steel changed little after 1986, employment levels had become stable. (Thinking Critically as You Read/Evaluating What You Read/Economics)

5. **(1)** This explanation is given in the third sentence of the second paragraph. (Comprehending What You Read/Understanding the Details/Geography)

6. **(3)** The second paragraph explains how people fill wetlands in to create land to live on, among other reasons. You can conclude that more land is needed because populations are growing. (Thinking Critically as You Read/Analyzing What You Read/Geography)

7. **(4)** The first paragraph explains how wetlands help keep seawater clean. If they disappear, seawater will be more polluted. (Thinking Critically as You Read/Analyzing What You Read/Geography)

8. **(4)** Economists are concerned with money, so commercial fishing and the value of seafood would be important to an economist. (Thinking Critically as You Read/Evaluating What You Read/Geography)

9. **(3)** In describing her job, the immigrant mentions the amount of work she had to do, the long hours, the speed at which she worked, and the accidents. (Comprehending What You Read/Preparing to Read/History)

10. **(5)** The smallest section of the graph represents teenage runaways. They make up 4 percent of the population of homeless people in the United States. (Comprehending What You Read/Understanding the Details/Behavioral Science)

11. **(2)** The parts of the graph that stand for single men and single women make up 60 percent of the homeless, or well over half. (Thinking Critically as You Read/ Evaluating What You Read/Behavioral Science)

12. **(1)** By inspecting meat, Morton maintains quality standards for food, a responsibility of the Department of Agriculture. (Thinking Critically as You Read/Applying What You Read/Political Science)

13. **(5)** By checking tax returns, Charmaine processes funds paid to the government, a responsibility of the Department of the Treasury. (Thinking Critically as You Read/ Applying What You Read/Political Science)

14. **(3)** As a ranger in a national forest, Deena helps to preserve federal land, a responsibility of the Department of the Interior. (Thinking Critically as You Read/Applying What You Read/Political Science)

15. **(4)** The map shows French ships. They must have played a key role in winning the Battle of Yorktown. (Thinking Critically as You Read/Evaluating What You Read/History)

16. **(5)** The British ships could not escape via the Chesapeake Bay because they were blocked at the mouth of the York River by French ships. In addition there were more French than British ships. (Thinking Critically as You Read/Evaluating What You Read/History)

17. **(5)** This question asked you to find an hypothesis. The hypothesis is given in the second paragraph. (Thinking Critically as You Read/Analyzing What You Read/Economics)

18. **(4)** The first paragraph explains how Ford's workers were seen as parts of machines. The last paragraph contrasts that with the way Japanese workers are viewed. Because Japanese workers are allowed to make decisions, you can infer that Ford's workers could not. (Inferring as You Read/Inferring Details/Economics)

19. **(3)** Assembly-line production can be used in manufacturing goods such as TVs. The industries in the other choices don't manufacture goods. (Thinking Critically as You Read/Applying What You Read/Economics)

20. **(2)** B is located in the middle of a moderate temperature zone, which would have a mild climate. Note that D, also in a moderate region, is very close to the polar region and would be colder. (Thinking Critically as You Read/Applying What You Read/Geography)

21. **(1)** The main idea is supported by each of the sentences in the paragraph. (Inferring As You Read/Inferring Unstated Main Ideas/Political Science)

22. **(4)** The paragraph mentions "colored troops." You can infer that African-American soldiers and white soldiers were assigned to separate troops. (Inferring as You Read/Inferring Details/History)

23. **(5)** The second paragraph explains how children identify with TV characters. Using the context, you can infer that *emulate their behavior* means "copy or imitate their behavior." (Inferring as You Read/Inferring Word Meanings/Behavioral Science)

24. **(2)** The researcher suggested that too much TV can keep a child from active play, which is important. So a parent might want to let a child watch just a little TV. (Thinking Critically as You Read/Applying What You Read/Behavioral Science)

25. **(3)** The fourth paragraph gives the conclusion that the California researcher came to. (Thinking Critically as You Read/Evaluating What You Read/Behavioral Science)

26. **(5)** Only damming Western rivers is not aiding other nations. (Thinking Critically as You Read/Applying What You Read/History)

27. **(2)** The word *right* signals an opinion. The statement cannot be proved true by checking reliable books or experts, as the others can. (Thinking Critically as You Read/Analyzing What You Read/History)

28. **(1)** The map shows that women had no right to vote in the states of the Southeast. Without that right, they could have had little say about the government. (Comprehending What You Read/Understanding The Details/Political Science)

29. **(5)** The map shows that women in Texas could vote only in local elections before 1920. (Thinking Critically as You Read/Analyzing What You Read/Political Science)

30. **(2)** After 1920 states had to allow women to vote. But before 1920, the western states had already given women that right. (Thinking Critically as You Read/Evaluating What You Read/Political Science)

31. **(3)** If the supply of something is great, its cost usually goes down. (Thinking Critically as You Read/Analyzing What You Read/Economics)

32. **(3)** Statement (3) suggests a reason for this generation's desire to save money. With further study, the hypothesis could be shown accurate or not. (Thinking Critically as You Read/Analyzing What You Read/History)

PHOTO AND ILLUSTRATION CREDITS

Page
1 Photo by Shirley Hinkamp.

3 *Left:* Data from Herbert H. Gross, *World Geography* (Newton, Mass.: Allyn and Bacon, 1986), p. 355. *Right:* Federal Reserve Bulletin.

4 Adapted from Clarence L. Ver Steeg, *American Spirit: A History of the American People* (Englewood Cliffs: Prentice Hall, 1990), p. 390.

5 Data from U.S. Department of Agriculture.

8 Data from Ford Motor Company and Wards Automotive Reports. Adapted from *The Chicago Tribune*, March 18, 1990.

11 Photo courtesy of the Nebraska Game Commission.

14 Translation: William Penn trades with the Indians, establishing the Province of Pennsylvania in America, September 1681. Benjamin West engraving. Courtesy of the Library of Congress.

15 Sygma photo by J.P. Laffont, courtesy of the United Nations.

17 Benjamin Franklin as engraved on U.S. legal tender.

20 Source: U.S Bureau of the Census.

21 *Top:* U. S. Bureau of the Census. *Bottom:* Department of Health and Human Services, National Center for Health Statistics.

22 Photo by Laimute Druskis.

26 Weather map courtesy of the National Oceanic and Atmospheric Administration.

28 Signatures to the Constitution of the United States, 1787. Courtesy of the National Archives.

33 U.S. Navy, from the Collections of the National Archives.

34 Photo by B. Lane, courtesy of the United Nations,

38 Mickey Mouse welcomes guests as the official mayor of Walt Disney's Magic Kingdom. Photo ©Walt Disney Productions.

47 U.S. Bureau of the Census.

48 Bureau of Labor Statistics.

49 Source: Department of Commerce, Bureau of Economic Analysis.

50 Department of Health and Human Services, National Center for Health Statistics.

54 Bureau of Labor Statistics.

55 Bureau of Labor Statistics.

56 Data from *World Book Encyclopedia*, 1988 edition ("World" entry).

57 Data from Ver Steeg, *American Spirit*, p. 725.

59 Data from Hammond *Medallion World Atlas*, p. 189.

61 Department of Labor, Bureau of Labor Statistics.

65 Based on data from Gross, *World Geography*, p. 70,

71 Photo by Page Poore.

74 Source: Department of Commerce, Bureau of the Census, *Current Population Survey*, November 1988.

77 Courtesy of the Architect of the Capital.

83 Courtesy of the Union Pacific Railroad Museum Collection.

87 Courtesy of the Library of Congress.

91 President Abraham Lincoln, courtesy of the Library of Congress.

94 Courtesy of the Library of Congress, from the Brady-Handy Collection.

97 Data from Gross, *World Geography*, p. 261.

98 (99, 100) Courtesy of Herblock Cartoons, The Washington Post, 1150 15th Street N.W., Washington, D.C. 20071.

101 Based on data from *Business Week*, June 8, 1992.

114 Bystanders pose for photographer S.J. Morrow. Courtesy of the National Archives.

124 U.S. Department of Energy.

125 Universal Press Syndicate.

127 U.S. Department of the Navy, courtesy of the National Archives.

128   Photo by Teri Leigh Stratford.

131   Squaw sitting in front of a Stoney Indian teepee. Note chief's headdress.

133   *Top and bottom:* Data from Meteorological Office, London; Jorge L. Tamayo, *Atlas Geográfico de México* (Instituto Mexicano de Investigaciones Económicas).

135   *Top:* Source: *Motor Vehicle Facts and Figures '86* (Detroit: Motor Vehicle Manufacturers Association of the United States).

136   Adapted from Gross, *World Geography,* p. 36.

137   Data from Gerald M. Pomper et al., *The Performance of American Government* (New York: The Free Press, 1972), p. 249.

140   Lordstown, Ohio, plant. Courtesy of the General Motors Corporation.

144   A preschool class. Photo by Ken Karp.

146   Cabrini Green Homes, Chicago, in 1982. Photo by Marc P. Anderson.

148   From the Collections of the Library of Congress.

149   A working mother and eight-month-old daughter. Photo by Ken Karp.

153   *Top:* Department of Health and Human Services, National Center for Health Statistics. *Bottom:* Department of Labor, Employment and Training Administration.

155   (156) Courtesy of New York State Department of Commerce.

158   Source: Department of Commerce, Bureau of the Census.

159   Source: Department of Commerce, Bureau of the Census, *Current Population Survey,* November 1988.

160   Source: Department of Labor, Bureau of Labor Statistics.

161   Data from *1990 Information Please Almanac* (Boston: Houghton Mifflin, 1989), p. 640.

162   Adapted from Gross, *World Geography,* p. 245.

164   Source: Department of Commerce, Bureau of the Census, *Current Population Survey,* November 1988.

165   Source: National Air Pollution Control Administration.

166   *Top:* U.S. Bureau of the Census. *Bottom:* Data from Irving L. Gordon, *American History: Review Text* (New York: Amsco School Publications, 1986), p. 648.

169   Source: Office of Industry and Trade Information, U.S. Department of Commerce.

170   Photo by UP staff photographer Frank Cancellare, courtesy of United Press International.

171   Source: Government of the District of Columbia, Department of Finance and Revenue, *Tax Rates and Tax Burdens in the District of Columbia: A Nationwide Comparison.*

172   Photo by Astronaut Russell L. Schweckart during Apollo 9 earth-orbital mission, March 6, 1969. Courtesy of NASA.

175   *Top:* Courtesy of the U.S. Department of Agriculture. *Bottom:* Hunter on left carries boomerangs; man on right, spear and spear thrower. Photo by W. Pederson, courtesy of Australian News and Information Bureau.

179   Source: Sol Holt and John R. O'Connor, *Exploring World History* (Englewood Cliffs: Globe Book Company, 1990), p. 584. Reprinted courtesy of Stephen Lewin, with permission.

180   Courtesy of the National Archives.

182   Adapted from *Pre-GED Social Studies* (Austin, Texas: Steck-Vaughn Publishing), p. 17.

185   Source: Federal Reserve System.

186   *Top and bottom:* Office of Management and Budget.

191   U.S. Bureau of the Census.

196   Source: Department of Commerce, Bureau of Economic Analysis.

199   Courtesy of RCA.

200   Sources: American Iron and Steel Institute, Congressional Research Service, AUS Consultants.

202   Source: U.S. Conference of Mayors.

203   Adapted from Ver Steeg, *American Spirit,* p. 195.

204   Based on data from Gross, *World Geography,* p. 70.

206   Data from Ver Steeg, *American Spirit,* p. 546.